MANAGEMENT OF ELEMENTARY SCHOOLS

MANAGEMENT OF ELEMENTARY SCHOOLS

Edited by

B.V. VERGHESE

ANMOL PUBLICATIONS PVT. LTD.
NEW DELHI - 110 002 (INDIA)

ANMOL PUBLICATIONS PVT. LTD.
4374/4B, Ansari Road, Daryaganj
New Delhi - 110 002
Ph.: 23261597, 23278000
Visit us at: www.anmolpublications.com

Management of Elementary Schools

ISBN 81-261-1048-1

PRINTED IN INDIA

Published by J.L. Kumar for Anmol Publications Pvt. Ltd., New Delhi - 110 002 and Printed at Mehra Offset Press, Delhi.

Contents

Preface

Management and administration like concepts in the area of education have often been considered as rather second-rate and consequently have been relegated to an inferior position behind the teaching function. This has been true particularly in case of primary school where head teachers have been offered even less in the way of management training than their secondary colleagues. What is often forgotten is that education, whether at national or classroom level, does not just happen but has to be carefully planned. Management should therefore be seen as indivisible from teaching, the two must complement each other if the education process is to be a success.

In the present book thought provoking readings are compiled for the benefit of teachers and policy planners. Topics like — nature of management in elementary schools, autonomy in teaching and management, education management in central and local government, school governors, primary school finance, teaching and non-teaching staff, management of special education, routine administration, organisational culture, collegial schools, school development plans, financial management and building etc. are given elaborate treatment.

I am grateful to all the scholars whose writings and fruits of painstaking research are cited or substantially made use of in this book. I am also thankful to all my friends who have assisted me while preparing the manuscript. Last but not the least I am grateful to Mr. J.L. Kumar, Managing Director, Anmol Publications Pvt. Ltd., New Delhi for undertaking the publication of this work.

—B.V. Verghese

Preface

1

The Nature of Management in Elementary Schools

MANAGEMENT AND ADMINISTRATION

In the educational world concepts such as management and administration have often been thought of as rather second-rate and consequently have been relegated to an inferior position behind the teaching function. This has been particularly true of the primary school where head teachers have been offered even less in the way of management training than their secondary colleagues. Many heads proudly, and quite rightly, claim that their first love and duty is the direct teaching of the children. Bureaucratic red tape is scorned as being at best time-consuming and at worst completely irrelevant. What is often forgotten is that education, whether at national or classroom level, does not just happen but has to be carefully planned. Management should therefore be seen as indivisible from teaching; the two must complement each other if the education process is to be a success.

It is as well to be clear about definitions at the outset. There is a world of difference between administration and management, although too often the words are thoughtlessly interchanged. Administration is a much more passive task than management and does not carry the same authority. It excludes the direction of resources and, more important, it excludes policy making. The administrator makes possible what has been planned; the manager plans the policy.

One of the growth areas of further education during the past few years has been management education, but primarily in the business and industrial fields. Educational management is far more complex than its counterpart in the industrial world so it is difficult to understand why acceptance of management training for new and prospective heads has only recently been established. It may have something to do with the Englishman's love of the amateur, coupled with the perceived professional role of the teacher. Failure in industrial management can often be dramatic, as shown almost weekly by press headlines. Educational mismanagement only rarely hits the headlines, as exemplified by the William Tyndale affair. Its results, however, though less immediately tangible, can be equally devastating in their long-term consequences for both individual and the state.

DECISION-MAKING

The central importance of decision-making for the educational manager cannot be over-emphasised: the headteacher has the authority and the responsibility to take decisions which will implement his policy. This process is complicated by factors which do not always appear directly relevant. Thus, effective decisions cannot be taken without effective management.

It would be pleasant to sit down and plan from scratch, with all decision-making constrained only by our personal prejudices. A head appointed to a school still in its construction phase initially may feel that he has this opportunity. Unfortunately the new head is not often in this fortunate position as all our decisions are affected by previous ones, usually taken by other people. The head of a new school will be affected by its design and by its very location in a certain catchment area; even his freedom to choose staff to implement his own policies will be limited by the employment market at the time and the probable continuing need in the 1980s for the redeployment of teaching staff.

One vital factor in decision-making is the consideration of its long-term effects. All too often decisions are made in isolation not only of constraining factors on implementation but also of likely consequences. A headteacher may, for example, have an enthusiastic teacher taking the third year juniors who, both at college and at an LEA language centre, has undergone training in primary French. The head agrees to the introduction of French in the third year but a year later may be frustrated if he has not made plans for its continuation into the fourth year. Consequently there may be further problems for the secondary school and its other feeder primary schools. So what seemed a simple and reasonable decision affecting one teacher and perhaps thirty children has consequences far beyond its original aim.

Nor are educational planners always as aware of the possible consequences of their decision-making as they should be. Too often decisions concentrate on the narrow view and ignore the wider possibilities. All education managers must accept that today's system is the result of previous decisions, some dating back many years. In turn decisions made today will have effects not only next year but possibly into the next century. The art of decision-making is therefore not simple; it is necessary to be aware of factors acting upon the decision-maker which will affect the decision while at the same time being aware of likely future consequences. As headteachers are in the business of making decisions daily it is essential to make them carefully.

THE NATURE OF MANAGEMENT

What do we mean by management? The word refers to the controlling process in any organisation; the managers are those who are concerned with achieving the objectives of the organisation and the use of resources to that end; in this case the resources are composed of the headteacher) his staff, capitation and other funds, equipment and, often forgotten but very important, time.

It is impossible to lay down a set of rules that an education manager can apply to all situations. In education there are no certainties although management guidelines can produce expectations and probabilities from particular courses of action. The head must manage effectively in an attempt to exclude as many of the uncertainties as possible.

Of course there are important differences between management in education and management in other walks of life and these will be detailed later. However, these differences become more evident in carrying out the non-management tasks rather than in the actual process of decision-making. The structure by which a primary head will reach a decision and follow it through will be similar to that of a chief executive or company manager; the differences will be in the constraints to be taken into account in arriving at the decision and the environment surrounding its implementation.

We can analyse the basic process of management and apply it to the school situation. A great deal has been written in this area but the main theorists would agree that the most central management elements are planning, organising, controlling and evaluating. This book is intended for the practical headteacher rather than the theorist but one must accept that sound management is more than common sense and experience. We will explore the nature of the management process a little more deeply but attempt to avoid the other extreme of accepting management as a pure science. There cannot be a set of true laws in management, therefore it cannot be a science. Management can be systematically practised but its application, particularly in the field of social provision such as education, must remain an art.

PLANNING

This is the basic function of management, the other functions being primarily the means through which the manager maximises his chances of making the plan a success Planning begins with setting objectives and specifying the steps needed to attain them. The head will be concerned with the school as an institution ; the head of infants will set her objectives within the overall plan, each class teacher will do the same for his class, groups or individual pupils.

Objectives can be either short-range or long-range, covering one term or the full six year primary school span. The shorter the range the more definite the plans can be and the less the risk of failure. Longer-range plans will need to be flexible to take into account changed circumstances. They also run the risk of non-completion unless definite commitments are made.

This can be illustrated by a plan to raise funds through a PTA. The time span is reasonable with plan completion in sight acting as a motivating force. Two thousand pounds over three years may be much more difficult to achieve as there is a greater risk that interest in the project will decrease and enthusiasm decline. However, provide a terminal commitment, purchase of a swimming pool or mini bus, and the,chances of success are improved.

The setting of the commitment illustrates another planning problem which has been hinted at already in the discussion on decision-making. If we are not careful our view can become so narrow that we lose sight of our overall objectives. It is as well from time to time to ask ourselves the fundamental question about objectives which is: 'What business are we really in?' To do this successfully we must stand outside our immediate frame of reference and tackle the problem in a fresh manner.

This planning technique is commonly known as management by objectives, or MBO. There are many examples which could be quoted from the world of industry. IBM, one of the biggest growth industries during the sixties, defined its objectives as supplying information rather than the production of office machines. In contrast the machine tool industry lost some ground, possibly as a result of defining its task as producing metal-forming machines rather than supplying the means of production.

Attempts to define the aims and objectives of education have always run into trouble and it is not a part of the present task to consider this in detail. The head must ensure, however, that he is working towards his overall objectives when he sets the purchase of a minibus or swimming pool as a commitment. It is all too easy to concentrate on a limited plan irrelevant to the main objective and thus waste valuable time while ignoring the real needs of the school.

ORGANISATION

It is often wrongly assumed that management is mainly concerned with organisation. Without a plan to implement, even the most efficient organisation would flounder in its own bureaucracy. It is only when objectives have been defined that one can move on to a consideration of the means of building up both the material and human resources required to implement the plan.

One part of the head teacher's task is to organise his school so that the various units are not working a cross purposes or so that two units are not overlapping. How many classes have 'done' a project on the Romans two or three times during their school career without any real advancement of knowledge or skills? How often do different classes use different assessment and recording techniques?

A further problem with organisation is that of the informal group. This can be particularly relevant to the usually friendly atmosphere of the primary school without the great substructure of hierarchy found more commonly in the secondary school. The informal organisation consists of a network of friendships, alliances and communication channels which do not follow the usual lines. Used well the informal organisation can encourage those who are enthusiastic and make everyone feel an important part of the decision-making process. Used without thought or tact, senior members of staff will bear grudges and harbour resentment.

CONTROL

Controlling involves translating one's plans into action through the organisation that has been built up. An important factor is the appointment of suitable staff, something which both headteachers and local authority administrators should regularly review. This is a continuing task since staff will be retiring, gaining promotion or resigning for other reasons from time to time. The fact that in a small school this may happen only once in every five years or so should not lead the head to become complacent about the appointing task; as should be self-evident the rarer and longer-term appointment in the small school can be more vital to the school as a whole than appointments in larger schools.

Controlling also means the improvement of staff through adequate training, much of which could be school-based. Heads should never become too preoccupied with day-to-day tasks so that they ignore the staff development needs of their teachers. Too often teachers choose to go on local authority courses for the wrong reasons; training courses are often made up of those who do not really need them while individuals who would benefit from some form of in-service work are ignored. Staff development and in-service education, for both individual career prospects and the needs of the school, should form a central part of the controlling task of every headteacher.

Controlling, directing or co-ordinating, puts together the plan and the organisation. Without a plan a happy and hardworking teaching staff could well be efficiently moving towards the wrong objective. Without organisation effective individual teachers could find their work being counteracted by others. The vital importance of control therefore becomes apparent.

Evaluation

Although evaluating education is extremely difficult it must be attempted. Whether heads like it or not they are currently open to public scrutiny under the general umbrella of accountability. It is important to ensure that those to whom we are accountable realise that education is not producing motor cars or tins of baked beans and that achievement cannot be measured in units produced per year or even on an accurate cost-benefit basis. The difficulty of achieving educational evaluation is compounded by the variable nature of the input to the system. Having said this, schools and local authorities must accept that they have a duty to monitor how well they are meeting their objectives.

Any conscious attempt to achieve some form of 'output measurement' is immediately open to cries of 'eleven-plus testing', 'payment by results' and so on. Obviously the measurement technique must remain the tool of the professional and not become his master. In any, case until objectives are defined it is useless to measure achievement against them.

Because educational evaluation is difficult there is the temptation to assume that objectives can only be met or 'output' improved by increases in resources, for example, improvements in pupil-teacher ratios. A degree of indulgent and misguided spending may result on the rather dubious and unproven grounds that 'it is a good thing'. While not arguing against the case for improved resources for education, particularly in the primary school, all heads should ask what they themselves can do through better management to improve their schools.

This must be the essential task of evaluation; to allow us to appraise and improve. Evaluation must be followed by further planning otherwise management becomes a sterile exercise which ends up like so many primary school schemes of work -in the bottom drawer of the filing cabinet. The essential nature of management is that it is cyclical and not linear; management never comes to an end but is always pursuing improvements.

Why is Education Management Different?

Although the general nature of management may be the same for the English primary school and the German steel industry there are some very distinctive features of education management which do not occur in business.

Education, unlike the business and industrial world, is not setting out to make a profit, even though the manpower theorists claim that it is an investment with a long-term return on capital. Nor are those who are engaged in the education service there to make personal fortunes. The reasons why people enter the teaching profession may vary from those who have a vocational call to those who in the words of the old saying 'teach because they cannot do'. The manager must accept that he is dealing with a group of professionally motivated people who, as a body, are both well-qualified and independent.

From this must come reinforcement of the point that education processes people and not goods. Thus the managerial relationship must be one of mutual trust and respect allowing, within flexible limits, considerable autonomy to the managed. The head's overall function must be to encourage purposeful activity without stifling individual initiative.

The difficulty for the head is that, lacking clearly accepted objectives or self-evident goals, the needs of his school must be determined in a context of continuous dialogue and competing demands. These demands and the dialogue can originate from outside the teaching profession and will therefore affect his freedom of action. Many of the constraints affecting decisions are not immediately apparent to the head who in many cases still feels he retains considerable freedom of action. It is now time to consider how much of a myth is the head's so-called freedom.

Autonomy in Teaching and Management

There can be few teachers who on visiting a school have not thought 'now if I were head of this school I would ...' In making such Utopian judgements we tend to forget the situational factors which might very well work against our plans, and when considering the success or lack of success of others we should bear in mind what autonomy they in fact have over their own curricula.

The pressures brought to bear upon the decision-maker in the school are both at a macro level (*e.g.*, governmental, local authority, teacher union) and at a micro level (*e.g.*, points allowances, retirement age), but we should commence our consideration with the individual. The head who wishes to alter the curriculum of his school should consider, if he is wise, his own personality. No two heads are alike in their authority but from their personal leadership will flow the bureaucratic structure of their schools. Apart from the variety of authority taken up by heads their very effectiveness will also vary. It is therefore as well to remember that the head's autonomy can be no greater than his own quality of leadership, no matter how large or small the other pressures upon him.

Let us assume that our hypothetical head has a certain charisma enabling him to encourage and lead his fellow members of staff. This is vital if he is to achieve any curriculum changes which are to become institutionalised, as opposed to those which die a lingering death in the stockroom—but it is not enough. Many pressures, both seen and unseen, are upon him. English schools and teachers pride themselves on their degree of freedom from central governmental control. However, that freedom may be something of a myth. A head who, for instance, wished to abolish a daily assembly or regular religious instruction, would find himself breaking the law. But it is in a more subtle manner that central control usually makes itself felt.

A decision by government to promote a particular piece of legislation is very likely to force LEAs and schools to divert resources away from their top priorities. The laudable 1970 Education Act brought mentally handicapped children into the school system but its affect in some areas was to slow down the development of other parts of special education. Even more insidious perhaps are the Employment Protection Act and the Health and Safety at Work Executive. Again these are praiseworthy attempts at improving the lot of individual employees but they restrict managerial flexibility and in the case of the Health Executive may even exert a direct force on the curriculum. As another example government policy during the late seventies was to transfer central grants towards metropolitan areas and this made the task of rural authorities much more difficult. The hidden hand of government will be seen in many of the constraints which follow.

What emerges is a complex and interwoven picture of constraints on a head's autonomy. Apart from central government the macro level of constraint could be subdivided into three main areas: resources, societal, and professional. However, these too are interlinked and can combine to restrict a head's freedom.

When considering resources, both financial as well as human resources must be taken into account. The local authority's ability and willingness to allow the school sufficient 'points' for adequate staff to be encouraged is important, as also is the head's flexibility in deploying his capitation allowance. It is in fact in the resource area that the local authority exerts its greatest pressure on the development of the curriculum. An LEA might have an expertise in, say, primary French, and extra money and equipment may be found for this area of the curriculum, while another is relatively starved. Pressure groups within an authority, whether officers, councillors or advisers, may also influence the resources available to the school, and hence the freedom of the head in determining the curriculum. As with the other constraints the two elements of human and financial resources are entwined and this can be seen in the field of in-service training. A head who wishes to introduce family grouping will want the staff who are to undertake it to be well trained. The LEA may have funds available and be willing to set up a course; it may have funds but divert them into other areas; or it may have no spare funds whatsoever.

Of course, the converse can also be true. External factors can often influence a head into undertaking curriculum changes which are not his own decision, and in so doing may prevent him from starting a more personal scheme. Such factors may be the arrival of the local authority's adviser bearing largess if the head will undertake such and such a scheme, or the provision of a high-powered in-service course in language development which persuades the head that the county 'believes in' language development, and therefore if the head introduces it he will do his promotion prospects no harm.

I have concentrated on resources as applied to in-service training, but a local authority can encourage or restrict the curriculum through the manipulation of resources in other areas. If the county architect builds new primary schools on an open plan basis, a curriculum suited to such schools will be encouraged. If a museum loan service operates it will help those heads who wish to encourage lively history teaching. Many other examples can be cited showing how authorities can encourage development in one field but restrict it in another.

The methods open to a head of influencing the decisions of an LEA in the resource area are limited. If he is fortunate he may be nominated as a representative member of the education committee and thereby gain a voice in direct decision-making. More possibly he may sit on a variety of working parties, the decisions of which influence the curriculum in his own school. Even more likely still, he may, as a member of a professional association, become part of a pressure group which has varying degrees of success. But it must be accepted that a head has more control over the constraints peculiar to his own school, than over a county-wide area.

Despite what some teachers might think, schools are provided for the benefit of society as a whole and not just to give employment to a work force of half a million. It is perhaps reasonable that society should exert some pressure on curriculum decisions, and this is done in both an overt and a covert way.

The labour market, as the employing section of the community, exerts a very real influence on the decisions of the headteacher. In general terms the employers' demands for certificates of competence have encouraged the extension of the examination system from GCE to CSE and now to GEE. The examinations themselves restrict considerably the options open for curriculum development in the upper secondary school, even with the introduction of Mode 3.

If the expectations of employers restrict options nationally, the very existence (or lack of it) of local industry can have a dramatic effect on individual schools. A head wishing to introduce business courses in a rural community is likely to encounter opposition as might the head of an East London comprehensive in attempting to introduce rural studies. The latter head may have excellent educational, even social, reasons for showing the children of Stepney that milk does not come from a bottle, but the relevance of such a course is bound to be questioned by the local community. Although the influence of examinations and employers is felt more directly by secondary schools, primary heads should not ignore completely their indirect and perhaps hidden influence on the primary curriculum.

The community may be concerned at a lack of literacy or numeracy in schools, and political capital can easily be made from this, developing the concern still further. In such a climate the headteacher might well think twice before introducing some aspect of the curriculum which might seem to trivialise 'real' learning. The impact and follow-up of Prime Minister Callaghan's 'Ruskin' speech at Oxford in 1976 is likely to be with us for some time. Communities are no more homogeneous than headteachers and thus the constraints of one area may be the enthusiasm of the next. The primary head wishing to start sex education may find great difficulty in persuading parents to agree to it while a neighbouring school is operating such a scheme very successfully.

Apart from numerous informal contacts with the community at large the head is likely to meet 'society' in two formal ways: through a parent-teacher association (PTA) or some other association of parents, if one exists at his school, and at meetings of governors, or managers. The PTA will provide the more articulate parents with a platform to voice their opinions on the curriculum, but at the same time will allow the head to display his curriculum wares to advantage. How many schools have held parents' evenings on 'Nuffield Maths'? A head can also use a PTA to encourage certain schemes positively by raising money for a kiln, or infant equipment, or a video-tape machine.

If heads are able to control PTAs more easily than they can the LEA, the same might also be said for the head's relationship with his governors. In theory at least the governors have responsibility for the curriculum, and a wise head can use his governors to get that little extra from resources which will turn his innovation into action.

Of very great importance to the head as a decision-maker will be the professional opinion of his colleagues outside, the school. Closest to hand will be the heads of neighbouring schools and the sensible head will work closely with them on curriculum innovation. He will steer clear of projects which will make transfer across the board or up the ladder difficult: an infant head should consult junior colleagues before introducing new reading methods and a tertiary principal would be unwise to demand British Constitution as a course entrance requirement if it is not taught in the feeder secondaries.

The influence of advisers will make itself felt and they can act as encouragers or dampeners of enthusiasm. As they often have small funds of their own they can influence the curriculum beyond the credibility of their own reputation.

Professional advisory bodies such as the Schools Council and the Council for Education Technology will also restrict the autonomy of the head, if only to suggest ideas which the head later regards as his own. A consensus of a sensible or relevant curriculum is handed down from such bodies and heads will think very carefully before going against such ideas. Professional acceptance is a weighy thing for the decision-maker to have on his side.

We have seen so far how many constraints conspire together to restrict the autonomy of the head. Take the simple example of a new reading scheme which a school wishes to introduce: there may not be enough money to buy it; there may not be teachers trained to use it effectively; the advisers may not like it; parents might not consider it relevant; the Schools Council may not give it their imprimatur. At the same time we must realise that education is a business and a head must be very strong to resist the pressures of all these groups if they are urging him to take up a particular scheme.

But let us assume that our head has gained the necessary resources, has convinced the parents and is in accordance with accepted educational opinion. He is all set to go: or is he? It is at this stage that he has to face the internal, micro factors which restrict his autonomous action. Unless the head is fortunate enough to have been consulted frequently on the design of his school, and to have chosen his complete staff, any changes he might make will have to be within an inherited framework.

The size of school and the buildings, the determinants of which lie largely outside the head's prerogative, can profoundly influence decision-making within the school. The very size of the establishment can limit the available number of allowances above Scale 1 and this affects the options open to the innovator. The architecture of the school strongly influences curricular decisions. A modern open-plan primary school will encourage cooperative teaching: a century-old school will make a different learning situation inevitable.

While both the size and shape of the school influence internal decision-making, just as important is its situation. A neighbourhood school in an urban area cannot sustain all the activities of a rural school. The local authority zoning system will determine the type of child who comes to the school, and hence the curriculum which is suitable.

When attempting to change curricula the head must be aware of the existing curriculum. Reading schemes in primary schools cannot be changed overnight; maths courses cannot be altered in mid-stream. If new concepts are to be accepted and made to work the head must bide his time.

A headteacher can manipulate to his advantage some buildings and he can also adjust his staffing and organisational structure to suit his own ideas, within the confines already suggested. However, if he fails to carry the teaching staff with him it is certain that his changes will fail. The experience of the teachers in working with the new methods, their personalities, their willingness to work as a team, will all contribute to the success or failure of new schemes. A wise head can convince his staff to alter their existing arrangements, but he will lead rather than force. He must be aware that some staff, perhaps as able and dedicated as himself, may themselves wish to make changes which conflict with his own views. Various groups may well form within a staff and need delicate handling. It may be a truism, but any curriculum development will only be as good as the teaching staff.

It is clear that the head's freedom to choose his curriculum is circumscribed, right from the type of pupil before him up to the Secretary of State. A head who is aware of these constraints will be able to manipulate the system and make compromises with, every chance of success. A head who attacks the problem directly may well decide never to become involved in controversial decision-making again. It is now appropriate to look in more detail at the primary school and its headteacher in relation to these constraints.

Education Management in Central and Local Government

Any primary teacher who has worked in more than one local authority will know that the experience of education can vary to quite a large degree from one place to another. This is the result of power and authority in education residing among a number of people and organisations, especially headteachers, local authorities, the Department of Education and Science, and Parliament. Teachers, but even more so parents, find it difficult to know who to turn to for decisions, advice and appeals. The aim of this chapter is to show who is responsible for what, and where the primary head fits into the scheme of things.

THE DEPARTMENT OF EDUCATION AND SCIENCE

The political chief of the DES is the Secretary of State, a senior member of the government with a seat in the cabinet. He is responsible for all functions of the education service in England as well as other aspects of the arts and science. Welsh schools are administered from the Welsh Office by the Secretary of State for Wales.

The administrative head of the DES is the Permanent Under-Secretary of State who, as his title suggests, is likely to be at the department longer than his minister. Departments within the DES deal with specific branches of the service and territorial teams deal with matters relating to the LEAs in their area.

The ears and eyes of the DES are, of course, Her Majesty's Inspectors, headed by a senior chief inspector. However, HMIs are jealous of their independence which is symbolised in their title and in their formal appointment by the monarch. About forty HMIs work at Elizabeth House, headquarters of the DES, and a few are seconded to other organisations such as the Schools Council or are posted abroad. The majority will be assigned to territorial divisions covering part of the country.

HMIs have as a basic function the advice and inspection of schools and in doing this they disseminate knowledge about curriculum and organisation. This is backed up by the many long and short courses organised by the inspectorate. They also meet regularly with LEA officers to act as an important, but not the sole, means of communication between the LEA and the DES.

Increasingly since Prime Minister Callaghan's speech at Ruskin College, Oxford, which started the 1977 great debate on education, the inspectorate has spent time on centrally based activities such as the 1978 survey of primary schools, and contributing to the growing collection of occasional papers on aspects of the education service. It is also involved with departmental working parties and other committees such as the National Foundation for Educational Research (NFER), Council for National Academic Awards (CNAA) and the Schools Council.

The 1944 Education Act instructs the Secretary of State 'to promote the education of people' and 'to secure the effective execution by local authorities, under his control and direction, of the national policy for providing a varied and comprehensive education service in every area'. But the DES does not build schools, it does not employ teachers and, despite ventures into the curriculum in the late seventies, it does not prescribe what should be taught.

In reality the Secretary of State has a regulating function, setting down minimum standards of provision and the context in which the service must be administered locally. He achieves this through the control of resources and through regulation. Resources are controlled via finance, buildings and teachers, and these are discussed in detail in other chapters of the book. It is worth spending a little time here considering the control of LEAs through regulations.

REGULATIONS

Acts of Parliament

It is through Parliament that all legislation must pass and since, in the end, our education is dependent on the law it is in Parliament that the ultimate control resides. Our present system is based upon the 1944 Education Act, amended and extended by a number of less comprehensive acts since. These acts determine what should happen by making it somebody's specific responsibility. Duties are imposed upon individuals or institutions and they are given the power to carry them out. In many cases there is an element of discretion between the duty of an authority and its power. Both central and local government are told what they must do, or may do, through the various acts; any action beyond this would be *ultra vires*, that is, beyond the law. This could include, for example, any LEA attempting to prescribe what mathematics books could be used in its schools.

Statutory Instruments

These are issued by the DES and have the force of law.

They normally detail the conditions necessary to adhere to a general clause in an Act of Parliament. The 1944 Act says education must be full-time for school children; the 1959 Regulation or Statutory Instrument details how many days and hours this in fact means.

Circulars

These set out in detail the government's policy on particular issues. Many of them are in fact non-party political, dealing with such things as school meals. However, the more well-known tend to be controversial, such as 10/65 on comprehensive reorganisation. The second set of figures on a circular identify the year in which it was issued.

Administrative Memoranda

These give advice to authorities on specific topics, usually interpretation of Education Acts.

The DES has in the past had a reputation for being isolationist, cut off from the rest of government thinking. This may have been partly because ministers and civil servants became almost totally involved in the educational world. We are now seeing a change of emphasis away from this detached view of education towards one of greater accountability and involvement in curriculum issues. Initiatives started under the Labour government of 1974-9 include the setting up of the Assessment of Performance Unit and the so called 'Great Debate'. The latter involved wide-ranging discussions on the curriculum at a series of conferences and set every LEA the task of completing a list of questions sent out in a DES circular. The department is, of course, still restricted to its role within legislative limits but it is now taking a stronger lead in collecting and disseminating examples of good practices. The role of central government is, therefore, being sharpened although, as we shall see, the local authorities, teacher associations and schools will not easily be subordinated to central control, particularly since many HMIs are reluctant to go too far along the centralist road.

LOCAL EDUCATION AUTHORITIES

The 1944 Act says in section 6 that: 'the local education authority for each county shall be the council of the county, and the local education authority of each county borough shall be the council of the county borough.' These councils derived their powers from the County Councils Act of 1888 and the Education Act of 1902, but a major change took place in 1965 when the Greater London Council took over the administration of Middlesex and parts of Kent, Essex, Hertfordshire and Surrey. The Outer London Boroughs were given responsibility for education but within the boundary of the new London County Council a special elected education authority was set up known as the Inner London Education Authority (ILEA).

The rest of England and Wales was reorganised in 1974. A Royal Commission set out the basic principles to be followed which were: that local authority areas should have a common purpose based on the interdependence of town and country; that the responsibility for personal services should be with the same authority (e.g., education, social services); that the new authorities should be normally larger than the old county boroughs, yet small enough to remain in touch with the public.

As a result of this the number of LEAs was reduced in 1974 from 163 to 104. The new local government system is basically two-tier with county and district councils. In metropolitan areas the district is responsible for education, in the remainder it is the responsibility of the county. Reorganisation had a profound effect on many parts of the country: proud county boroughs became parts of a shire county and lost their educational independence; new counties such as Avon tried to consolidate the educational provision made previously by four authorities (Somerset, Gloucestershire, Bristol and Bath); a few counties disappeared or became rumps of their former selves, *e.g.*, Somerset.

At the same time reorganisation took place in the Health Service, and Area Health Authorities (AHA) took over many of the responsibilities of the School Health Service previously exercised by local authorities. Understandably the AH As were based on hospital provision but this has caused boundary problems in some parts of the country. A quarter of the Somerset LEA is administered by the Wiltshire AHA with consequent problems of coordination and liaison.

All is not well with these reorganisations, although it should be said that they have had only a few years to prove themselves during a time of rapid inflation and scarce resources. However, another health service reorganisation is quite likely and the ten major cities in the country may eventually gain control of some personal services, possibly including education, as a result of so-called 'organic change'.

Members

In the main there are three groups of people who work in the administration of a local education authority: elected members, officers and advisers or inspectors. It is the elected members, the councillors, who are ultimately responsible for the decisions of the local education authority, and they are elected by us, the public, at the regular local elections.

If is important for the headteacher to remember that a council has other functions beyond education, and members of the council may have other interests beyond education, or indeed no interest in education at all. However, before deciding on any educational matter a council must consider a report from its education committee to which it may delegate any educational functions apart from the levying of a rate.

The education committee will have a majority of elected laymen, but it will be augmented by co-opted members who must have experience in education or be acquainted with the educational conditions in the area. The education committee will set up a number of sub-committees charged with specific tasks or the overseeing of specific areas of policy or management. The structure of sub-committees varies from one authority to another but a typical example is shown in the diagram overleaf.

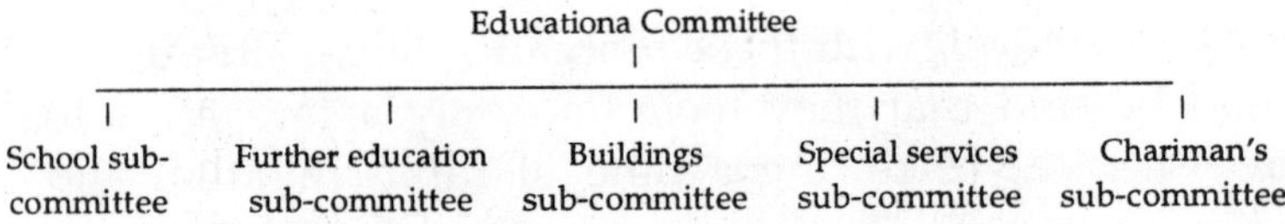

The schools' sub-committee will consider policy relating to the statutory parts of the school system and in some authorities there are separate primary and secondary committees. 'Schools sub' tends to be prestigious and there can be a heavy work-load for members. The further education (FE) sub-committee is concerned with post-school education and may cover youth and adult education, although these areas are sometimes separate committees or combined into a community sub-committee. Local education authorities are among the largest estate managers in the country and the buildings sub-committee will be involved in all aspects of site purchase and disposal, as well as liaising with schools and FE sub over building programmes. The special services sub-committee will have responsibility for the education of handicapped children and it is likely that the recommendations of the Warnock Report will cause some changes in the make-up and responsibilities of this committee. Frequently special services will also encompass more general services such as transport, school meals and crossing patrol duties. Finally, some authorities have an executive committee known as chairman's sub-committee which allows sub-committee chairmen to discuss issues of a broad policy nature before meetings of the full education committee.

The committee structure may appear cumbersome even though there have been some attempts at streamlining since reorganisation in 1974. It does enable the more important policy issues to be discussed in detail several times before the policy is confirmed by full council although urgent matters can be undertaken by the chairman through 'chairman's action', and reported at the next sub-committee meeting, or by officers under delegated powers.

Matters of detail or policy will go before the appropriate sub-committee and any decision will be recommended in a report to the full education committee. Here decisions can be questioned and if the full committee is not satisfied the matter can be referred back to the sub-committee for further discussion. If expenditure is involved the decision may be passed to a finance committee (comprising members who may be apathetic to, or even anti-education, as well as the pro-education lobby) and then to full council. In some authorities the finance committee, or the policy and resources committee, acts as a type of Cabinet, but it must be remembered that before any council, in its capacity as the local education authority, takes a decision on any education matter, it must by law ask for a report from its education committee.

Officers

It is the elected members of the council who carry the ultimate responsibility for the LEA's service but delegate the day-to-day administration to, and are advised by, professional education officers. The professional staff are headed by a chief education officer and he is assisted by a number of officers with specific responsibilities, usually relating to sub-committee areas. In many parts of the country the education service is the biggest local enterprise, with an annual budget, even in a small area, of £80 million, and therefore the task of the education officer is similar to that of a manager in a large company. Even third tier officers, only a few years from their last teaching post, can find themselves responsible for budgets of £10 million or more. Education officers are recruited from qualified, honours graduate teachers and have their own professional association, the Society of Education Officers, and their own trade union, the Association of Education Officers.

Just as the sub-committee structure varies from one authority to another so does the education officer hierarchy and indeed the nomenclature. However, a typical structure is:

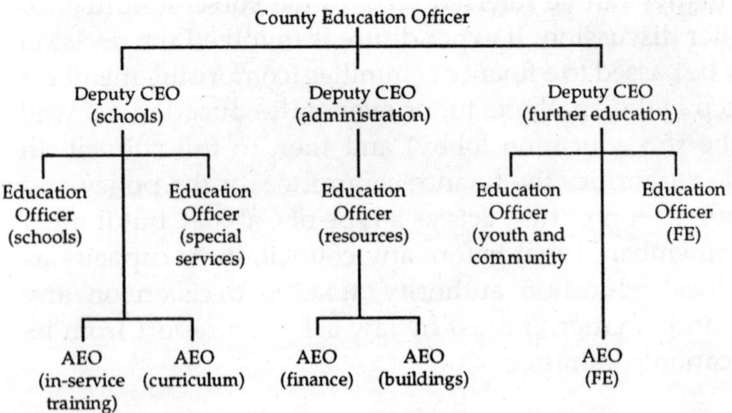

In recent years an increasing number of CEOs have moved towards a multiple deputy arrangement, with each deputy taking charge of a branch of the service; this is a more effective means of management than having a line deputy.

The professional education officers, recruited from a teaching background, are supported by administrative and clerical staff, the more senior of whom will have graduate, or graduate equivalent, qualifications in management or administration. The services of the treasurer and the architect will usually be shared with the rest of the authority.

The precise relationship between elected member and education officer will vary with the structure of the authority, the political make-up and motivation of the majority party, and the individual character and personality of chief officer and chairman of committee. Generally the members will agree the policy, officers will implement it. The policy may often be decided on the basis of a report from the CEO but the officers are not the sole repositories of policy ideas. In essence the officer represents the 'educational' constituency based on a knowledge of, and expertise in, the teaching profession. The member represents the wider needs of the community and if a primary head wishes to fight a policy decision he must direct his criticisms to member as well as to officer.

Advisers

Each LEA will have a larger or smaller force of educational advisers with a dual, and sometimes conflicting, role. The adviser's job is to support and advise individual schools and heads, and also to advise the chief education officer on specific parts of his service. In doing this he may take on some degree of an inspectorial function. In 1968 Sir W. Houghton identified seven major tasks of a local adviser:

1. help with staff requirements and promotion;
2. encouragement and help to young teachers;
3. development of in-service and induction training;
4. transmission of current educational thinking;
5. advice on new buildings and equipment;
6. appraisal of individual schools as a whole;
7. channel of communication between school and administration.

The HMI has a brief to ensure that local educational standards are adequate, and to monitor the nation's provision as a whole. The local adviser will be concerned to gain sufficient resources for his own subject for the schools in his area and to make certain that their needs are presented at 'court'. A head can seek the support of an adviser for his particular requirements but he should not forget that the adviser also has a duty to make sure that LEA policies are being carried out.

Local advisers may have an area, or pastoral function; they may have a specialist function, such as mathematics, language development or music; or they may have a phase function, such as primary, infant or special. They will usually report to the chief education officer via a chief adviser, and they may have the support of a number of advisory teachers whose job will entail more direct work within the classroom, often of an in-service training nature.

If a primary head is to manage his school effectively he needs to know his key advisers. Contrary to popular mythology most advisers are not refugees from the classroom. They have held senior positions in schools at head of department or headship level, and their acquaintance with a large number of schools enables them to offer fair and objective support. The advisory service offers a head the opportunity to make the most of his resources, human and financial, and it offers, him an entree to the decision-making world of the authority.

PRESSURE GROUPS

An increasing influence on the decision-making processes of our modern democracy has been exerted by the various pressure groups representing the collective and sometimes sectionalised interests of their members. It is possible to distinguish between those groups which are accepted as an almost formal part of the policy machinery bureaucracy and those which operate outside the system but with sometimes surprisingly effective results. Examples of the latter are the teachers' campaign against corporal punishment (STOPP) and the National Federation of Parent Teacher Associations.

Although the informal groups may well cause headaches for a headteacher from time to time, or although he may in fact be a member of one of them, the longer-term effects of the pressure groups' action will come from those that are accepted as part of the consultative process. These groups fall into two main sections: those which act as the collective voice of the local authority employers, and those which act for the teachers. A third section which may well have an increasing influence on headteachers and the management of education generally comprise other public sector unions, notably the National Association of Local Government Officers (NALGO) and the National Union of Public Employees (NUPE). At this stage we are more concerned with teachers and employers.

Until 1973 there were six local authority associations covering England and Wales including the Association of Education Committees (AEC). The AEC, under the energetic leadership of Lord Alexander, kept the influence of education high within the local authority structure but soon after the reorganisation of local government in 1974 the new authorities claimed that local government educational interests should represent education *authorities* and not education committees. With fewer committees continuing in membership the AEG was forced to disband and the most dominant voice on the education scene since the war went into well-earned retirement.

This meant that after reorganisation three national groups represented local authorities and one of these (the Association of District Councils) was not involved in education. The other two remain—the Association of County Councils (ACC) and the Association of Metropolitan Authorities (AMA) covering metropolitan counties, metropolitan districts, the GLC, the London Boroughs and the City of London. The AMA and the ACC have set up their own joint educational organisation, the Central Council of Local Education Authorities (CLEA).

The local authority associations have a continuing dialogue with government and are formally consulted on legislation, circulars and other issues of relevance to local education authorities. They have a statutory rights to be involved in the determination of the rate support grant (RSG) and of teachers' salaries. Their evidence is sought on every committee affecting education and they have members on all educational councils and consultative committees. They also have a close relationship with a significant number of MPs. Therefore, when you vote in your local elections your vote not only goes to determine the eventual policy of your own education authority, but also, by extension, wields an influence on the national, scene.

The teachers' unions would not see themselves as part of the establishment but they are perhaps more involved than they recognise. They cannot work from the same base as other trade unions because they represent among their membership headteachers who manage the institutions which collectively form the establishment. They also represent rank and file teachers who are concerned with working in a system which is part of the establishment. Their day-to-day negotiations are with education officers most of whom are teachers themselves and some of whom may still be 'left profession' members of the union. Furthermore, the broad membership of the unions makes it difficult to get agreement except on fairly wide issues such as working conditions and salaries. Despite some industrial action in the seventies and a more militant stance on individual issues the teacher unions remain essentially soft in their relationships with government and basically conservative in outlook.

However, the unions are powerful bodies with a joint membership of around half a million. In consultative status they are very close to the local authority associations and they are consulted about most of the issues which affect the interest of their members or educational policy in general. At local level a Teachers Consultative Committee, comprising LEA members and representatives of the recognised teacher unions, will offer advice and comment to the education committee. The unions have a dual function: to act in a usual trade union role by advancing the conditions of their members (and making the assumption that what is good for teachers is good for education as a whole) and to act as a force in creating opinion about the organisation and content of education.

As is the case with most union—employer relations the differences get far more publicity than the agreements. The unions have frequent meetings with local officials and on many issues the local authority will share the union view rather than the view of the DES. On some of these issues education officers will identify with the teachers' interests. And where differences remain, there is at least a shared understanding of the problems involved.

In the last fifteen years the influence and behaviour of the teachers' unions has broadened. As government has become more involved in the economic functioning of the country through such means as pay and prices policies, the teachers' unions have sought an entry to the powerful economic departments of government. This has led to the National Union of Teachers (NUT), the National Association of Schoolmasters/Union of Women Teachers (NAS/UWT) and the former Association of Teachers in Technical Institutions (ATTI) becoming full and active members of the TUC. At the same time teachers have found themselves, with doctors and nurses, as part of a more financially aware group of vocationally oriented professionals, as they see economic and social values changing around them.

Government in education is, therefore, a complex business and the unwary head can be caught out by the confusing and sometimes ambiguous nature of the relationships. The sensible head will be aware of the constraints upon him through the central and local government system but he will also know how to use the system through its policy of checks and balances and through its formal and informal set up to bring his own influence to bear.

School Governors

School governors, or managers as those in primary schools used to be known, are a tier of educational administration peculiar to England and Wales. No similar body exists in the rest of the world and their presence reflects the evolution of English education which has combined community and political involvement with the devolution of as much power as possible to local level.

County Schools

Maintained schools comprise all schools run by local education authorities and this sector includes both county and voluntary schools. The whole cost of running a maintained school is met by the LEA and this includes maintenance of all the fabric in the case of county schools. At the moment two-thirds of the governors are appointed by the LEA and one-third by the minor authority ('the Council of any borough, or district or rural parish in the area served by the school and where the school serves more than one area then all these minor authorities acting jointly'). In a county school religious education and worship must be undenominational and in accordance with the agreed syllabus.

Aided Schools

An aided school is a voluntary school provided by a

religious denomination or an educational trust. The governors must be able and willing to find 15 per cent of the cost of any enlargement or improvement to bring the school up to regulations' standards. Two-thirds of the governors are called foundation managers, appointed by the body controlling the school and having a particular duty to ensure that the school is run in accordance with the trust deed.

Religious education is controlled by the governors and must be in accordance with the trust deed. Secular instruction remains under the control of the local education authority.

Teachers are appointed by the governors and remain their 'servants', subject to the establishment set by the LEA and the authority's acceptance of their ability and qualifications to teach secular subjects. School meals staff are appointed by the LEA, but non-teaching staff, subject to the authority's requirements, are appointed by governors.

The governors are responsible for the exterior maintenance and repair of the building, with an 85 per cent contribution from the DES. The LEA is responsible for the interior.

Controlled Schools

These are voluntary schools where the governors have surrendered their responsibility for finding 15 per cent of the cost of improving or enlarging the school. This has passed to the LEA who accept the whole cost of such improvements. In return the LEA controls the appointment of teachers, although the governors must be involved in the appointment of the head and the authority must agree to a percentage of the teaching staff being 'reserved teachers' for religious education. This must be in accordance with the agreed syllabus but denominational instruction may be provided twice a week.

The Instrument of Government

This defines the membership and contribution of governing bodies and although instruments vary they generally include the provisions shown overleaf.

1. The constitution and the appointment of any *ex officio* member (*i.e.,* the parish incumbent).
2. The tenure of appointment of members, generally speaking for the life of the local education authority, though foundation governors often have a life of five years.
3. Method of appointing the chairman and vice-chairman (unless stated in the instrument the incumbent is not *ex officio* chairman in a voluntary school).
4. Provision for preventing the appointment of governors having a financial interest in the school.
5. Arrangements to end the tenure of a member for bankruptcy, incapacity or resignation, and to fill such casual vacancies.
6. Provision for calling and recording meetings, and their frequency.

Usually the instrument for county schools is a general one; each voluntary school has its own.

Articles of Government

Again these vary from place to place but they are designed to guide governors and heads in the management of schools. Their central purpose is to define the function of the governors and set limits to the authority and relationship of governors *vis-a-vis* the head and the LEA. The articles will normally include:,

1. the place of the school in the educational system;
2. the general conduct of the school, *i.e.*, in accordance with provisions of Parliament, the articles of government and the LEA regulations;
3. the financial responsibilities of governors. This is generally limited to having general financial oversight in the case of primary schools although most governors are able to authorise minor repairs. Governors usually happily accept their task of informing the LEA when, in their belief, financial resources have failed to meet the school's needs. Some authorities are devolving more financial responsibility to schools and in these areas the governors' role will be enhanced;
4 the upkeep of premises, including the carrying out of minor repairs, informing the LEA of the needs of the school for changes in accommodation, and the use of school premises outside school hours subject to the provision of the LEA and the Education Acts;
5 the appointment, suspension or dismissal of non-teaching staff;
6 the organisation of the school, including conduct and curriculum;
7 the fixing of occasional holidays;
8 dealing with leave of absence requests from staff, subject to the LEA's regulations;
9 the suspension of pupils.

Provision is made for full consultation between the head, governors and local education authority and opportunity is given for assistant staff to make their views known either through the head or in some cases by attendance at the meeting. Heads are entitled to attend governors' meetings unless excluded for good reason during the discussion of specific business.

Copies of the articles must be given to every teacher upon appointment, or facilities made available to them for reading the articles. Few teachers take up the opportunity to read them but the advice to all new heads is, read and understand your articles of government.

The Education Bill, 1978

In April 1975 the government set up a Committee of Inquiry under Councillor Tom Taylor to 'review the arrangements for the management and government of maintained primary and secondary schools in England and Wales, including the composition and function of bodies of managers and governors, and their relationships with local education authorities, with new teachers and staff of schools, with parents of pupils and the local community at large; and to make recommendations.'

The committee reported in 1977 under the title, 'A New Partnership for our Schools' and the recommendations included a four-way governing body of LEA representatives, school staff, parents (and where appropriate pupils) and the local community. Minor authority representation would be abolished and the headteacher would be an *ex officio* governor. The new Taylor governors would set the aims of the school and review progress towards meeting these aims. Systematic training for governors was also recommended.

Reaction to Taylor's proposals was swift. Some authorities claimed that they were already meeting many of the recommendations; a survey in 1979 showed that most authorities already made provision for parent and teacher governors. The minor 'authorities naturally resented losing their direct representation and most headteachers felt their position as an adviser to the governors was stronger than being an *ex officio* member. In the area of the 'secret garden of the curriculum' one of teachers' leader claimed that the proposals were 'a busybodies' charter'. One of the strongest arguments against Taylor was the cost of the proposals: one authority estimated a doubling of administrative costs attributable to 'Taylor' governors.

After due consultation the Secretary of State introduced a bill into the 1978 session of Parliament which included sections on the government of schools. The main features of the bill relating to governing bodies were:

1. All primary schools were to have 'governors' in place of managers (throughout this book the term 'governor' has been used).
2. The Secretary of State was to be enabled by regulations to determine the composition and site of all governing bodies but would be required to ensure that they included:
   (a) those appointed by the local education authority;
   (b) those who are teachers in the school (elected by the teachers);
   (c) those who are parents of children in the school (elected by the parents);
   (d) representatives of the community in the case of secondary schools.

   The sections of the 1944 Act dealing with the prescriptions on the composition of governing bodies were due for repeal. The White Paper published after the bill outlined the regulations by which 2 would have been achieved and they were far more flexible than the original Taylor proposals.

3. Elections for teachers and parents were to be under rules made by the Secretary of State.
4. Provision for voluntary schools to be included in the general arrangements with the current one-third proportions being changed.

The fall of the Labour government in March 1979 meant that the bill was lost in the 1978-9 session of Parliament. However, the Conservative government elected in May 1979 promised legislation in due course to safeguard parental rights and reform school governing bodies.

Working with Governors

Some heads are afraid to make a decision without the consent of their governors while others hold governors in contempt. The wise run their own ship but enter into a partnership with governors and keep them fully informed. If governors are expected to play a central and active part in the life of the school, and to discuss, although not control, professional as well as procedural matters, a partnership of benefit to both parties can be established.

It can be very frustrating to explain educational matters to a committee of laymen, but it can bring the head back to earth. If the governors cannot understand the head's policies, are they good policies? If used well a governing body can be of a great source of strength for the head, especially in his relations with County Hall. Used badly splits will develop, which in a small village community can have catastrophic results.

The key governor is the chairman, so arrange to meet him fairly regularly between meetings. Ask his advice on community matters and show him the work of the school.

Invite all the governors to make regular visits to the school; indeed it is fair to tell them that you expect them to show such an interest. Ask the governors to invite members of your staff to occasional meetings so that they can explain the work of their classes or the area of the curriculum for which they have responsibility.

If governors are to feel part of the school they should be known well both by staff as well as by parents. If they are prepared to work hard and conscientiously, and if you as head are prepared to work with them, they will be a source of encouragement and assistance in what can often be a lonely job.

5

Primary School Finance

Heads of primary schools, particularly the smaller ones, often feel themselves to be the Cinderellas of the education service. The source of much of this feeling can be traced back to the apparent inadequate funding of primary education. Although the head's major and immediate problems may be the stretching of his capitation allowance it is worth reflecting on where the primary school fits into the set-up of education and the economy. If the headteacher can understand how the budget is compiled he has taken a major step in recognising his financial responsibility.

Education is by far the most expensive local government service and this can cause jealousy from other services and make it the first target of the treasurer's department in any cutbacks. It is not just the size of the education budget which causes comment but also its rapid growth. Although the comparison of statistics is always open to question (and there is not even agreement over what contributes education in total) it is clear that the service now has a much larger share of national resources than it did at the beginning of the century.

One reason for this is the increase of pupil numbers due to bulges in the birthrate, the raising of the school leaving age (ROSLA), better take-up rates in further education and so on. Many local politicians and economists would argue that the present dramatic decline in the birthrate should lead to a lessening of the demand for resources but as we shall see later the reverse is just the case; educationalists argue that not only does a slump in the birthrate give us an opportunity to improve matters but, *pro rata,* more must be pumped into the system merely for it to stand still.

Other reasons contributing to increased educational expenditure are the general growth of the economy as a whole, and major policy changes. It is in these areas that primary schools appear to have suffered relative to secondary, further and even special education. As an economy expands so does the demand for skilled manpower but it is to the secondary sector that resources are sent to meet the demand. The education acts of this century have been concerned with expansion at the upper end of schooling and resource allocation has reflected this. Secondary reorganisation and ROSLA have both been looked at enviously by primary heads, at least in terms of resource provision. On the other hand it seems that recent cuts have relatively improved the position of primary education.

When headteachers complain about the inadequacy of primary staffing ratios or capitation allowances they are often bewildered by the range of reasons given by the LEA. Building allocations, RSG, Public Expenditure Surveys, the Pool (see p. 62), and so on, seem to put up a smoke screen beyond which it is difficult to see.

Capital

There are, first of all, two major financial budgets of local councils—capital and revenue. Capital expenditure goes on the building and remodelling of schools. Each LEA submits to the DES a bid for a building allocation and is then notified before the beginning of the financial year how much it has been allocated. The DES allocation is in fact only permission for the LEA to spend its own money; it is not, as is often thought, an actual cash grant to the authority. The government uses these allocations as one way of regulating the national economy. After an authority has been notified of its allocation it will decide which projects can go forward and it will then set about borrowing the money required, usually through the Local Government Loan Board.

Revenue

Revenue is quite separate from capital and is the money which is used each year to cope with running costs. This expenditure includes the salaries of all employees, including teachers, capitation allowances, maintenance of school premises, in-service education, school meals, school transport and so on. Salaries and wages form the major part of the LBA's expenditure with teachers' salaries taking nearly 50 per cent of the total. In such a labour-intensive business this is not surprising although in recent years the proportion of teachers' salaries to non-teachers' has altered in the latter's favour. Now nearly 50 per cent of the people employed by an LEA are non-teachers and this has caused some criticism of an over-bureaucratic service. In fact the majority of these people are welfare assistants, clerical assistants in schools, school meals staff, cleaners etc. All of these services are provided by the local authority but if we look not just at how the money is spent but also at where it comes from we shall see that central government plays a substantial part.

The Budget

The budget-making process of any LEA is a very complicated business starting many months and often years before the beginning of the financial year. Estimates have to be made about the cost of continuing existing policies, allowing for different pupil numbers and any changes in the number of days a school is open during the year. Budgets for development items such as improved pupil-teacher ratios will be prepared in the hope that sufficient resources will be available to implement them. The budget then has to be prepared alongside the resources likely to be available and political decisions may have to be taken between raising the rate or contracting the service. But where do the resources come from?

Rates

The basic source of local authority income is the rate, although it is not the largest source. There has been much criticism in recent years about the inequitable system of levying rates and changes are likely in the not too distant future. However, the final result will be similar—money will be raised locally for local purposes.

Many people judge how well or badly a council is doing by the size of the rate demand each May. While most constituents are prepared for a modest 1 per cent or 2 per cent rise to improve services they have been horrified at the large increases of 15-20 per cent during the last few years due almost entirely to inflation. Council members are, therefore, very cautious about approving additional rate increases even when they are told that 100 extra teachers could be employed for just an extra penny on the rates.

There are other problems in justifying rate increases for education. What is a trifling sum in the education budget could make a major improvement in other services and, therefore, non-education committee members are likely to be sceptical of education's claims. Furthermore, there is little tangible evidence of 'value for money' in education as the service is one of the most difficult to quantify. Even if reasonable measuring tools could be agreed the results could not be seen in the short term. Council members have to rely in a large part, therefore, on the professional expertise and prejudice of teachers and education officers.

On the other hand, education has had, at least until recently, an emotional pull, and tends to be a good vote catcher. Education costs themselves are rarely criticised by the public although the distribution of resources within the service might be. There does not seem to be a trend, however, towards greater financial accountability, accentuated no doubt by the difficult financial situation generally, the sheer size of the education budget, and the inability of education to be the cure for all the social and economic ills we were told it would be in the sixties.

Education policy, whether the primary head likes it or not, has to be considered in the light of resources. As the revenue from rates has at least the virtue of some flexibility the limiting factor is not so much any proposed new policy itself but the political advisability of rate increases. Unfortunately, as we have seen, education is labour intensive. This, when added to the mandatory nature of much educational expenditure, means that anything other than basic provision is at risk. However, it is in these 'at risk' areas where educational progress can best be achieved.

Local authorities have not been able to raise enough from the rates even to cover basic services, however, and the bulk of the difference is provided by the government under a very complicated formula.

Rate Support Grant

The system of the rate support grant is meant to supplement the cash which an authority receives from the rates. RSG was introduced in 1966 as a refinement of the general grant which had been paid since 1958. The grant covers all services except housing subsidies. The Secretary of State for the Environment is required to consult with local authority associations and to take account of:

1. Current levels of prices, costs and wage awards and any likely variation in these during the period of the grant. This allows the government to determine cash limits in order to ensure that local government adheres to government pay policies.
2. Any likely change in the demand for services which might affect the grant, e.g., the declining birthrate, will affect the demand for education.
3. The need for developments and the extent to which it is reasonable to develop them. Thus the Secretary of State for Education and Science can claim to have included an extra 10,000 teachers in the RSG negotiations to develop in-service education. As we shall see, the equation is not as simple as that.

After negotiation the extent of central government aid is calculated as a percentage of the relevant expenditure and in recent years has been around 60 per cent. Specific grants, mainly to the police, are subtracted and the remainder is distributed under a complicated tripartite formula.

The three elements of this formula are 'domestic', 'resources' and 'needs'. The domestic element is distributed not to the spending authorities but to the rating authority (in a county that will be the district council) to cushion the householder against rising costs. This element is common to all authorities but the resources and needs elements can have a different effect in different authorities. The resources element is meant to help the poorer authorities without penalising the richer. The government provides sufficient resources to bring those authorities with a below average rate product up to the average. There are criticisms of the way this works in practice; for instance, rateable values tend to be poor indications of the real wealth of an authority.

The needs element, which makes up about 80 per cent of the total, is distributed on the basis of so-called objective factors such as pupil numbers and road mileage. It attempts to relate the income of an authority to the claims upon it. The largest part of the needs element is based upon population with the next most important being the 'education units'.

There is one factor in all of this which is crucial; despite arguments in RSG negotiations for extra teachers, in-service education and so on, the resulting grant is to the authority as a whole and education has to fight with other services for its share of the cake. It is, of course, unlikely that an individual authority would get completely out of line but it is impossible to tell how much education expenditure comes from the rates and how much comes from RSG. However, as education features highly in the needs element the RSG will tend to finance a larger part of education than over services and as a very rough guide it could be said that only about 25 per cent of education spending comes from the rates.

Controlling Public Expenditure

Great concern has been expressed recently about the percentage of gross national product devoted to public expenditure and the comment is frequently made that the country cannot spend more than it is prepared to earn. Public expenditure has risen from about 5 per cent of GNP in 1900 to a little under 50 per cent at the present time. It is understandable therefore that the government should wish to control such expenditure, particularly in inflationary times. Careful planning is essential in order to ensure that public spending as a whole can be financed, that services meet real social and demographical needs and that priorities between services are reviewed.

In 1958 the other 'Powden Committee' on the 'Control of Public Expenditure' recommended that there should be regular surveys of expenditure as a whole, including that of local authorities, looking at a period several years in the future in relation to likely resources. Ten years later a white paper set out a new system of presenting estimates to Parliament and the Public Expenditure Survey Committee (PESC) was born.

This committee reviews expenditure on the basis of continuing current policies and then takes into account bids from service ministries for development, a similar process to that going on in the local authorities. This process is completed by mid-summer and it is then up to the cabinet to decide what policy changes the government desires and what level of expenditure the country can afford. Towards the end of the year the Public Expenditure. White Paper will be published.

We have now reached a point where the local authority has guidance from the Public Expenditure Paper about the level of growth or reductions envisaged in its services, it knows in total the RSG being allowed and it has prepared total estimates based on continuation policies and developments. Before the full council meets to decide on the level of expenditure for the following year, the developments or cuts necessary and the rate demand, one other item must be fed into the financial equation—recoupment.

Recoupment

Recoupment is a process by which one authority pays

another for the use of its services, usually the cost of providing education for children across a border. It would be difficult to gauge the total cost of every individual place, therefore agreed standard rates are suggested by an inter-authority payments committee. Other sums of money may be recovered by 'recharging' other departments for their services, notably social services and area health authorities.

There remain three areas where local authorities share expenditure by paying a set sum according to children population into a 'pool' and then drawing from it according to need. These pools are for initial and some in-service training of teachers, advanced further education and the 'no area pool' which covers students who have no 'home' authority, such as the children of travellers or whose parents live abroad.

Where Does the Money Go?

It should now be clear that, although a refusal to grant a headteacher more money to improve his remedial provision might seem to be a naive and heartless attitude on the part of the LEA, the constraining factors on expenditure are both detailed and complicated. The individual primary head might only want £500 but, in total with all the other heads, who require £500 across the country, this could represent a considerable drain on the nation's resources.

Furthermore the budgetary discretion of LEAs is limited. The total percentage spent on primary education nationally is about 29 per cent compared with 23 per cent for secondary education. Administration and inspection account for a further 4 per cent and FE, teacher training, and related expenditure (meals, transport, etc) account for all but 12 per cent of the remainder.

However, that 12 per cent comprises debt charges, or interest, on schools already built and is, therefore, an area over which the LEA has no discretion. We have seen that education is a major employer, therefore nationally agreed salaries have to be paid. Other parts of the service are provided by statute, eg, transport, school meals, mandatory awards, and in effect only something like 15 per cent of the education budget is truly discretionary.

It is in this area that cuts are usually made and LEAs can be as mean or as generous as they like. Unfortunately it is also from this area that many of the essential components that make a school or education service effective are financed. An LEA has discretion about where on the Burnham range it fixes the number of points available to a school, with obvious effects on staff recruitment and school organisation. It also has discretion over the amount of maintenance given to its properties and the strength of its advisory and support services. In particular it has discretion over the level of capitation allowances.

School Income

The procedures outlined above will settle the overall level of resources in any one education authority and will determine the staffing allocation of a school and other centrally controlled expenditure. However, when it comes to cash in hand the head is usually faced with his capitation allowance, possibly supplemented by 'unofficial' school funds, with which to implement his curriculum policies. Traditionally, and in many cases remaining so today, the development of policy and its implementation financially has been solely in the hands of the headteacher. Too often scarce resources are not taken into consideration when making decisions about policy and yet it is surely impossible to separate a school's objectives from the money available to fulfil those objectives. At the very least, therefore, it is essential for heads to think of their capitation as a means to an end and not as a piggy bank which can be dipped into from time to time.

Capitation allowances are allocated to schools according to a scale determined by the LEA. It is a source of irritation to primary heads that an infant child is often worth only 50 per cent of a sixth former although when the specialist expenditure needs of secondary schools are considered the differential appears a little more reasonable. Nevertheless there are signs that the gap is beginning to narrow a little. The amounts allocated for day-to-day expenditures vary from LEA to LEA and as they may be intended for different specific functions it is difficult to compare one part of the country with another. Schools usually have discretion over spending on such things as textbooks, equipment and materials, consumable goods, servicing and hire of equipment, games visits and special expenses. Sometimes library books and furniture are included, and sometimes specific grants are made for these items. In some areas cleaning materials and even postage are included within capitation allowances on the assumption that heads are more likely to control such expenditure if directly educational needs might benefit. Occasionally additional allowances are given to individual schools to cater for specific needs.

Most LEAs give heads detailed advice about their expenditure from capitation but it is worth bearing in mind that purchase through consortium or authorised suppliers can sometimes be at a discount and that VAT can often be reclaimed through the LEA. Schools are usually given regular, often monthly, computer tabulations of their expenditure as an aid to financial control.

Although capitation is the main source of income for a school, LEAs will probably retain some funds centrally for curriculum development. This may be disbursed through the advisory service, or schools may be able to make direct bids for planned expenditure.

In addition to the funds provided by the local authority, there are usually other funds created for the benefit of the school and its pupils known as 'unofficial school funds'. These will usually be raised by PTAs, school functions, sponsored walks and so on, although a few schools ask parents to make a termly or annual donation to the school fund. If carried too far the latter practice is difficult to support as education is a 'free service' apart from rates and taxes.

The responsibility for such funds rests with the head and governors as the recipients or custodians of the money. Usually the only requirement of the LEA is that a certificate of audit be submitted annually to the chief education officer covering all such funds, certifying that normal approved audit practices have been followed. In the case of voluntary schools there may be other funds available for the benefit of the school and its pupils which are held by the trustees of the fund. These are administered quite separately from the local authority and an audit certificate for these funds is not normally required by the authority.

Much of the unofficial school fund will be raised in one way or another from the parents but it often seems that the same parents dig deeply into their pockets time and time again and repeatedly man the stalls at the summer fete or the Christmas fayre. It is worth reflecting on how many times in a year parents are asked to contribute to the school for such things as Christmas parties, school photographs, summer camp or visits, touring theatres, collections for the blind, Miss Smith's leaving present and so on. The list seems endless and not only is the cost to the individual sometimes large but regular demands can be irritating and counter-productive. It may be better, therefore, to have one or two major fund-raising events each year, keeping other financial requests to a minimum.

Most schools receive relatively little income other than capitation, school fund and the very occasional donation. Official income usually occurs under the following headings:

1. Sales of work, materials, etc. Materials not brought to school or purchased by pupils for practical work are charged against capitation allowance so finished articles which pupils wish to take home can be charged for and the income set against expenditure.
2. School meals: funds collected for this purpose should be banked promptly.
3. Private telephone calls: if postage and telephone charges are set against capitation, private calls should be charged for to offset the school's expenditure.
4. Bettings: the letting regulations of some LEAs allow governors to levy additional charges in appropriate cases to provide additional income for school purposes.

School Expenditure

In reviewing his expenditure the primary head will be grappling in miniature with the same problems faced by the LEA and the DES administrator: how can scarce resources be best allocated to forward the chosen policies of the school? As with central resources one cherished project, a staff library for instance, can only be afforded at the expense of something else, for example, new PE equipment. Priorities have to be decided and decisions made. How a head does this will depend on his style of leadership. The head carries great responsibility for establishing priorities between competing claims and some heads prefer to share this decision-making with their colleagues, or at least consult them before the final decision is taken.

However, in other schools a head will remain secretive about his resources, perhaps asking staff at some stage in the year what they would like and then deciding in an arbitrary fashion whether or not they can have it. In other schools staff will only be given resources if they actually take the initiative. Not only does such a management policy build up frustration and jealousies among staff but it also makes a nonsense of sensible planning and financial responsibility.

An alternative strategy employed by heads is to allocate a set amount to each teacher per term or year, possibly weighted to allow for class sizes or specialist responsibilities. This has the advantage of fairness and openness but if carried out too rigidly it can stifle experimentation and innovation and leads to a situation where no teacher can purchase major items for re-equipping his classroom. It also has the danger of allowing teachers to purchase conflicting schemes or projects and filling stockrooms with science kits which are only used for one year before the teacher concerned is promoted.

There is really no substitute for a regular review, with staff, of school policies and resource allocation. Before this is done funds should be set aside for consumable items, although there is also room for review with regard to this category. An 'emergency' fund should also be allocated to cover any unforeseen expenditure during the year. Sufficient money will also have to be set aside for any projects which are to be carried forward from previous years and which require continuing expenditure. These items can be seen as the school's continuation budget, allowing present policies to be carried forward for a further year.

What remains is the development budget and it is in this area in particular that staff discussion is essential. Much of this investment will have long-term implications and will have an effect on future policy decisions. Many of the projects considered for this money will be on a continuing basis needing injection of materials or equipment over a period of several years. A carefully planned and timetabled programme is desirable if the investment is to be fully effective. When these programmes are being considered the aims and objectives of the school must be central to the discussion. When resources are limited priorities have to be decided which are consistent with overall aims.

One of the basic management dilemmas is the amount of freedom that should be given to junior colleagues. We have seen in an earlier chapter how educational management differs from some other forms of management in the degree of professionalism involved in personal relationships. Too much freedom results in stock being purchased and rarely used; too little freedom leads to a dulling of initiative and a lack of personal involvement. What is necessary is participation in the setting of aims, and in resource decisions to reach those aims, while at the same time allowing for individual initiative and enthusiasm.

There is one final point for consideration about the question of allocating financial resources within primary schools, and that is in-service education. Teachers tend to 'spot' courses during the year which they would find useful and frequently return from them fired with new ideas and anxious to purchase the materials to put their ideas into practice. However, they find when back in school that no money is available and the ideas generated by the course never take hold. If in-service education is planned in a coherent way as part of overall staff development and policy implementation then the right courses would be attended and resources would be planned accordingly. Sometimes schools are allocated extra resources from the LEA when a member of staff returns from a course but unless attendance at the course has been considered as part of the school's policy the situation might arise that the school's aims are being unduly influenced from without. To be effective in-service training needs to be planned and the follow-up needs to be resourced.

Devolution of Financial Responsibility

So far we have been mainly concerned with how a head should deploy the capitation resources at his disposal. However, it is becoming more common for LEAs to give greater flexibility and discretion to head teachers to transfer expenditure from one budget heading to another. In this way heads have more control over the total resources available to their school. Such 'alternative use of resources' or 'virement' schemes should be discussed with and have the cooperation of the staff, especially where savings made through the deferment of appointments are 'vired' for materials or equipment. Used with care virement can allow a head to become a more effective manager provided that colleagues are aware of its reasons and understand the principles by which the decision was reached. Most authorities running virement schemes expect savings to be planned in one heading before they can be allocated to another. Fortuitous and retrospective savings are not usually entertained.

6

The Teaching Staff

Without doubt it is the teachers in a school who are the key to its success or failure. The best manager in a head's position is only as good as his staff will allow him to be, and despite the well-worn catch-phrase 'Johnny learned maths in spite of his teacher', even the brightest children need their work programmes developed, analysed and evaluated. To achieve the maximum results a head has two options:

1. To appoint new staff to suit his aims and objectives.
2. To develop existing staff to work towards the agreed policy.

The first choice seems the easier option but with falling school rolls and decreasing mobility on the part of teachers there will probably be fewer vacancies over the next few years, unless public expenditure is significantly increased to create more jobs. Even if you are fortunate enough to have vacancies to fill there is still a long road to travel before the successful appointment can be made.

Advertising

Whenever there is a vacancy in your school you should consider very carefully whether the new incumbent should be given the same responsibility as.his predecessor. This will provide you with an opportunity to give flexibility to curriculum innovation and to the composition of the staff. Before the existing teacher leaves it is important to carry out with him a review of his basic teaching job and any extra responsibilities which he has undertaken. The aim of this review is to see which parts of the job can perhaps be discontinued, which parts are essential, and which parts can be dealt with more appropriately by another member of staff. The job should then be put into the context of the school's developing policy and from this some idea of the responsibilities of the new post can be discerned, together with the qualifications and experience that the ideal candidate should have.

Far too often a vacancy is filled without any real thought about the type of teacher required, the job specification, and how the job fits in to the school organisation. Not only should these points be clear to the head, but also to other senior staff and the governing body, especially the interviewing panel. The panel at the very least should be equipped with a specification for the job to be done and the sort of person who can do it. Without this the members have no means of objectively evaluating the candidates., Remember that a Scale 1 teacher aged twenty-five can cost an LEA £4,000 to employ which, multiplied over forty years, means a total investment of £160,000. This is a lot of money to throw away on a careless twenty-minute interview.

Once the job itself has been assessed the next stage is to attract a good field of suitable candidates. Although this might seem straightforward it can be quite difficult. The aim is to dissuade those without the necessary qualifications or experience from applying without putting off those who would do a good job.

Candidates are attracted through two separate but interlocking actions, the advertisement and the job description. Often the nature of the advertisement will be taken out of the headteachcr's hands and the journals in which it is placed will be specified by the LEA, as will its format. Even if this is the case make sure you know what your LEA's policy is regarding advertisements. Which papers does it advertise in, does it circulate all LEA schools with current vacancies, does it run a mailing list and are you permitted to advertise locally?

If you are allowed to compose your own advertisement remember that 'in just a few words you must both inform the candidates about the nature of the post and at the same time impress them that the job is for them. It is perhaps wise at this stage not to put off candidates with phrases such as 'special diploma essential' but to concentrate instead on a general impression of the vacancy.

It is in the job specification sent to candidates that fuller information can be given which will allow for a form of self-selection by the candidates. The basic policy is honesty: be accurate about the opportunities and problems of the job, the school and the area. The job specification should leave no doubt about the exact nature of the job, its responsibilities and where it fits into the school's overall philosophy, because the aim at this stage is to attract those who are genuinely interested in the vacancy. For the same reason it is helpful to give some guidance as to the son of experience and additional qualifications which would be an advantage to the candidate.

Selecting the Short-List

It is a daunting task to reduce fifty or more applications to a short-list of six. This is usually done in two stages: a long list of candidates for whom references are taken up and from this a final short-list to be interviewed.

During the job analysis stage you will no doubt have formed an impression of the ideal candidate for the job and your long list should reflect this. Occasionally heads will proudly boast about how they reduce the candidates list by discarding the bad writers, the poor spellers and so on but the task should really be done in a more systematic way. One way of achieving this is to use a simple points system for various factors which are seen as relevant to the vacancy. If nothing else this ensures that each application is carefully read and analysed. It is time-consuming, but then the appointment of staff is one of the most important tasks a headteacher undertakes.

It will be necessary to amend the points system for each job but typical factors might be:

Age

21-25	(2 points)
26-35	(3 points)
35-40	(2 points)
over 40	(1 points)

Qualifications

B.Ed.	(2 points)
Open University degree	(3 points)
Open University diploma	(2 points)
Special education diploma	(2 points)
One term secondment	(1 points)

Experience

More than five years in primary	(2 points)
Scale 2 experience	(3 points)
Special education experience	(2 points)
Urban experience	(2 points)
Large school experience	(2 points)

When the scores are added up the more suitable candidates should be apparent. However, always be careful not to ignore the border-line cases or those whose scores are reduced significantly by one factor such as age.

Having reviewed the applications and agreed a long list the next stage is to seek references on the chosen candidates. The most important references are, of course, from the head of the candidate's previous school or, where appropriate, a reference from the LEA. You should always be doubtful about a candidate who does not wish to include his existing employer as a referee. Although character references from the vicar, youth club leader, or bank manager can be used as supporting evidence, it is highly unlikely that a candidate would use one of these as a referee if they were expected to express a poor opinion of him.

Very occasionally a good reference will be written to get rid of a poor candidate, or a poor one written to keep a good teacher, but fortunately these cases are rare. The vast majority of references are honest and meant to be helpful, although the reader must be prepared to dig deeply into what might be meant between the lines of the reference, and what might have been omitted. A good reference will always be relevant to the job description (which should be sent to referees for their guidance) and caution should be exercised over a reference full of the good timekeeping and good health' of a candidate but lacking anything about his ability actually to do the job. Ideally a reference should confirm what the candidate has already written in his application and should also provide additional relevant information. References should be written, but the telephone can be used to discuss a particular point or to ask for more information.

Many authorities no longer request testimonials. The difference between a testimonial and a reference should be clearly understood. A testimonial is an open letter setting out a candidate's strengths whereas the reference is a confidential appraisal of, his ability to perform the job for which he has applied. While the testimonial might be helpful in drawing up the long list it cannot substitute for the reference at the shortlist stage.

So the chosen few have been selected and have been invited for interview. The next stage begins.

The Interview

The day of the interview can be stressful for both the applicant and the interviewing panel. Your main aim should be, therefore, to leave as little to chance as possible. Applicants should be given clear instructions about the reporting time and how to find the school plus, if necessary, information on where to stay overnight. A little thought here can pay a large dividend; if three candidates are coming from the Home Counties don't ask them to arrive ten minutes before the London train is due at the station.

It is important that candidates should be given the opportunity to see the school, ask questions of the staff, and get an idea of the school's structure and organisation. Invite them to report during the morning and arrange lunch for them at the school. This morning session can be valuable in a number of ways. Interviews should be a two-way process and it is reasonable that candidates should themselves be able to assess whether or not the job is for them. This can save time during the formal interview and may avoid the making of a disastrous appointment. On the other hand a lot can be seen of a person's personality and his rapport with children and staff as he is shown around. Allow the candidates time to talk to teachers and children as well as time to themselves. Research has shown that the best predictors of a person's performance are his potential colleagues so it can be useful at least to have an idea of which candidates 'click' with your staff.

The organisation of the day should be made clear to the applicants—the order of interview, who will be on the panel and so on. Remember that the members of the panel may be as tense as the candidates and possibly more unsure of themselves. Invite them to attend before the interview day for a briefing or, if that is not possible, leave a reasonable period of time before the interview itself to have a discussion with the panel.

The composition of the panel will depend on the regulations laid down by the LEA and the articles of government. If possible avoid an over-large panel and try to dissuade every member of the governing body turning up for a Scale 1 interview. Not only is this intimidating to a young teacher but much time can be wasted by asking irrelevant or duplicated questions.

Arrange to have available for the briefing a duplicated curriculum vitae of each candidate for all the panel members. Go through each one briefly so that the panel has an overall view of the people to be seen. Do not discuss any in detail at this stage, or read references, or suggest who the favourite might be try to keep the appraisal as objective as possible all the way through. Next decide who will chair the panel and who will do fetching and carrying. Finally, and most important, lay own the ground rules for questions. The aim of this is to give all members the chance to ask a key question, to make sure that all important issues are covered, to avoid people asking the same question in different ways, and to persuade the panel not to waste time asking such questions as, 'will you live in the village?' It is, of course, quite reasonable to allow panel members to come in with supplementaries but a basic framework should be agreed upon.

A small but important factor is the layout of the interviewing room. The candidate must be made the centre of attention without having the room look like an interrogation cell. If possible remove surplus furniture and avoid having panel members sitting behind bookshelves or desks. A simple semicircle arrangement is better than a formal straight line. The light should be considered as it is quite unfair to expect a candidate to concentrate while blinking in strong sunlight, which is also silhouetting the people against the window.

When the candidate comes in the chairman should put her or him at ease; a couple of minutes can be spent breaking the ice through informal conversation, but it should be made clear that this is not part of the main interview. After this the major part of the time should be spent in listening to the candidate talking about her experience, how she views the job, and her opinion on other relevant matters. Some panel members like the sound of their own voices more than the candidates' so the chairman must be tactful but firm if this happens. Two things are important at the conclusion of the interview. Allow the candidate a few moments to ask questions of the panel which are relevant to the job. You should avoid getting into a long discussion about job prospects for the candidate's spouse, or the price of houses—these questions can be answered by your deputy. Second, ask the candidate if, after seeing the school, meeting the staff, being interviewed and given the opportunity of asking questions she still wants the job, if it is offered. This can save an embarrassing time later in the afternoon for all parties.

At the conclusion of each interview give the panel time to write down brief notes. It is much better that they do this rather than rely on memory. Full discussion and the reading out of references is best left to the end. When all the candidates have been seen the chairman should relate their strengths and weaknesses to the vacancy and all the members should be expected to comments. Often a consensus will quickly emerge but the paramount view must, of course, be given to the headteacher. One cardinal rule is, however, if in any doubt do not appoint. The time lost and the cost involved in re-advertising is small compared with that of making the wrong appointment.

Staff Development

A school's manpower should not be left to their own devices whether they are newly appointed members of staff or teachers of many years' standing in a school. A head must accept the responsibility for staff appraisal, guidance and development even if in practice the operation of this is delegated to another senior member of staff. Such guidance and development is particularly essential in the case of probationary teachers although the assistance of LEA advisers is more likely to be available in that instance.

New teachers, whether new to the profession or not, must be guided through a period of induction into the school, the local authority and its resources. They should been encouraged to feel part of the organisation as quickly as possible and they should be shown that they have a particular contribution to make to the philosophy and objectives of the school. Probationers will also need additional pastoral help in the early terms although it is better if this is unobtrusive. Most probationers are better off staying away from any intensive in-service education during the first year; they have enough to do in relating their initial training to the demands of their first job.

Headteachers should undertake a continuous evaluation of an individual's training needs but a formal annual appraisal interview is very advantageous. This will allow the teacher to discuss, without prejudice, any problems he is having in pursuing the school's objectives, and his personal hopes for the future. The head will be able to assess, with his help, areas in need of improvement and areas of strength which may be of benefit to other members of staff. Suitable in-service education can be discussed for the coming year, together with ways in which the teacher can continue to make a positive contribution to the school as a whole, beyond his own classroom. The aim of the appraisal should be to build on existing strengths and to agree where extra help could be valuable.

In-service education can be of value to three different groups, although often the advantages are interwoven. An LEA can. promote training to institutionalise new policies, such as secondary reorganisation, assessment or mathematics guidelines. A head can encourage teachers to attend courses which will be of direct benefit to the school, either in adopting common policies and philosophies among staff or in filling existing gaps. Third, individual teachers may wish to attend courses for promotional purposes.

The reasons why teachers attend courses should be clearly analysed and the benefits to school and individual assessed. Sometimes the disruption caused to routine is not worth the course because even if your LEA has a generous supply cover a regular change of teacher may not be in the children's interests. All these things are-pan of the managerial responsibility of a head. -

It is a truism to say that those who go on courses do-not need to, and those who never attend a course should. Regular and frank, appraisal interviews will help to overcome this problem by setting the correct development objectives for each teacher.

If the aim of a course is to improve school or classroom

performance, what happens at the conclusion of the course is even more important than its content. Heads should be aware of the content of the courses which staff are attending and should recognise any resource or organisational implications of follow-up. Ideally courses which are to benefit the school as a whole should be school-based or, in the case of small isolated schools, federally based. If this is not possible ample time should be allowed for staff discussions at the conclusion of the course and resources should be allocated to put ideas into practice. Above all, in-service education should not be carried on in isolation but should be firmly rooted in staff and school development.

As suggested earlier staff development is a continuing process and the provision of a small but carefully selected staff library can encourage new developments and introduce points for discussion. A feature should be made of any new books purchased and teachers should be encouraged to read and discuss them. A staff subscription to *Junior Education* or *Child Education* can also promote discussion of articles in the staffroom.

Visits to other schools should be encouraged, including those in other phases of education. This can be particularly helpful to teachers in isolated areas, offering them a comparison of practices and the chance to discuss their problems with colleagues.

Consultation

An earlier chapter emphasised that it was necessary for all teachers to pull in the same direction if common objectives were to be achieved. Consultation is part of the process of ensuring that everyone feels part of a team, and each individual knows what is expected of him. It can be achieved through informal contact and discussion and through the more formal forum of a staff meeting.

Informal consultation has its place but it is open to abuse unless its use is limited and the dangers clearly understood. A head will often wish to discuss a matter with his deputy but sometimes other teachers would be able to contribute meaningfully to the debate if given the opportunity. Even more dangerous, but an easy trap to fall into, is the consultative use of informal hierarchy where a teacher senior in age, or years of service, becomes the head's sounding board. This 'will inevitably lead to frustration and jealousy on the part of other members of staff.

In the end there is nothing that can replace a regular, formal staff meeting. Even in the smallest schools the setting of a regular time, with an agenda, can ensure more effective communication than relying on a chat over the mid-morning cuppa.

The content of staff meetings varies from the trivial, which sometimes takes up the bulk of the time, to the setting of long-term aims. One way of overcoming the *ad hoc* nature of so many staff meetings is, to fix a regular fortnightly or monthly time, after school, or possibly during an evening at home, for the discussion of major items. The agenda should be prepared and circulated in advance, and everyone should have the opportunity to place an item on it. If necessary supporting papers can also be circulated.

Such a process would ensure that time is set aside for major items and that teachers are aware of their commitments. It avoids the rush to find a time when everyone is available at short notice. The trivial items can still be discussed al more informal lunch-time staff meetings.

The setting of such a regular commitment, especially if extended occasionally as a social event, can go a long way to encouraging a team feeling among teachers and thus keeping morale high. It is quite likely that, as the commitment is accepted, small groups will wish to explore more important themes in depth and the sense of one school pursuing a common goal will be strengthened.

Staff Deployment

The number of senior posts in a school will be determined by its size and the local education authority's generosity on the points range. However, when the opportunity occurs to review the responsibilities of senior staff the head should start from the basis of what is in the best interests of the school. Whether or not additional responsibilities are given to teachers not receiving Scale 2 or above will depend upon the particular circumstances of the school, but the nature of all delegated responsibilities should be relevant to the school's aims and objectives, and the relative priorities should be within these objectives.

An NFER survey of Nottinghamshire primary teachers published in 1978 showed that the most common additional responsibility was for the organisation of the school library (72 per cent of respondent schools) followed by language consultants (67 per cent). Music responsibilities led mathematics by 61 per cent to 48 per cent; needlework at 37 per cent was well ahead of science at 21 per cent, and tuck shop organisation not far behind at 18 per cent. The 1978 Primary Survey of HMI showed a similar high percentage for music and low percentage for science.

Now it may well be that scale posts should be used to attract musicians and that the place of science in the curriculum can be safeguarded without delegating specific responsibilities to an individual teacher. What is important is that heads do not accept these assumptions without careful thought and discussions with colleagues.

The position of the deputy head is a difficult one. In a sense he sits in a no-man's-land but if he acts wisely he can be a major force in the staffroom. It is important that he, more than any other teacher, is given a clear job description and responsibilities, and these must extend beyond organising the duty rota. In the sudden prolonged absence of the head he would be expected to take charge of the school so he should be as fully involved in policy and problems as possible. Responsibility for a major area of the curriculum will involve him in day-to-day contact with all the staff; this becomes important if he is to be seen as more than the head's personal assistant.

Discipline

Many of the readers of this book, taking up their first headships, will have received their initial training during the mid- and late sixties. This was a period of rapid expansion in training colleges with the result that this generation of teachers has been given a reputation for low standards. This seems to be quite unfair, as any close look at the teaching profession will show that it is among the older generation that problems can be found, resulting from a, failure to meet new challenges, or frustration at seeing the opportunities for promotion passing them by. Any profession has its black sheep and its less-than-average practitioners, but demands for greater accountability are highlighting the situation among teachers. The problem is compounded by the declining birthrate affecting the size of the primary teaching force for the next ten years at least, resulting in redeployment of staff and demands for higher teaching standards. It is almost certain, therefore, that primary heads will need to face up to issues of discipline, redeployment or premature retirement with their teachers and this section looks at this problem in some detail.

LEAs will have written into articles of government the procedure to be followed in the event of a teacher being in danger of discipline or suspension. Before such a stage is reached the head should have attempted a number of things to improve the teacher's performance. This is not only good management but also common sense in observing the rules of the Employment Protection Act and the recommendations of the Advisory, Conciliation and Arbitration Services (ACAS).

Your local authority should have a written disciplinary procedure available for consultation by all teachers and it is essential to follow this in practice. The ACAS code emphasises that employees should be told clearly the conduct expected of them and the consequents of breaking the rules.

Disciplinary procedures should not be viewed primarily as a means of imposing sanctions but more as a way of encouraging improvement in ensuring that acceptable standards of conduct and capability are maintained. Normally discipline can be effectively maintained by example, advice, job training and informal reprimand. If a difficult situation arises, and they usually arise gradually, a detached look should be taken at the problem; can the teacher be held entirely to blame or are there circumstances in the environment or organisation which aggravate the difficulty? After a frank discussion, either some in-service education, a change of class or responsibility, or an opportunity to try something new may suffice for an improvement to occur. Such discussions, including informal reprimands, do not usually constitute part of a formal disciplinary procedure. However, the teacher should be advised of the conduct or standard expected in the future and of the probable consequences of a further breach of discipline or act of omission.

If after a reasonable period of time the informal reprimand and other positive measures have not succeeded in obtaining an improvement, the formal procedure as laid down by the LEA should be followed. Asking for help from an adviser or education officer at an early moment is essential as they may be able to offer a solution which eludes the head. At all events their early involvement will make the process easier to bear for all concerned.

Occasionally a teacher may have a grievance against one of his colleagues or even against you as the headteacher. The Contract of Employment Act legislates that every employee must be given a note specifying the manner by which he can seek redress. A standard procedure is how common in most of the country, with some local variations, and all heads should be aware of it and be knowledgeable about its provisions.

Redeployment

We all hope that as pupil numbers in primary schools decline, pupil-teacher ratios can be improved and standards of education enhanced. However, even if LEAs act generously in this way some redeployment of teaching staff between schools is going to be a common feature of primary education for a number of years. By early 1979 there were signs of a 5 per cent rise in the birthrate, but this will not begin to affect schools until 1984. During the previous decade the decline was 25 per cent in some parts of the country which means that the overall reduction in primary pupil numbers is not likely to be balanced out before 1990 at the earliest.

Again all LEAs will have redeployment policies, discussed and agreed with teacher associations, and the method of deciding which teachers should be redeployed will be agreed locally. There are some common factors: the credibility of a redeployment policy will fail if schools only wish to take advantage of the situation to transfer their least able teacher. The overall needs of the school should be looked at in determining who should be nominated and this must be matched against known or likely vacancies in the area. The experience and aptitude of the teacher are also very relevant here.

If you have a vacancy it is likely that you will be approached by the authority to accept a redeployed teacher. Quite naturally you will be reluctant to give up your freedom to appoint from a short-list and you will probably be supported by your governors in this. Bear in mind, however, the personal plight of a teacher redeployed in mid-career through no fault of her own, and be as sympathetic as possible within the overall needs and organisation of your school.

More often than not redeploying teachers is solved amicably and quickly through volunteers, promotions, retirements or 'natural wastage'. If not, and the problem remains intractable, the new premature retirement scheme for teachers may be the answer.

Premature Retirement

Regulations have now been approved which allow teachers who retire before the age of sixty to receive, in certain circumstances, their pensions on retirement. Before this no allowances, other than invalidity benefits, were payable before sixty. To qualify for premature retirement compensation (PRC) the local authority must agree that the retirement is attributable to redundancy or else is 'in the interest of the efficiency of the service'.

Teachers accepting PRC must be at least fifty and must have completed five years' reckonable service. They are then paid immediately the pension and lump sum to which their superannuation contributions entitle them, and this may be augmented by the local authority to cover a notional addition of years of service up to a maximum often. Some authorities only pay a percentage of the maximum, which in any case must not:

1. be more than the teacher's pensionable service;
2. bring the total pensionable service to more than forty years;
3. have the effect of extending pensionable service contributions beyond the age of sixty-five, *i.e.*, a teacher receiving PRC at fifty-eight could only get a maximum of seven added years.

Industrial Action

It is a pity to close a staffing chapter on a note of discord but all managers have, to accept the responsibilities as well as the powers of leadership. The 1970s saw a rise in industrial action among public sector workers, including health and education. Teachers in a number of areas were on strike at various times in the decade but perhaps the worst disruption came early in 1979 as a result of National Union of Public Employees' (NUPE) action by caretakers, cleaners, lunchtime supervisors and canteen staff. Working to contract by teachers in May 1979 brought further difficulties.

As headteachers you will probably be members of a teachers' union or association and in the event of industrial action by teaching or non-teaching staff your own union will usually offer guidance. At the same time your LEA may give you guidance or instructions which might conflict with union advice.

Your own personal views should be relegated in favour of the long-term needs of the school. Two things should be borne in mind and the action taken should depend on a consideration of them. Most important—what action is in the best interest of the children? The safety of each pupil must be secured and advance notice of any exclusions must be given to parents. Heads should assume responsibility for any children who arrive at school through a misunderstanding of the situation.

The second consideration is the long-term effect of the action on the school, and the need here is to ensure as far as possible that normal routines are re-established in an atmosphere of goodwill. Actions which will aggravate the situation should, therefore, be avoided, unless the safety of children is at risk or the loss of their education is becoming intolerable. With proper consultation at all levels it is surprising what agreements can be reached even during a period of industrial action. Heads should not undertake anything which can be construed as black-legging as this is certain to cause long-term bitterness. If possible, discussions held before the action takes place should determine what is or is not permissible One should note here, however, that most LEAs regard it as the headteacher's responsibility to open the school, even though this may be delegated to caretakers for practical purposes.

It is the teaching staff who are in the front line of education and it is their work which is crucial to the whole process. Careful selection of staff, successful deployment to make the most of their various abilities, good consultation with them, together with an overall caring attitude towards their work are key tasks for the manager. If he is successful in this his school is off to a good start.

Remember also, staff will be judging the head—by his compassion, his sense of humour, his attitude towards the children and by his sense of purpose.

7

Non-Teaching Staff

Schools exist for children to learn and this demand a close relationship between pupil and teacher. However, some critics of the education service point to the fact that only 50 per cent of the employees in the service are teachers, accusing schools and education departments of bureaucratic mismanagement. In fact less than 5 per cent of the salary bill is spent on central administration by LEAs, including advisory services; the rest goes on essential support to teachers in keeping classrooms clean and in meeting legislation in respect of school meals. In a primary school, therefore, it is likely that there will be as many non-teaching staff as teachers. Headteachers come from the ranks of assistants and it is natural for you to be more concerned with the actions of teachers than with the actions of other members of staff, but if a school is to run smoothly it is important for you to accept your responsibility as a manager, regardless of profession.

The Caretaker and Cleaning Staff

'The power behind the throne' is a phrase sometimes used about school keepers, or caretakers, and it is true that some caretakers seem to exert more influence on the running of a school than the head. As in all walks of life there is a range of interest and ability among caretakers. Some can be particularly cantankerous, making life a misery for cleaning and teaching staff. If this is the case a headteacher must be prepared to make a stand for good management. But it is more often the case that a caretaker will not only do his allotted tasks in an efficient and friendly manner, but will also do a variety of extra jobs for the school at no extra charge. Such a man is worth his weight in gold.

The relationship between head and caretaker must be based upon mutual trust and as full an understanding as possible of each other's functions in the school, including their respective tasks, frustrations and expertise. Heads should avoid a 'know-it-all' attitude; an approach recognising the particular knowledge of the caretaker will always be more effective. The recognition of the key role of the caretaker is important; in the day-to-day running of the school he is perhaps second in authority only to the headteacher. A possible source of conflict may arise in this connection because of different perceptions of authority with regard to role importance. It is not unknown for Scale 1 probationers to give orders to caretakers of many years' experience, and children will not be slow to play one member of staff off against another. Heads must be on the watch for any developments of this sort and they should be tactfully nipped in the bud.

The caretaker's main tasks are probably carried out when the academic staff are not on the premises, before 8.30 am and after 5 pm. At these times he becomes the representative of the school and the LEA, in effect the acting headteacher. Visitors are as likely to come to school at these times as any other, telephones will ring, crises will occur. Caretakers should therefore be aware of the importance of this role and the occasional discussion on meeting school visitors and dealing with telephone calls would not come amiss.

Under the caretaker, or cleaner in charge, there may well be other assistant staff. He is responsible for their deployment and has an important managerial function to perform in this connection. If he is wise he will want to be able to give his staff a 'pat on the back' and in the same way he also likes to know that his own efforts are appreciated. A regular 'thank you' or 'well done' goes a long way to encourage him to do that little bit extra the next time the school hall is used for a pet show.

It is possible that more time than should be will be spent by the caretaker on vandalism and damage. He will have a good deal of daily contact with the children and it is natural that he might see their presence in the school as being the only thing preventing it from always being clean and tidy. A broken window or blocked toilet can sometimes be the last straw. A good head will recognise this and will attempt a positive approach in using the caretaker to get through to pupils the problems, costs and inconvenience of vandalism.

Teachers, too, can unwittingly cause extra work for caretakers. Is it really sensible to leave pieces of clay all over the floor at the end of the last lesson on a Friday? Can little Johnny really be trusted not to empty the waste bin all over the junior playground? This is not to say that caretakers should determine curriculum or discipline, but merely that they should be one of the factors considered in reaching an operational decision.

To overcome these minor difficulties, which sometimes reach major proportions, personal contact is vital. An hour or so put aside each week for a cup of tea and a chat with the caretaker is well worth it. This might seem a large investment of time but can be seen in proportion when set against the total number of hours available. It is much better than hoping for a word at an odd moment. It is surprising how many things need to be discussed: how much cash is available for cleaning materials; how the cleaners are performing; what areas of the school or members of staff are creating cleaning problems; what planned school activities could intrude on the cleaning of the school; what repairs and minor building alterations are necessary;.how can the central heating system be made more effective, and last but by no means least, how is his wife's lumbago.

Such an approach will foster a communal spirit, and it should be the aim of every head to have his staff working as one for the good of the school. The main function of the school in educating children will be achieved much more pleasantly if the surroundings are clean, tidy and well cared for, and if an 'us and them' approach between manual and non-manual staff is avoided.

The activities of the caretaker and cleaners should be outlined to the pupils to give them some idea of what is involved in maintaining a clean, warm school for their use and comfort. Not only will this make them more appreciative of the caretaker's work and hence more responsible in their use of the premises but it will also give the older ones some idea of the world of work. The caretaker's job and responsibilities can also be used as a teaching point.

Many LEAs already appoint teaching staff to their governing bodies and just a few include such non-teaching staff as caretakers. In any case the caretaker should be invited to the occasional governors' or PTA meeting, to see and be seen, to ask and answer questions and to state his views should any problem or query arise. He will be seen as, and will feel, a full member of the school staff.

The caretaker and his staff are a vital part of the school's day-to-day life. Should they fail in their duties, at best life in the school will be uncomfortable, at worst the school could be a health hazard. The head who accepts this and goes out of his way to encourage the spirit of belonging in *all* his staff will have a happy and clean school. A 'good evening' costs nothing but it does mean a lot.

School Meals Staff

As long as schools operate a full day, a catering service of some description will continue to be necessary. Some parts of the country have experimented with one-session days on the continental pattern but it is unlikely that such a practice will become common in view of this country's employment pattern for working mothers. Suggestions are also made, especially at times of economic difficulty, that the meals service should be transferred to social services departments. If this happened it is unlikely that the education budget would see any financial benefit, as the demand for the service would still need to be met. Neither would the management structure be made easier; school kitchens are expensive plant and in my view it is essential for a head to have overall responsibility for all the workers in his school, and all parts of the school, even if the canteen is linked to a county catering officer.

Many of the points made about caretakers and cleaning staff are also appropriate to the 'canteen and dinner ladies'. The staff employed to provide the meals service have a vital job to do and they are just as important as other staff. Because they provide a service they need motivation and if a head is to get the best out of these members of staff he must give them some daily attention, whatever his personal feelings.

This attention can be in various forms. A daily look into the kitchen to say 'good morning' is always appreciated, while sitting down for morning coffee with the meals staff once a week shows a real interest in their work. It is also important to help the children understand the work of meals staff by taking time to show and explain to them what the staff have to do to ensure that the meals are ready in time. Again, many teaching points can arise from this involvement; indeed a project on 'The working of the school' can be of more benefit than other themes more remote in time or place. Great use can be made of the kitchen when discussing food and foodstuffs with pupils. The opportunity should be grasped to illustrate what is 'good' and what is 'bad', why certain foods are offered and others not, etc. Why not take *organised* groups into the kitchen?

Contact made in ways such as these will encourage two-way communication between teachers and pupils on the one hand and non-teaching staff on the other. High morale and motivation for all must be the direct benefit of this.

Once a year, perhaps, the cook, like the caretaker, could be invited to a PTA or governors' meeting so that parents or governors can put their questions and worries directly to her. So often complaints about school meals, are secondhand and coloured by a person's own school experience of twenty-five years ago: The opportunity to discuss difficulties at first-hand can do much to relieve problems.

Ancillary Help

The concept of ancillary assistance is not new in an educational context although, mainly because of financial constraints, their use is perhaps not as widespread as it could be. These helpers have a variety of titles — auxiliary, teachers' aide, etc.—but whatever the name the idea refers to persons who can aid professional teachers in their daily encounters with children in the classroom. The impetus for this move has come from teachers wanting relief from the more time-consuming and repetitive tasks reinforced by objective studies of how teachers spend their time. There are still a few heads and teachers who see the aides as a threat to the teacher's position in the classroom and there are others who feel unease at sharing a class with another adult. Those who feel threatened should reflect on their training and experience: they are the professional educators, the directors of programmes, the evaluators of work. Seen in this context aides can be a source of help by relieving teachers of routine non-teaching tasks and so increasing their direct contact with children. Unease at sharing a room with another adult is understandable, although it can stem from a sense of insecurity. Given time and good personal relationships on both sides it can usually be overcome.

It is clearly important that ancillaries do not cross the line between non-teaching and teaching work. They should not be used as substitute teachers, or on duties involving the organisation and management of classrooms, the planning of learning strategies, the assessment of pupils' needs or the evaluation of their progress. However, they can be of immense use in helping pupils with problems in using materials, especially giving encouragement during activity lessons. The preparation of work cards, paint and so on can also, save the teacher a great deal of time.

One thorny problem is that of reading. Generally it seems quite appropriate for ancillaries to hear adequate readers when there is unlikely to be a fundamental learning problem. It is a different matter with a remedial group who will need specific help, attack skills and learning strategies.

The key to success in using ancillaries is the attitude of the head. Where the role is defined and made clear to all, including pupilsi, there is an even greater chance of real effectiveness. Teachers will have their own views about the amount of ancillary time that should be allocated to them and they should be consulted about their needs. Larger blocks of time do, however, seem to be more effective than shorter ones. It can be helpful to leave a couple of hours each week free from class responsibilities for the helper to be used on specific and irregular tasks.

The ancillary helper, like all non-teaching staff, should be regarded as a full member of the school staff. Use of the teachers' room (if the school has one!) can cause difficulties and teachers sometimes worry that their conversation and discussion will be inhibited by non-teachers being present. In the end the solution will depend on the size of the staff and the staffroom and the relationships which have been built up. However, a shared common room helps to create a better understanding and allows teachers to discuss their needs with the helpers.

All non-teaching staff—cleaning, cooking, ancillary, secretarial (of which more is said later)—need in-service training if they are to perform their duties to the best of their abilities. Often the opportunities for this training are rare. Heads should encourage their LEAs to mount relevant courses and facilitate the attendance at these courses by their manual staff. If no LEA course is available the occasional school-based course can do much to increase commitment to the job and is well worth a headteacher's time. He will often find that local authority staff are willing to help, especially superintendents of caretakers, catering officers, and nursery/infant advisers.

The emphasis in this chapter has been that to manage a school a head must be interested in the whole exercise and not just the educational side. This may be the end and the reason for the school's existence: however, the rest is part of the means of achieving that end.

8

Management of Special Education

In May, 1978 the first major government committee to consider the needs of the handicapped child produced its report. The recommendations made under the chairmanship of Mrs Mary Warnock will certainly shape special education for the rest of this century and will also have a significant impact on the organisation of ordinary schools. One of the more emotive parts of the special education debate has been the question of integrating handicapped children into the mainstream. This argument was legislated for in the 1976 Education Act which, in Section 10, states that all children should be educated in ordinary schools where it is in their best interests provided that this does not act to the detriment of the non-handicapped pupils and does not take an unreasonable amount of public expenditure.

The Warnock Report accepted the principle of 'Section 10' but was more concerned with the practical difficulties of integration. The consultations undertaken since the publication of the report seem to show that most authorities are pressing on with programmes for more integration but that the need for special schools will remain for the foreseeable future and their status enhanced by their development as resource centres. It is not only the individual child who needs to be integrated into the normal system but special education as a whole, and this is one of the main features of the report. Furthermore Warnock identified a large percentage of children as in need of special support, and most of these children are integrated already into ordinary schools. Which children are therefore in need of this special help, how can they be identified, and how are their needs to be met?

Who Needs Special Help?

Children in need of special help, and formally ascertained under -procedures laid, down by the DES, are still categorised within the Schools Regulations made following the 1944 Education Act. These categories are:

Educationally subnormal (mild and severe);
Maladjusted;
Physically handicapped;
Delicate;
Partially hearing;
Deaf;
Partially sighted;
Blind;
Epileptic;
Speech defects,.

After ascertainment by medical and psychological officers, a child is found a place in a school with the appropriate label. It has become quite apparent that such a system is restrictive m the opportunities it offers to the handicapped child and the emphasis, strongly backed by Warnock, is now to determine the environmental and curriculum needs of a child and to educate him in the most suitable way. Needs therefore become more ımportant than the basic handicapping condition.

This is less than half the story, however, as the categories outlined above, and which Warnock is anxious to modify, cover less than 3 per cent of the school population. That 3 per cent has needs which require special teaching, a special curriculum, a special medical or social environment, or a particular form of treatment. This teaching may be provided in a special school or in an ordinary school but it is likely to be long-term with implications well beyond normal school leaving age.

It is proposed that the rather obscene label 'educationally subnormal' should be replaced by 'children with special learning difficulties', and these difficulties should be seen as severe (mentally handicapped children), moderate (children presently in the ESN(M) area) and mild (children in need of remedial help). The size and needs of the latter group are larger than was once appreciated and although the demand may be for relatively short-term help, limited to fairly specific objectives, nevertheless it has to be met. Among the school population as a whole one child in five might need some form of special educational treatment at some time during his school life, or compensation to make up for an inadequate educational environment outside school. Thus, the real demand for special education is much higher than the formal ascertainment of 3 per cent would suggest.

Identification and Referral

The sooner a child's special needs are identified the better the chances of making adequate educational provision for them. A severely mentally handicapped child, and children with physical or sensory handicaps, will be recognised by parents or doctors well before school age. For some of these children a decision will be made to start schooling in the mainstream, possibly with extra support from ancillary helpers. The child's progress will then have to be carefully monitored to ensure that his needs really are being met in the ordinary school.

Children with less severe handicaps, and those with learning difficulties, may not be identified until the infant stage, or possibly even later. It is sound practice to use some form of screening device, such as a developmental checklist, which will assist teachers in deciding whether or not a child has a particular difficulty. A good checklist will include the observation of physical factors (eyesight, hearing, speech, coordination), perceptual difficulties (visual and auditory discrimination), linguistic problems (understanding stories and instructions), social/emotional demands (confidence, peer group difficulties) and direct responses to learning situations (interest, distraction, perseverance). The checklist should not only assist teachers in the identification of children with special needs but should also be diagnostic in pointing out how these needs can be met, and who should be approached for help.

It cannot be emphasised too often that a child's particular needs must be monitored throughout his school career. After careful assessment it may be decided that his education can be provided quite adequately in an ordinary class, but this must be a positive decision. It is quite wrong to let a child struggle in the mainstream when the school is not really able to meet his needs. With falling pupil numbers in primary schools it is true that their ability to cope with special problems will be improved; nevertheless this must 'be set against alternative forms of provision.

The use of a sophisticated developmental checklist, together with other school-based screening procedures, should lead to the identification of most difficulties. Some authorities are also taking up the recommendations of both Bullock and Warnock in starting the screening of whole age-groups of children, first at about seven, again towards the end of the junior stage, and sometimes at the options stage in the secondary school. Not only does this scheme provide another fail-safe device but it also enables a linear profile to be kept on each child, and allows for the comparison of reading quotients to be made across school boundaries. This can be particularly helpful at the transfer stage.

If a teacher is concerned about a child's progress, and this is confirmed by screening, the first step is to discuss with the headteacher whether the school can cope. If there is any doubt about this an advisory teacher or educational psychologist should be contacted for further advice. This is especially true for children with social or emotional problems which aggravate their learning difficulties. If it is thought that special education (SE) should be considered then the appropriate procedures, usually involving the completion of SE forms, should be set in motion. If continued placement in the ordinary school is thought best the psychologist and adviser should recommend learning programmes and strategies that can be used.

Two small points may have a significant part to play in success. If parents can be involved at an early stage, listened to, and shown how they can help, the chances of educational improvement are greatly enhanced. On the other hand the structure of the school, the curriculum, the attitude of staff to the child, should all be reviewed. This is not to say that a perfectly good organisation should be turned upside down to allow one child to settle. However, quite often a minor change on the part of the school can make a considerable difference to the child with special problems.

Support Services

Advisory and support services are there to be used, despite lengthy waiting lists. Educational psychologists, social workers, medical officers, advisory teachers, all have a part to play in diagnosing difficulties and offering solutions. But they can only analyse a difficulty in proportion to the information they have. Before asking a psychologist or other adviser to see a child be sure to have discussed his problems internally. Prepare a brief report including in it all relevant test scores, the ways in which the problem has manifested itself and the strategies which have so far been applied. This will give the psychologist a sound base from which to approach the difficulty. You are then more likely to get back detailed suggestions for further help than a mere quotation of test scores and repetition of a problem you already know.

Special Education Provision

The Warnock Report advocates a continuum of special education provision from total integration in an ordinary school classroom to residential special school. Although many of the children in a school for the mentally handicapped, and to a lesser extent the physically handicapped, will never have attended an ordinary primary school, the wise headteacher will recognise that he is but a part of the education system. He will try to be aware of local special schools, arrange visits or even staff exchanges and encourage links between children. Physically handicapped children could, for example, be invited to share a touring theatre company's production with primary children. This will help the non-handicapped children to accept the problem of handicap in society. Such a venture must always be done very carefully and selectively, as a sudden influx of severely handicapped children can be very disturbing emotionally to the primary child.

The less severely handicapped child may be placed in a specialist class attached to an ordinary school. Such a class will be staffed by a specialist teacher of the handicapped (*e.g.*, the hearing impaired) and will be equipped with suitable aids and equipment (loops, speech trainers, phonic ears). Depending on their handicap, the children will spend part of the day in the special class and part in the ordinary school. Such classes are now widely available for the hearing impaired, but are much fewer in number for the visually and physically handicapped. A handful of LEAs are experimenting with special classes for mentally handicapped children.

A more radical type of provision is total integration with extra support if necessary. This is most common with physically handicapped children where specialist equipment is provided, building alterations are made, and welfare assistants are appointed to look after the physical needs of the children.

It should never be taken for granted that just because a handicapped child is educated in a special class attached to an ordinary school, or even directly in the ordinary school, he is totally integrated. By being given different work to do, or being especially protected from normal rough and tumble, his particular difficulty can be highlighted. Heads must be quite clear that any handicapped -child in their school is fully benefiting from the experience. Integration in the sense of location and placement is only part of the answer; integration must also be considered from the social and educational point of view. Furthermore the integration of pupils is not enough: the integration of specialist and main school staff must be complete, and the integration of the parents of the handicapped, who may come from a much wider catchment area than the main school parents, is also essential.

Dyslexia

One of the most emotive types of handicap which the primary head may have to deal with is 'dyslexia'. Not only is the handicap itself open to some question but its particular links with the so-called 'middle class parent' tend to hide the real problem. Some headteachers, psychologists and educational administrators believe that it is only a question of such parents trying to make their child's reading problem sound respectable. One correspondent to a national paper went so far as to suggest that the only way to get dyslexia accepted by the authorities was to 'visit the Child Guidance Clinic, hair in rollers and dog end in mouth, reeking of stout and saying as loudly and coarsely as possible that Wayne (a less dyslexic name than Rupert) can't read because he's thick and you haven't got time to keep bringing him to the clinic because you are missing bingo'.

Be that as it may it is clear that there are some children, of apparently good intelligence, who suffer from a specific reading problem. The literal meaning of the word dyslexia is 'difficulty with reading' but a neurologist would define it as a 'disorder which, despite conventional classroom experience, prevents children from attaining skills in reading, writing and spelling', thus implying an underlying neurological cause.

The argument between medical and non-medical opinion about the existence of an identifiable dyslexic condition has been continuing since 1890 and there seems little sign of it abating. The basic error made by many people is to assume that dyslexia is not simply a word which describes a problem but rather a diagnosis indicating the underlying cause of the problem. The busy class teacher, or primary headteacher, just does not have the time to enter into such a philosophical discussion. When a child shows classic 'dyslexic symptoms' (b-d confusions; letters in the wrong order; leaving letters out of a word; apparently 'careless' reading errors; difficulty in coping with arithmetical tables, etc) the teacher should be more concerned with helping than labelling.

Redding failure of itself cannot be a disease as reading is a process of modifying behaviour and learning a skill. Failure to learn that skill is not an organic disability. The basic causes of reading failure are so complex that one single term for it is a gross oversimplification, ignoring many other contributory factors such as personality, emotions and motivation.

A child with apparent 'dyslexia' should be given the same support as any other child with a learning difficulty. If it helps the parents to call their son 'dyslexic' then so be it, but the job of the school is to identify the problem, propose and implement suitable remedial action, and if necessary refer the child for specialist help. Parents of ''dyslexic' children often rush to the media to claim that their local authority does not recognise dyslexia. What they really mean is that their LEA will not pay for their child to attend an independent school. Many authorities have well-structured channels for dealing with this difficulty and heads are advised to acquaint themselves with local practice.

The Gifted Child

Special help seems sometimes to be more than adequate for the less able pupil but a common feeling is that the brightest child can take care of himself. Increasing concern has been shown recently at the curriculum offered to gifted children in comprehensive schools and the 1978 HMI Primary School Survey suggested that bright children were not stretched enough. There is now an increasing awareness that these children have special educational needs and they are becoming a greater focus of concern among teachers.

There is probably a significant number of gifted children who remain unrecognised in the primary school. This is likely to be more common among schools in deprived areas as environmental deprivation has been shown to have its greatest effects on the academic attainment of the brightest children, not the average or dull ones.

There is no common consensus about the definition of a gifted child. A generally agreed baseline is an IQ of 145 in a reliable test, but the abilities of the specifically gifted, especially the creative, must not be ignored. Furthermore, a child could well be gifted without the fact being made evident either generally or specifically. Teachers should therefore be alert to signs of specific ability and be prepared to investigate further. They should also be willing to give a reliable test to any child who has shown himself generally gifted during whole age-group monitoring. This is why a screening exercise should have a high cut-off point to suggest the most able as well as a low one to identify the least able.

A gifted child may have problems with personal relationships as well. Close cooperation is required between parent and school and the head should strive to establish an understanding and sympathetic relationship. Within the school attempts should be made to allow the child to maintain normal contact in everyday activities with children of his own age range. The gifted child should not beset apart, but should be given the opportunity to work alone on occasions, and to join with children of comparable ability on special courses if these are available. Above all he should be subject to a high level of expectation and he and his parents should have regular counselling available through school and from other specialists. To meet these particular needs the school must be willing to tap all the available resources which will allow the child to carry out a sophisticated programme while the internal organisation must be sufficiently flexible to allow him the opportunity of sufficient enrichment within everyday school life.

A school which develops an ethos in which qualities of leadership, creative thinking and artistic ability are nurtured will set itself high standards and will encourage the gifted child. A school which develops a philosophy of caring for all whatever their difficulties or handicaps will set itself compassionate standards and will encourage the less able or disabled child. There is no reason why these two should not go together in embracing the needs of all children within a general policy of considering them as individuals. In this way every child will be a special case, and those with special needs will be adequately provided for.

9

Outside the School

Despite moves, towards more open forms of democracy and attempts by many schools to become more involved in community life there still remains an us-and-them attitude between laymen and those involved professionally in education. Such a feeling even exists between some secondary schools and their feeder primaries. The Taylor Committee proposed basing governing bodies more firmly in the community but how far this exercise will go remains to be seen; far more is needed than a statutory parent and industrialist on the board of governors.

The only real and lasting way of overcoming this attitude is 'by involving the school in the life of the community, and the community in school activities. What happens beyond the school gates is of vital importance to the health and success of a school. External relationships should be encouraged, nurtured and monitored. Those who fear undue interference on the grounds that a little learning is a dangerous thing should recognise that the alternative is frustration and ignorance which can prove to be a much more explosive mixture. External relations must be carefully controlled to avoid cliques, favouritism and prejudice but if managed with sensitivity they can help to ensure a smoothly running school. Like all other management activities external relations must be planned, organised, controlled and evaluated.

The world beyond the school gates can be conveniently divided into three areas (relationships with LEA, teachers' unions, etc, have already been discussed). These are parents; the educational community; and the non-educational community.

WORKING WITH PARENTS

Reports ranging from Hadow[1] in 1931 to Warnock[2] in 1978 have emphasised that deprived homes can seriously prejudice a child's knowledge of language and communication skills, and thus the whole foundation of education, while on the other hand supportive homes help children to enter school with the foundations well laid. Researchers such as Douglas[3] have backed these reports, suggesting that children can, acquire at home almost as much information about the world as they can at school. Thus every opportunity should be taken to make clear to parents the very great importance of supportive altitudes in the first five and subsequent years of a child's life.

The first five years are of crucial importance, and the good primary school can play a central role in guiding parents through these difficult years. Good contact with local playgroups can be a great advantage and some schools have arranged meetings of parents with the cooperation of maternity and health clinics. If parents can be encouraged to have a supportive attitude to school when their child is a 'pre-five' it is likely that they will work for the school's good when their child attends full-time. Schools can still be forbidding places for young parents so it helps if early meetings with head and staff can be on neutral premises, such as at a playgroup or clinic.

Great care is now taken over the medical needs of babies but much less over their educational needs. 'Mother and Toddler' groups have proved to be successful in encouraging mothers to talk and play with their children and if a primary school can encourage and assist in this sort of activity it will reap benefits from both parents and children at the time of school admission.

Even when a child is. attending school full-time he only spends about 27 per cent of his waking hours there. Unless there is cooperation and support from, home the work of the school can be quite useless. But it is all too easy for a head to complain that he has no cooperation, or that 'the parents you want never come'. There will be many frustrating times when no meaningful dialogue can be opened, but in general good cooperation will come only from hard work.

The obvious way adopted by many schools is to set up a parent-teacher association and provided the PTA does not attempt to dominate the situation but is based on a harmonious relationship between the head, staff and governors, such organisations can be a source of strength and support to the school.

A parent-teacher association should not infringe on the professional rights of the head and his colleagues in the matter of the curriculum, syllabus, teaching methods, etc. On the other hand a parent-teacher association which is only involved in social activities may not justify the devotion by teachers of their energies and spare time to it. More fruitful is the middle way in PTA act useful information about the school's aims and how it fits into the educational pattern of the area is disseminated, as well as information about what the school is trying to achieve. This should by no means be a one-way process but truly professional teachers can often gain insights into their job by listening to parents; listening is perhaps not ingrained in all of us.

In any case the aims of the association should be carefully set out so that everybody knows what can be done, and what cannot. If a formal association is to be set up some form of constitution will be necessary, if only to ensure the orderly conduct of meetings and the democratic election of officers. The National Federation of Parent-Teacher Associations can offer advice about this. It is best to avoid too formalised a structure otherwise bureaucracy will take over and the association will die a lengthy but definite death. Some associations spend endless time arguing about their name; should it include or exclude parents and teachers. It really is not worthwhile wasting time on this; call it the 'School Association' or 'Friends of the School'—presumably all teachers and parents will want to be friends of, or associated with, the school'.

PTAs can be very valuable, but they are not necessarily the best means of fostering close relations between home and school. They can be valuable where good leadership is given by the head, but they may do harm if in the hands of a small group. There is also some evidence to suggest that certain parents are not good attenders at PTA meetings, so that may not be the best method of involving all concerned.

Above all parents need information — information about the school but particularly about their child's place in it. Comments on communicating with parents are made elsewhere in this book but a headteacher should never take significant action regarding a child or class without informing the parents and giving them the reasons. This is especially so when a child's class is changed, or where a new organisation is adopted, eg, vertical grouping. Parents' conception of school is based on their primary school days perhaps twenty years earlier and they may well not appreciate the organisation or curriculum of the 1980s.

Whatever device is adopted to suit local circumstances—a PTA, a parent association, friends of the school-or simply very active involvement with school affairs, the essentials are: to get parents into the school; for parents to meet teachers and see what the children are doing and why; to ensure that parents are well informed about the school in general and their own children in particular?

The following is a not exclusive list of the more obvious ways of stimulating parental involvement, with or without a PTA.

General Information

The national survey undertaken by the Plowden Committee showed that more than 30 per cent of parents did not see the headteacher before their children started school. The more information available to parents about the general organisation and running of the school the better (see A-Z section 'Admissions' p. 141 and 'Information for Parents' p. 146), but this is much more valuable if head and staff can take the time to meet new parents and allow children to visit the school before admission.

Educational Meetings

These meetings notoriously encourage only those parents with a special interest in their children's work, but they should not be ignored purely on this basis. It is precisely these parents with a little knowledge of education who can be most critical of the school's performance. Every way of giving them more information about the aims and methods of the school should therefore be used Sessions can be held not only on curriculum matters but also on how parents can help their own children with reading and number, and what other activities can be encouraged at horned. From time to time educational clinics could be held with teachers and others answering educational questions on an individual basis.

School Reports

The value of reports is often underestimated as this can be the only way in which a parent is given some indication of how a child is progressing. Reports should be informative and should contain much more than just grades for performance. Comments on progress and development and suggestions about the ways in which parents can help to overcome their child's difficulties can involve them in the academic side of school. Some teachers present reports much more as a letter to parents rather than a forbidding pro forma, and add space at the bottom for parents to write their own comments. All this takes tune of course and therefore the report writing needs to be limited; there is no reason why this should be at the end of each term, or even at the end of the year. A report written, for instance, at the spring half-term can be used as a teaching tool in encouraging a dialogue between parent and teacher, rather than being just a certificate of course completion.

Open Evenings

Reports will be much more meaningful if allied to a reasonable system of 'open evenings'. These again are time-consuming but can be a very positive help to the teacher. Appointment systems seem to work best, provided times are kept to and queues of parents are avoided. It is also wise to avoid leaving children's books on display all over the room; parents are naturally inquisitive and will want to compare their child's work with other class members. However, an opportunity should be given to see the work of the school displayed, and possibly some activities actually in progress. It is impossible to find a time 'suitable for everyone so flexibility must be the key note. Remember that fathers form 50 per cent of parents and times should be chosen when they can attend. Not all of them finish work at 3.30: on the other hand some may do shift work in the evenings. If the amount of time spent on this exercise seems inordinate remember that parents, in the long run, will exert more influence on their children's development than even the best teacher.

School Magazine

This can form a welcome link between school and parents and can also be a useful teaching point for lessons and activities. Why not invite parents to contribute to the articles, which can include programmes of events, information on developments and changes in staff and buildings, organisational and curriculum changes, expeditions and school success in sport, cycling proficiency etc, and examples of children's worker?

School Functions

The range of activities to which parents can be invited is endless—sports, music, carol festivals, plays and so on. The only danger is that the audience becomes more important than the performance. A slick production is all very creditable but parents should understand that they are seeing the culmination of primary school learning activities and not a performance by the Royal Shakespeare Company.

Personal Support

There are many ways in which individual parents can support the school and at the same time feel tha+ they are partners in education. These include contributing materials, expertise on building projects, clerical and non-teaching chores, supervision of swimming pool or playground and serving on governing bodies. Corporately parents can be encouraged to organise money-raising and social activities including bazaars, fetes, raffles, jumble sales, dances, and second-hand shops.

A school with a dynamic and balanced programme for encouraging and controlling parental cooperation will probably be working well in other respects. If there is distance between school and parents the task of the teacher in the classroom will be made that much more difficult.

THE EDUCATIONAL COMMUNITY

It is sometimes more common for a school to ignore the educational community outside its own gates than it is for it to ignore parents. What is happening in other schools and institutions is bound to exert an influence on the school decision-maker, even if he is unaware of it. Keeping in touch with this community is the very least that should be done.

Most headteachers meet fairly regularly with their primary school colleagues, and perhaps less often with their secondary colleagues. Such meetings can be very useful forums for discussing problems and initiatives but they sometimes go little further than being mutual support groups for discussing organisational or transfer difficulties. The kernel of school life is the curriculum so time should be set aside to debate with one's colleagues the pros and cons of adopting a particular pattern. Discussions on these lines with secondary colleagues is especially helpful in promoting increased understanding about what each sector is trying to achieve.

More than isolated discussion is necessary, however, school visits and exchanges should be encouraged. Teachers are, by and large, a conservative group and often find it difficult to accept even fellow professionals in their classrooms, but it is surprising how much can be achieved by a joint exploration of a problem and ways of solving it. The problem of time and class disruption can make such exchanges difficult to achieve but if they are carefully planned, organised, and evaluated they can be a source of strength to individual teachers and promote inter-school harmony.

Schools outside the primary sector should not be forgotten. Exchanges with secondary schools can often be arranged after the Whitsun half-term, and this can be particularly beneficial to the primary school leavers. The opportunity to let the children meet some of their new teachers should be taken if offered, or even better should be taken to the secondary school to see a play, school sports or possibly share in PE or home economics lessons. Ways of enabling parents to see something of the secondary school before transfer should also be explored.

How many primary heads know what is offered in a tertiary college or college of further education? Yet these institutions are influential in shaping the education system itself and the eventual life style of their students. Lecturers in FE can be heard criticising 'modern methods' when their most recent direct knowledge of a primary school was 1940, or secondhand when their children attended in 1960. Why not arrange to visit your local college and encourage some two-way interchange of ideas? The spin-off in expertise suddenly made available to you from both staff and students could be surprising.

Special schools have already been mentioned. It is a salutary experience to visit a hospital school for the mentally handicapped or a residential school for the visually impaired.

These schools are part of our education service and as such all primary heads should at least have some knowledge of their functioning. Many of these schools will be developing as resource centres to help ordinary schools with special problems, while visits to them may open up new career opportunities for teachers in mainstream education.

Some of the most common 'whipping boys' of the education service during the seventies were the colleges of education. Newly qualified teachers who could not keep discipline, had no idea of how to teach literacy and numeracy, and were themselves poor spellers — these complaints were commonplace. There may well have been an element of truth in these allegations as colleges tried to come to terms with rapidly reducing intakes after ten years of unparalleled expansion. Most of the comments were pretty subjective however and few heads went to the trouble of checking the actual situation in the colleges. Take the opportunity therefore of visiting your local college, or joining an in-service working party, and if you are still dissatisfied with the product of the college tell them so from a position of real knowledge.

The importance of good links with playgroups has been emphasised. Not only will this provide a useful forum for making contact with parents but it will also be directly helpful to the playgroup supervisor and her staff, provided that the impression of the school making a takeover bid is avoided.

THE WIDER COMMUNITY

It might be thought that local businesses and industries are more relevant to secondary schools. Despite this and welcome moves to improve liaison between secondary education and industry, the primary school still gets its share of criticism from the world of work. We are constantly being told that the basic skills are not being taught or that all would be well if we took a leaf out of the industrial managers' book. The only way to overcome these difficulties in communication is to invite the critics to see for themselves, and to go and visit them. The response will probably be mixed—some firms will ignore you completely but others may be keen to enter a period of close collaboration which will be of benefit to both sides.

Using the media, press, radio and television is an art in itself. Some authorities employ public relations officers and they can offer sound advice on what is possible and what should be avoided. Nothing can be more boring or irritating than seeing one school constantly in the headlines, presenting proficiency certificates, winning swimming shields, having its fete opened by the Prime Minister. On the other hand good but balanced press relations can be a great advantage if a problem should ever arise at your school which might involve adverse comments.

Establishing strong relationships with the world beyond the school is time-consuming. Care obviously has to be taken not to undervalue the basic needs of the school. However, those needs are likely to be better met if a carefully planned community programme is operated. In the rapidly changing eighties, with micro processors bringing a new industrial revolution and a changing work ethic, no school can afford to ignore the wider community. Everything should be done to gain an understanding of that community and to encourage it to be understanding about the primary school's own objectives.

NOTES & REFERENCES

1. *Primary School Report by the Consultative Committee of the Board of Education:* its brief was "To inquire into and report on courses of

study suitable for children (other than infants) up to 11 in elementary schools, with special reference to needs of children in rural areas."

2. *Special Educational Needs: report of the Committee of Enquiry into the Education of Handicapped Children and Young People.*
3. *Home and the School* by James William Bruce Douglas (MacGibbon & Ace, 1964).

10

Routine Administration

The distinction between management and administration has already been made.(Management is concerned with decision-making, administration with implementation) Much of this book has been concerned with making heads aware,of the context within which they manage, of the constraints upon their freedom, and of the measures likely to produce an atmosphere that will maximise the chances of successful management. Nevertheless administration itself is important as the most carefully designed plans can flounder if not properly administered.

There is the very real danger that administrative tasks assume too much significance or else are almost completely ignored. This seems more frequently the case in the small rural school where a head has to manage his time to cope with both a full timetable and administrative tasks. Carefully thought-out procedures are therefore needed to keep the paperwork in hand without it being relegated to the waste paper bin. Equally important is an attitude of mind which recognises that administration is part of successful educational management and not something beneath a head's dignity.

It is possible to identify the main components of good administration which can then be applied in the appropriate circumstances. Standard procedures are needed so that confusion and mistakes are avoided. If the administrator knows what is required to achieve a certain action it is less likely that in an emergency an important detail will be forgotten. Such procedures will also ensure a continuity of action and avoid 'one-off' reactions to sudden demands and requests.

Clear channels of communication and consultation will be established by sound administration. If everyone has clearly defined responsibilities, and is aware of them, school life, will function smoothly and teaching will be efficient. Good administration will take care that skills are used properly, that time is devoted to key tasks and not to irrelevant operations, and that energies are used in the right places. Above all the administration will be organised so as to be unobtrusive, *serving* teaching rather than constraining it, and flexible, meeting situations appropriately with planned responses but with the capacity to adapt.

If the planned use of procedures is important in relation to paperwork and manpower, so too are they in relation to time. Administration should be concerned with spreading the workload of the school effectively both in day-to-day activities and in more unusual circumstances.

Planning the hall and television timetables are examples of the day-to-day activities. Not only is it necessary to be fair to all classes, but also to ensure that the time spans are appropriate to the age group and activity being pursued and that, for instance, a thirty minute hall period is not followed immediately by a twenty minute television programme. The allocation of time is perhaps one of the most important functions of the head as an administrator.

Avoiding a clash of dates, or a conglomeration of activities at the same time, are functions of good

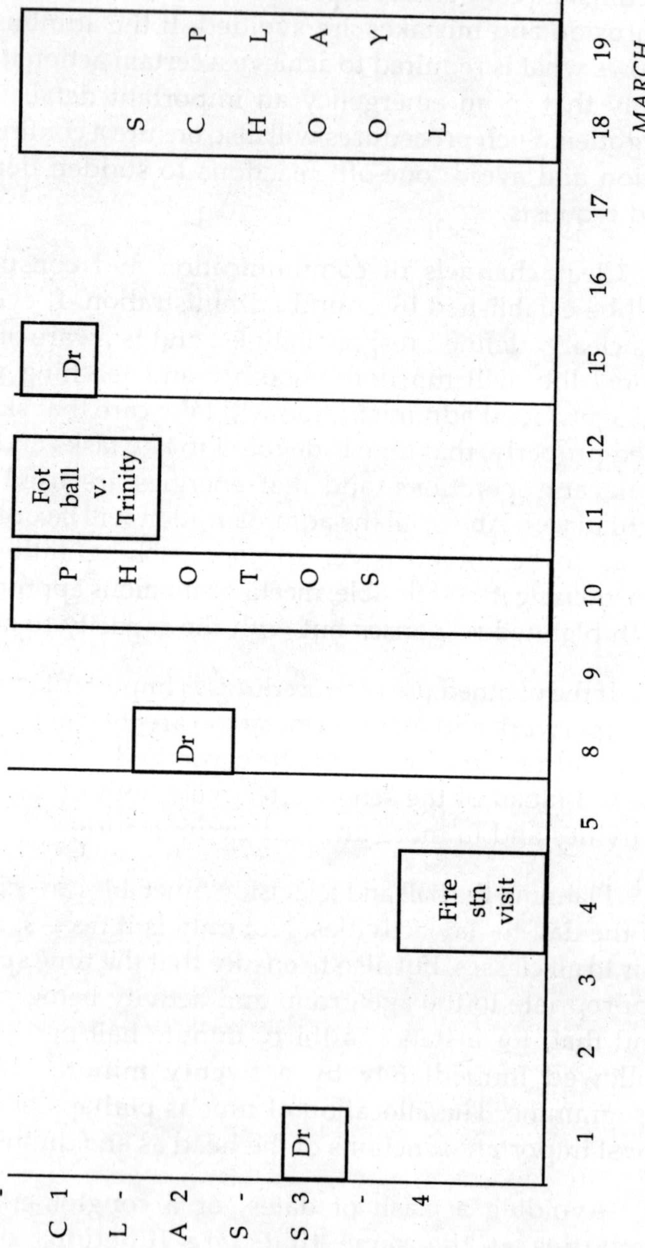
CLASS
1
2
3
4
Dr
Fire stn visit
Dr
PHOTOS
Fot ball v. Trinity
Dr
SCHOOL PLAY
1
2
3
4
5
8
9
10
11
12
15
16
17
18
19
MARCH

administration. In many primary schools the end of term sees a rush of activities many of which could easily have been spread over the previous weeks. Sometimes these dates are not even placed in diaries and often all that is done is to place them on a convenient year planner in the staffroom. However, with a little more thought a flow chart or critical path diary can be prepared and time problems seen at a glance. Particularly helpful is a chart which shows the classes involved at any particular time. An example is shown overleaf. Different colour shading can be used for each class.

Procedures, communication and planning of time will all improve a school's administration but there still remain some key areas where a little thought will pay an excellent dividend.

Information

The passing of information is often done lightly with little thought about procedures or timing. First of all decide what different types of information are most needed in the school, who needs the information and when is it needed. The most likely recipients are staff, children and parents. Can the information safely be delivered orally and individually or are more standard procedures appropriate? Should it be given out in assembly or at a staff meeting or will a circular have more effect?

Parents should be, and need to be, kept well-informed about special activities or particular problems at school. Often this saves misunderstanding or even ill-will later. The information must be carefully presented. It is unlikely that parents will bother to read till the end of a two-page, closely typed and poorly duplicated letter. The information should be clearly sub-headed and relate to what parents need to know. Too much detail leads to boredom, too little to confusion. The letter should be worded so as not to insult the readers' intelligence but, at the same time, should take into account the reading limitations of some parents. It should not be written in official jargon but it should avoid being too chatty and informal. The head should keep a file of all circular letters sent home and a simple numbering system on the letters can be a help also to any bureaucratic minded parent.

Information for children can either be presented directly to them at the conclusion of morning assembly or can be delivered via a note to class teachers. Most heads will have their own views about the sanctity of assembly but many will want to take advantage of this communal time to present information which is of value to the whole school. Provided this is kept in check it should not upset the religious aspect of the assembly.

From time to lime, however, recourse has to be made to the traditional note sent to the classes. There are some fairly obvious points to watch. A simple ticking system on the note will make sure that each class has received it and it will be particularly necessary to observe this if the missive concerns the supervision of children. Before the note is sent be absolutely certain that it is necessary. Nothing is more infuriating than to break off a story, the explanation of a maths concept, or a scientific experiment, to read a note which could have been left until playtime. Many heads find that sending an exercise book round containing the notes, each one dated, is a better system than using separate pieces of paper.

The staffroom notice board if your school is fortunate enough to have one should be the centre of the information system. Too often, however, the board is a jumble of out-of-date notices, often completely irrelevant to the running of the school. Thought, therefore, should be given both to notices and the board.

Notices should be attractive, readable and, if important, eye-catching. If they are not important should they be on the board at all? A simple colour banding system can identify the main categories of notice, *e.g.*, orange hatching for in-service training announcements (which frequently never get past the head), blue hatching for teaching vacancies, red hatching for PTA news.

The board itself should be kept in a tidy state. Notices of similar categories should be kept together and out-of-date ones removed and kept in a simple filing system in the staffroom. One part of the board could be labelled TODAY or THIS WEEK and reserved for the most immediate notices. Some large and long-term notices such as BBC and ITV timetables could perhaps be removed to another place completely.

The running of the staffroom noticeboard is an ideal task for delegation to a teacher with a flair for design and order. This teacher could also be responsible for keeping the school's other information systems up to date, including the staff handbook, fire precautions, etc.

Finally if the staffroom is used as it should be, as part of the information system, it is important that every teacher visits it at least once during the day. They should be encouraged to have their mid-morning coffee there with their colleagues and not in the isolation of their own room.

Forms

When administration is discussed at heads' meetings the mind immediately leaps to the vexed question of forms. Most heads would agree that there are too many and that most of them are useless. As always there is a mixture of truth and exaggeration in this. However, if the filling in of forms is seen as a time-consuming and unnecessary exercise there is something wrong with the head's attitude, his procedures, or external demands upon him, and the reasons should be sought.

Forms mainly originate from one of three places: the DES, the LEA, or the school, with the LEA probably being the biggest offender. Forms seek information to ensure that manpower is being used efficiently and rewarded suitably, to ensure that statutory procedures are being carried out, or to elicit information which may be of help in improving the service. If the reason for having the form is understood a head is more likely to cooperate in filling it in.

Forms from the DES are not all that frequent, the most common being Form 7, upon which much of the statistical information about the nation's education is based. DES and NFER questionnaires are sometimes sent to primary schools and despite the chore involved it is worth filling them in carefully because the evidence produced can well have a long-term effect on educational planning.

It is the LEA forms which generate the most friction. Sometimes they seem unrelated; they are frequently changed. Nil returns are requested which may seem counter-productive. Many LEA forms, are required to ensure that the authority is carrying out its financial commitments responsibly, including the payment of teachers. The forms should allow the local government administration to meet the demands of the auditor but most education departments will listen sympathetically if you question the need for a form. Most people working in local government are as disenchanted with forms as headteachers.

Like the DES some LEA forms ask for information on how well the service is functioning as one of the steps towards making improvements. This evaluation process may be time-consuming, and when several questionnaires arrive together it can be aggravating, but as we have seen it is an important component of management.

It is unlikely that the primary head will need to produce many forms but if he does there are a few golden rules:

1. Make sure that the information you want cannot be collected in a better way.
2. Be clear about the use to be made of the information collected.
3. Consult the customer about the design and be sure he understands the need for it.
4. Make it clear and concise, and if it is to be a repetitive form ask for returns with the longest possible intervals.
5. When the form has outlived its usefulness abandon it.

Procedures

The desirability of establishing sound and known administrative procedures has already been acknowledged in this chapter. Equally important is the setting of procedures dealing with the day-to-day life of the school. All teachers should be aware of the procedures for registration, dinner money collection and assembly. Procedures for dealing with more, irregular happenings should also be made clear; what happens to children at wet playtime or lunchtime for example? It is far better to have a plan which can swing into action at the wave of a hand than to invite indecision and delay. Such procedures reduce the opportunities for confusion and indiscipline among children. These should be known and understood by all teachers and some schools might find the production of a simple staff handbook helpful provided it is updated when necessary.

Filing

All efficient administrators need a simple but effective filing system. The system should meet the demands of the school, so commercial systems should not be adopted without careful thought and adaptation. The main reason for having a filing system is, of course, to ensure that papers can be put away and then retrieved with a minimum of fuss and delay.

There are some common pointers to an effective retrieval system, whichever form of filing is eventually used. Precise definitions are important and although the number of files used should be kept to a minimum too wide a definition can easily lead to endless confusion. Each part of the system should be given a common number and the files within that part given an appropriate sub-number. Thus language development could be 40; staffing 60; accommodation 10; governors 50; and so on. Within one sector the system can be further divided:

60	Staffing-teachers	61	Staffing-non-teaching
60.1	Salary scales	61.1	Salary scales
60.2	Grouping documents	61.2	Canteen: establishment
60.3	Establishment	61.3	Cleaning: establishment
60.4	Advertisements	61.4	Advertisements

An index should be kept of the filing system, available to all who need to use it.

Sometimes effective use can be made of different colours for filing purposes which increases the speed of identification. However, when a new system is started begin in pencil so that adjustments can be made in the light of experience and errors and omissions corrected. For the same reason gaps should be left in the numbering system so that new files can be inserted without upsetting the number sequence.

One of the functions of a good clerical assistant, or school secretary, even if part-time, should be the maintenance of the filing system. If the part-timer's hours are properly arranged filing should not wait too long. It does help if the head, when passing paper on for filing, marks a clear 'F' at the lop of the paper, and gives some indication of the appropriate file to be used. This is perhaps the proper point to move on to the key to successful administration.

The School Secretary

It is clear that a number of local authorities undervalue the assistance given to a school by a secretary, or, as she is more often called in the primary school, the clerical assistant. Only the largest primaries have one available full-time and smaller schools may have to make do with help on only one or two mornings each week. If more clerical help was available it would reduce the routine administrative load on the head and free her for the more professional duties of management and teaching.

However, even when a school has a reasonable allocation of clerical hours the secretary is not used as effectively as she should be. Too often her only basic task is dinner money and register collection and the rest of her time is taken up with items that tend to arise on the spur of the moment. A well-thought-out job description is, therefore, a must and the exercise of doing this will force the head to appraise the use that is made of his secretary.

A good secretary can be one of the most effective public relations officers a school has. She should be, well-turned out with a pleasant manner. This is especially necessary for dealing with parents, for some of whom a visit to the school is still little better than a trip to the dentist. With more aggressive parents a sympathetic secretary can often calm ruffled edges before the head's door is reached and in many cases the problem can be solved without recourse to the head. On the other hand, it is important that the secretary does not act as an immovable object between visitor and head but as a flexible and helpful mentor to both.

If the secretary is to perform this function properly her siting is important. Clearly the design of the school, the space available and heating arrangements all constrain where a secretary can be accommodated. However, a careful analysis of the available space may yield some surprising results. It is unsatisfactory for a secretary to share the head's room unless this is inescapable; he, or she, does not want to be disturbed by the typewriter; the secretary does not want to be sent out every time a confidential visitor arrives. It is equally unsatisfactory if visitors have to run the gauntlet of remedial room, staff toilets and staffroom before coming to the secretary's office.

Whenever possible, therefore, the secretary should be sited near to the main entrance, in a space of her own, and with a clear sign welcoming visitors. If her office is enclosed a sliding window system can do a lot to provide a more intimate relationship with the visitor. If a separate office is unavailable a welcoming reception area could be made in the entrance hall, or a cloakroom adapted to serve as a reception concourse. The equipment needed actually at a secretary's fingertips is not as great as sometimes imagined. In harsh financial times LEAs will not be keen to spend money on administrative accommodation but the wise head, in his bid for a minor works allocation, will emphasise the advantages accruing to the professional side of the school.

An efficient secretary, given the opportunity and invited to use her initiative, can make the head's task easier in many small ways. As a 'telephone sifter' she can answer many queries herself, passing to the head those which he should deal with. Files can be made ready in advance of meetings, and papers arranged for conferences. Not only will this save time but it will promote an air of efficiency in the school. She will also know when the head can be disturbed and when not; quite reasonably most heads want to make themselves available to children but there are times when a stretch of peace and quiet is essential.

If the secretary is part-time a profile of the week's pressure points should be established and arrangements made for her to attend at those times; if necessary messages and letters can be stored on a dictaphone to await her return. Her secretarial tasks should also be specified; is it her job to make the staff their morning coffee and wash up after them? Should she always be the one to run off carol sheets on the duplicator or should a teacher in charge of audio-visual aids accept this as one of his or her responsibilities?

The secretary is close to the main holder of authority in the school and she is often among the longest serving members of staff of the establishment. This probably means that some reflected authority is invested in her. This can lead to a situation of potential conflict, for while the secretary is seen as professionally junior to any member of the teaching staff her central place in the organisation can sometimes lead to a contradiction of this relationship. Provided heads recognise this danger it can be avoided with tact and sensitivity.

Day-to-day Administration

One of the most difficult tasks facing any headteacher is how to cope with the multitude of day-to-day problems that face him or her, and how to leave time for the really important decisions; in short, how to sort the wood from the trees. Any single day can bring decisions or actions on stock ordering, room allocation, supply teachers, difficult parents, maintenance, the education officer, school meals, in-service training, curriculum development, transport—to name only a few. How can the head deal with the administrative priorities and leave herself time for management?

Running an efficient administrative structure through the filing system, use of secretary and so on, as discussed above, is part of the answer. So is knowing how to deal with the letters and other pieces of paper; which ones need an immediate answer, which can be referred; which items can be dealt with on the telephone, which need further research?

Broadly speaking a headteacher has four main perspectives: her role as the main curriculum developer and evaluator in the school; her personnel role; her tasks as community relations and public relations officer; and her role as resource provider. It is obvious that few problems will be exclusive to one category but it may be useful to identify the main category to which an individual situation belongs. Without realising it a head may be concentrating on the task of curriculum developer at the expense of the personnel needs of the school. Staff tensions will build up and these will create further problems to reduce overall the time available for management.

Research tends to show that heads are either people-orientated or process-orientated. Thus one style of headship can be very different from another. A basic difficulty for both types is freeing oneself from the small decisions which it is necessary to take. The only answer is delegation and this involves a careful review of school objectives combined with job evaluation and description.

Delegation

Some administrative problems can be referred upwards to someone of a higher status, the chief adviser or the chief education officer. Other items can be deferred as the head decides that although action may be necessary its urgency is not essential. Sometimes the item is deferred while further information is sought. This leaves items which must either be dealt with by the head or delegated.

Delegation is a power which most managers are afraid to use to the full. However, the advantages can be considerable, freeing time for the head, involving a subordinate in higher status work and, not infrequently, arriving at a better decision from someone closer to the problem.

How far down the line should the delegation be pushed? Deputy head, secretary, Scale 1 teacher, caretaker? This depends on three things:

1. At what point does the person in the line have access to all the information necessary to tackle the job? For instance, a probationer cannot be expected to make a judgement on the introduction of a new reading scheme.
2. At what point can the person delegated decide what is best for the whole school? Tied up with this is the question of status, one of the differences that we have seen between educational management and business management. Can a Scale 2 teacher with responsibility for language development make operational decisions about the annual school play, or should these be made at a higher level?
3. Can the individual exercise good judgement on the item in question?

The first two criteria are easy to apply but the last one

is difficult and involves staff appraisal. However, when the decision to delegate is made the incumbent should be given the resources to complete the job and the terms of reference should be clearly understood by all concerned. Avoid the temptation to think you could do the job better yourself; you probably could but can you use your time better?—that is.the crucial question. Finally allow the person doing the job the chance to show his initiative; this is not the same as abrogating responsibility.

Am I Effective?

One way of deciding whether your routine administration is effective is to compare what you think you do with what happens in practice. If your answers to the following questions are 'no' you are spending too much time on administration and not enough on management.

1. Do you organise your week and day according to pre-determined priorities?
2. Are you balancing out your time efficiently between the main aspects of the job?
3. Are you giving adequate time to reviewing the past, evaluating the present and planning for the future?
4. Are you doing only that work which cannot be delegated?
5. Are you seeing all the people you should be seeing, including non-teaching staff?
6. Are you able to complete tasks?
7. Are you making time for your own professional improvement through reading and in-service education?
8. Are you keeping in touch with what is happening in the classrooms in your school?

11

The Small Elementary School

Most of this book is applicable to primary schools whatever their size. Each school has its own particular circumstances and environment which makes it unique. The needs of the inner city primary school are very different from those of the school in the wealthy suburbs of a country town. Less often recognised are the problems of managing the smallest of primary schools, often situated in an isolated village community.

The thought of being head of such a school, with few staff to control and a small number of children to worry about, situated in the middle of beautiful countryside, may seem appealing to the teacher grappling with remedial problems in Birmingham or Manchester. The truth can be very different, for running such a village school has its own particular difficulties.

The school may have fifty children on roll, staffed by a head and one assistant. The children will be divided into two classes, infant and junior, with a widespread of ages in each. The head might be supported with five hours' clerical assistance and seven hours' cleaning time, but inevitably this support will not be available when it is most needed. Much of the head's time may be spent therefore on non-teaching or non-managerial duties. The building is likely to be small and old, and it maybe difficult to organise the environment to suit modern teaching techniques.

The small school faces a number of difficulties which can restrict the curriculum and the development of the school, including the head's personal training. The amount of money available through capitation will restrict the equipment and resources available to the small school, although more enlightened authorities attempt to bolster small schools' capitation with a special allowance. The lack of contact with other adults in the school will mean that the primary head will not be able to test new ideas or activities against other people. It is quite likely that the nearest other primary school is several miles away.

The particular difficulties of the small school head are time, resources and contact.

The newly-appointed head will quickly discover that, in a small school, he must be an administrator, a manager, a leader and organiser, and a manual worker, at the same time as being a full-time teacher. Immediate solutions could be to stay at school later than usual, to take work home, to arrive at about 8.00 am or to double up classes if possible for certain periods of the week.

The last suggestion is rarely practical, nor in the children's interests, so most heads are forced into a combination of working late and early. Fortunately many authorities now provide some part-time teaching help for the small school and this can be used in a number of ways to make the head's task easier and more effective.

The most straightforward use of the part-timer is to relieve the head of teaching responsibilities, freeing him for other things. This can certainly be helpful for part of the week but other ways of using part-time help in the interests of the whole school should be considered. The part-timer might be able to extract small groups of children for special help or might offer a particular speciality to groups of children. One problem in a small school is to establish a wide but balanced curriculum with only a small number of adults. It is important therefore for all strengths to be fully used and the part-timer should be considered as much more than a child minder for the head's class.

If, however, the head has been able to plan the timetable of the school to give himself a free afternoon he must consider very carefully the most effective ways of using it. Teachers are professionals and they recognise that there are certain tasks which can be done after school hours when the children are not present. Few headteachers would maintain that their job is only from 9 am to 3.30 pm for 190 days a year. Time free from teaching in the small school will therefore be used most effectively in tasks which require the presence of children or other members of staff.

This time might be profitably spent in working with individual children, by team-teaching with a colleague as part of a staff development and in-service training programme, or by visiting neighbouring schools to make contact with colleagues and see them in action. The evaluation of children's work and teaching programmes could also take place during this time.

It is quite natural when a school has only a head and one assistant teacher, for them to assume that their teaching is complementary and that there is no need for written aims and objectives. What is discussed in formal meetings in larger schools can be sorted out over a cup of tea at lunch-time in the smaller school. One must of course have a reasonable attitude to consultation in the small school but the danger of assuming things will happen without proper consideration must be avoided. Even if the sessions only involve two teachers, time should be set aside for planning work and setting the objectives of the school.

All schools, whatever their size, need a basic amount of equipment and this can be a severe strain on the resources of the smaller primary school. Thought could therefore be given to jointly purchasing a piece of equipment and sharing its use with colleagues, on a mutual help basis. This idea need not be restricted to equipment. Arrangements could be made to share and exchange teachers who can offer specialist subjects to children or expertise to other colleagues.

The likely development of special schools as resource centres should not be ignored. Many secondary schools are anxious to improve contacts with primaries and they may have equipment, resources and even staff that can be borrowed.

Every opportunity should be taken for teachers in small schools to meet together, despite the practical difficulties, for in-service training and the sharing of ideas. Teachers will also want to maximise the use of voluntary help in the village to help with the one hundred and one tasks which are necessary to keep the small school running.

The most frustrating thing for the headteacher of a small school is the constant disruption of his teaching programme, even if he has managed to timetable himself some 'free' time. There are a number of things which can be done to minimise these disruptions. Parents can be contacted and asked to call before morning school or after school closes in the afternoon. Exceptions can be made for real emergencies but otherwise parents should not be allowed to disrupt teaching. If other visitors arrive unannounced and want to see the head they should be asked to make an appointment, unless it is an emergency.

The telephone in a small school can be a lifesaver but it can also be an irritating nuisance. If it is in the classroom lessons will be interrupted while it rings and is answered. If it is elsewhere the class must be left while it is attended to. Regular callers could be asked to call before or after school, or during the head's non-teaching time. Telephone answering machines can also be hired at reasonable cost and it might be worth investigating the possibility of using one to solve some of the problems. Use of a tape recorder for dictation has already been suggested and this practice can be very useful for the head of a small school.

If the organisation and administration of a small school is carefully planned the job of the head teacher can be one of the most rewarding in the education service. It cannot however be thought of as a sinecure as it is without doubt one of the most demanding posts.

12

Organisational Culture

What is Organisational Culture?

Here are two attempts at defining organisational culture.

> Culture is an informal understanding of the 'way we do things around here.' The elements of culture are shared values and beliefs, rituals and ceremonies and an informal network of storytellers, spies and gossips.
>
> (Deal & Kennedy, 1983)

> Central to the concept of culture is the idea of value, that which is regarded as worthwhile by members of some group. These values are manifest in the norms which govern behaviour and the symbols — language, actions, artefacts — which express these values. Thus, in a school with an academic culture there will be norms which emphasise academic endeavour perhaps symbolised through dress, honours boards, staff qualifications etc.
>
> (Hoyle, 1986)

It can be seen from these two quotations that culture is about values which are both implicit and explicit to the school.

What Makes a Culture?

Obviously people make a culture, but culture is really the way people interact. Interactions are affected by several things.

1. Buildings

They affect how staff interact and work together. Temporary classrooms, split sites, corridors, halls, staffrooms, cellular classrooms, open-plan areas—all of these influence how staff meet and what opportunities they have to learn about each other.

2. Coordination

Arrangements to coordinate the work of staff affect the culture. By deciding how far headteachers want to coordinate the work of colleagues they are affecting the extent and nature of formal interaction.

3. Social Events and Incidents

The ways in which staff interact socially have a bearing upon the general ways in which they 'work' together. Over a period of time patterns can be detected which are frequently highly stable. Social encounters are concentrated at play-times, lunch-times, and before and after school. Therefore, who meets with whom, when and where are matters which might reveal patterns.

4. History

A school's history and traditions affect and often explain behaviour. Things we have tried in the past, crises we have survived, adversity we have overcome, all have an influence on the way we do things now.

Traditions are most visible at Christmas but also at other times of the year (for example, May Day, Fayres, Easter and other festivals, Sports Day, charity events).

5. *Rituals and Ceremonies*

Often these are linked to eating and drinking: staff meals, cakes (for birthdays or saying thank you), glasses of wine, tea and coffee arrangements, going to the pub.

School assemblies are significant events—often when the unity and community of the school is implicitly celebrated.

Leave-takings and farewells (to staff moving on or retiring) are also important ceremonies.

How Do You Find Out About Culture?

It takes time to find out about a school's culture, not least because it is often implicit. However, newcomers often 'blunder' into the culture and are most sensitive to it because they and the culture are strange to one another.

Culture can be seen through in-jokes, mottoes, sayings, stories about the school's past, the values which are celebrated in assemblies, and what staff say to each other (see Nias, Southworth & Yeomans, 1989).

Nevertheless, culture is difficult to see since it is both a process and product. You may be interested to look at some of the exercises suggested by Pollard & Tann (1987), which provide useful ways of looking and thinking about culture. The best way is to try to observe one's own school's culture.

Why is Culture Important?

Two responses might serve as answers to this. First, since culture is to do with values, it is important to try and discern what a school's culture is since the values which underpin the culture are likely to affect not only how the staff behave but also the children. Although the connection between culture and curriculum is likely to be indirect, children will nevertheless learn things from the school's culture (for example, how adults relate to each other; consideration and courtesy).

Second, there is a belief that when a school's culture is strong and positive this will contribute to the effectiveness of the school. Mortimore et al. (1988) say: 'an effective school has a positive ethos. Overall, we found the atmosphere to be more pleasant in the effective schools.'

This is also supported by Deal (1985) who has devised a chart comparing the characteristics of effective schools with strong organisational cultures. Deal's chart is shown overleaf.

Characteristics of Effective Schools	*Characteristics of Strong Organisational Cultures*
Coherent ethos with agreed-upon ways of doing things: agreement on instructional goals	Strong culture with shared values and a consensus on "how we do things around here"
Importance of principal as leader	Importance of principal as hero or heroine who embodies core values or who anoints other heroic figures
Strong beliefs about teaching and learning	Widely shared beliefs reflected in distinctive practices or rituals
Teachers as role models: students with positions of responsibility	Employees as situational heroes or heroines who represent core values
Staff training on schoolwide basis	Rituals of acculturation and cultural renewal
Effective meetings to plan jointly and solve problems	Potent rituals to celebrate and transform core values
Orderly atmosphere without rigidity, guilt without oppression	Balance between innovation and tradition, autonomy and authority
Joint participation in technical decision making	Widespread participation in cultural rituals

Finally, culture also shows us that although schools can be structured and planned it is how the people inside them interact together and what they value and believe, which really makes the place distinctive and alive. Schools are organisations full of people, not robots. Schools are value-laden places.

THE ENVIRONMENTAL CONTEXT

Every school exists in an environment. Environment can be thought of in terms of *level:* the macro level which is common to all schools, and the micro level which is more closely linked to the individual school. Factors which affect the environment include:

Macro Level	**Micro Level**
Department of Education and Science (DES), National Curriculum Council (NCC), Schools Examination and Assessment Council (SEAC), central government legislation, teachers' salaries, unions and associations, H.M. Inspectors	School's catchment and local community, policies of LEA, school site and buildings, community use and involvements, governors.

A school is, in part, influenced by the environment in which it is situated. This is most obvious in terms of the micro context. Individual governors may affect the school's aims; fund-raising schemes and PTA/PA support generate greater or lesser financial help. Thus, staff are usually well aware of the micro context.

This awareness is possibly because staff perceive

themselves as able to affect the micro level. The constituents of the micro level are things we know, people we meet, groups we can contact and negotiate with. By comparison, the macro level is much more remote.

Two things are interesting about the environmental context. The first is the way in which each school is a product of both levels. For example, staffing quotas will be determined by LEA policies whilst, at the same time, salaries and allowances are determined at the macro level. Any school is a blend of macro and micro environmental contexts. Since schools have greater opportunity to 'negotiate' with the micro level, schools might also be able to affect, and in a sense manage, the environment in which they exist. The section on External Relations (pp. 206-219) picks up this theme with its attention to school image, and 'selling' the school. Second, the context is always changing. At the micro level this might be the influx of 'new' parents because of housing developments, because of alterations in LEA policies or changes in national policies. Indeed, schools are most likely to be most sensitive to the environment when it is changing.

Turbulent Environment

The 1980s were a time of considerable environmental change. The 1980, 1981,1986 and 1988 Education Acts show just how turbulent the macro level became. Moreover, the turbulence was made greater because each of these Acts altered the micro context, especially in respect of school governance and accountabilities and the role of the LEA (*see*, Sallis 1988).

Turbulent environments make life more difficult for those inside the school. For one thing staff cannot focus purely on the internal organisation—they must also be alert to the external. This dual focus is something headteachers have had to develop.

However, headteachers are not unique in having to remain alert to the school and its context. Most managers in most organisations also have to do so. What headteachers (and others) need to recognise as a result of the 1980s, is that the post-1988 period makes it imperative that they are as knowledgeable about and as sensitive to the environment as possible. Headteachers work at the interface of the school and its environmental context. While, previously, headteachers needed only to manage the environment in a token way, today they need to see the school's environmental context as one of their main arenas of activity.

KEY MANAGEMENT ISSUES

ANCILLARY STAFF

In recent years there has been an increasing emphasis on the need for primary schools to function as *whole* schools. Usually this has caused headteachers and deputy heads to consider issues of coordination or continuity, while many schools have worked hard to improve staff communication and to increase the amount of teacher collaboration. Although much valuable work has taken place, the bulk of the work appears to have either emphasised or been aimed at *teachers*. Therefore, while in many schools teachers have become less independent and more collaborative, there may also have been an underemphasis, perhaps even an underestimation, of the roles and responsibilities of ancillary staff. If whole schools are to be a reality we need to think seriously about how all staff—both teachers and ancillaries -work together.

Who are Ancillary Staff?

Naming these people is something of a problem because their titles sometimes vary from LEA to LEA. We list below some of the more common titles (with alternatives in brackets):

- school secretary (clerical assistant)
- welfare assistants (non-teaching assistants)
- Section 11 assistants (dealing with ethnic minorities; mother tongue teaching; EFL)
- caretakers (school keeper/cleaner-in-charge)
- cleaners
- midday supervisors (midday assistants/dinner ladies)
- kitchen staff(cook, meals staff)
- National Nursery Education Board Assistants (NNEB assistants).

However, another way of answering this question is to think about how they are referred to in your school. Are they regarded warmly or not? Who uses the staffroom? Who attends meetings? How many teachers do they talk to? How do the children regard them? How has the school kept them informed about recent changes and developments? Does the caretaker know about LMS, for example? Which of these individuals are *naturally* regarded as members of staff and which (if any) are perhaps marginalised?

How are they Involved in the School?

One thing seems quite obvious from looking at this list of ancillary staff: they undertake a range of tasks and make very significant contributions to the work of the teachers, the children's work and the life of the school as a whole. One way of illustrating this is to list just some examples of what these individuals actually do:

- act as receptionist/telephonist/typist (secretaries/ancillary assistants)
- manage school finances and funds (secretaries)
- control stock and paper resources (ancillary assistants)
- provide classroom support (ancillary/NNEB assistants)
- work with individual children (ancillary/NNEB assistants/midday supervisors)
- support children with special educational needs (ancillary/NNEB assistants/midday supervisors)
- deal with behaviour problems (ancillary/NNEB assistants/midday supervisors/kitchen staff).

And these are only a few examples! In fact, what emerges from drawing up such a list is the realisation that all these ancillary staff deal with children. For example, all will have important conversations with children, and in this way the adults will affect the children's language development because all these adults play a part, albeit 'informally', in the school's language curriculum. Yet how far has the school involved these important members of staff in the planning, implementation, review and development of the language curriculum? Questions like this need to be asked for all aspects of the curriculum, especially social, moral and personal education. How, for example, do ancillary staff influence the school's policies on equal opportunities?

Some schools ignore such staff altogether; this seems to be unsound management. Some schools involve such staff very well; we know of schools where caretakers, secretaries and ancillaries take part in staff meetings and/ or attend regular meetings with the headteacher and deputy; schools where welfare assistants for children with special educational needs are offered regular meetings to talk about their work and how they feel they and the children are getting on; schools where ancillary staff are offered in-service and development activities.

Looking Forward

When schools undertake development plans they need to think about how to make best use of the ancillary staff. When schools look forward they need to try to embrace *all* the staff. That is fairly obvious but what about how their roles and responsibilities might change? Two things come to mind here.

First, over the last 15 years the 'number' of ancillary staff in schools has generally increased: either in terms of the numbers of persons in school or the amounts of time in school. There are now more midday supervisors, Section 11 assistants,, welfare helpers (especially for children with special educational needs). In acknowledging that there has been an increase in ancillary support, we are not saying whether this is sufficient or adequate—only that there are more today than there used to be yesterday! However, we also believe that this increase will continue. As LMS is applied to more and more schools we anticipate that some schools will expand their ancillary staff force. In which case it becomes even more imperative that they are fully integrated into the life of the school and perform roles which truly support the intentions of the school.

Secondly, LMS is likely to affect the work of secretaries quite significantly. During the 1990s school secretaries will become, in part at least, *bursars.* Of course they will need help in this—they may also need to work longer (paid!) hours. Also, since some LMS schemes rely on computerised programmes, secretaries will need to be increasingly familiar with information technology. For some secretaries this will be a dramatic change.

Moreover, if secretaries are to spend more time as bursars, who will take on their typing or receptionist work? They surely cannot be expected to absorb all the 'new' work while continuing with all their previous work. Thus the secretary's new role will have implications for others.

A final point to bear in mind when thinking about ancillary staff concerns the fact that they are often part-time workers—present on site for only a part of each day or week. Some will not see others because they are never present at the same time. Some may not see the headteacher or deputy head if their timetables never coincide. In a sense, one challenge for schools is to try to ensure that part-time workers *feel* they are full members of staff.

TEACHER APPRAISAL

The formal appraisal of teachers, on a widespread scale, has been a relatively recent development in education. While some individual schools have operated appraisal schemes for several years, it was not until the Department of Education and Science commissioned pilot work in teacher appraisal in 1987 that LEAs became involved. Prior to this activity appraisal tended to be informal and covert. With the government requiring all LEAs to introduce appraisal schemes from September 1989 appraisal has the opportunity to become more formal, open and systematic.

Although each LEA will have adopted a scheme best suited to its perceived needs and preferences, there are certain principles, aims and elements which schools need to keep in mind and, from time to time, apply to their own practices and the LBA's.

Basic Principles

(a) Teacher appraisal is on-going. It is a continuous process, not an isolated (even if regularly-repeated) event. Teacher appraisal is not 'hit and run'.

(b) Teacher appraisal is only a part of staff development; it is neither the whole of staff development nor a substitute for it.

(c) Teacher appraisal should make a positive difference to each teacher's classroom practice. Although appraisal will review other aspects of a teacher's work, appraisal should affect for the better teaching and learning in the school.

(d) Teacher appraisal should be a supportive process for *all* teachers. Appraisal is not simply for those whose performance is deemed to be poor; appraisal should also help the creative, imaginative and gifted teachers.

(e) Teacher appraisal should be 'two way': it should benefit the school and the individual.

(f) Resource implications should be reviewed periodically. Local Education Authority Training Grant Schemes, LMS, INSET and time spent on the process of appraisal should all be given full consideration and synchronised so as to facilitate the best possible approach to teacher appraisal and staff development.

Aims of Teacher Appraisal

Different schemes may have differing aims but the following might be common to many schemes. They are offered since it may be helpful to compare them against those adopted by the school. Appraisal should seek to:

(a) help teachers develop as teachers and as professionals;

(b) encourage teachers to engage in self-appraisal and in the discussion of their work;

(c) enable teachers to know how they are doing;

(d) clarify the teacher's responsibilities and tasks in the light of present and changing circumstances;

(e) identify the support the teacher may need inside and beyond the school.

Key Elements of an Appraisal Process

(N.B. The sequence of these elements is, at best, notional and not prescribed.)

Preparation: appraisal should not be a surprise event. Prior to a teacher's appraisal there should be a rather informal (but not casual) meeting to discuss the appraisal process. A time schedule and specific focus might be agreed and a review reflecting upon the previous appraisal shared.

Job descriptions: appraisal should be related to the teacher's job description which, in turn, must be fully negotiated, understood and agreed in detail by both appraisee and appraiser. The job description is effectively a working document and should be a tool for considering teachers' responsibilities in their various tasks (curricular, managerial, pastoral, etc.).

Classroom observation: there is a clear need to observe

the teacher's work in the classroom. Suitable times for observation should be mutually agreed. More than a single session and activity should be observed.

Self-appraisal: teachers should undertake a review of the period since the last appraisal. Using an agreed approach (for example, checklist, prompt list) successes, failures, developments and disappointments could be itemised prior to discussion with the appraiser.

Initial review discussion: some days before the appraisal discussion an agenda for this discussion should be agreed and any relevant notes exchanged (for example, the appraiser could receive the teacher's self-appraisal; the teacher might receive the appraiser's review of the same period and classroom observation notes).

The appraisal discussion or interview: a time for formalised sharing of points of view, information, hopes, aspirations, expectations and targets for the future.

The appraisal report: this should be produced by the appraiser and be a concise summary of the appraisal discussion based upon notes taken during the discussion.

Follow-up: there is a need to check that agreed actions do happen and for the appraiser to ensure that individual teachers' professional development takes place.

Some further questions which each scheme and perhaps school will need to answer:

- Who appraises whom?
- How frequently should each individual teacher be appraised?

- How much classroom observation should take place?
- Are there any special circumstances to take into account (for example, children with special needs, critical incidents in the teacher's life)?
- What happens if judgements cannot be mutually agreed?
- What happens to the report?
- How long is the shelf life of a teacher's record?

Appraisal is not a guaranteed method of improving relationships, abilities, self-esteem or the health of your school. There is a real danger that education will follow sections of industry in believing that the existence of an appraisal scheme is enough in itself and that, once set up, the scheme will be self-running and self-determining.

Unfortunately, nothing could be further from the truth. The problems involved in talking with colleagues about strengths and weaknesses, about making classroom visits, about being the appraiser without apparently ever being the appraisee, about linking promotion and the allocation of posts with appraisal interviews and so on are enormous.

There is some evidence which indicates that in the majority of cases where appraisal has been introduced in organisations performance, relationships and self-confidence have all taken a dive.

If education is to avoid this, then both those conducting the appraisal and those being appraised need to work out beforehand exactly what is going to happen and need to feel confident that the theoretical benefits of appraisal have at least a chance of materialising in the real day-to-day life of their schools.

Those conducting the appraisal need to be particularly self-critical. An appraisal is—and should be—more than a friendly chat, but it requires skill and understanding to operate successfully. It requires the understanding of all participants, crucial abilities in the appraisers and a process which is clear to all.

So, don't take appraisal for granted. Organised effectively within your school it *can* bring dramatic improvements. However, it will only be effective if the process of appraisal is itself continually appraised.

LEADERSHIP—1

A considerable number of studies have been conducted into leadership. Consequently there is no shortage of analyses and theories which attempt to portray what leaders do, what makes some leaders more effective than others and which factors influence leaders. Leadership has been studied in commercial and industrial organisations as well as education; we can all benefit from this research.

The Key Elements

Let's look at six key elements:

- leaders provide structures
- leaders need to be considerate
- leaders affect the way decisions are taken
- leaders provide an example
- leaders work in particular contexts
- leaders provide their organisation with a mission.

1. Leaders Provide Structures

Structures are the basic organisational building blocks of your school. When we act as leaders in schools we set up structures. For example, there are timetables, communication networks and the organisation of colleagues and children into various groups.

Timetables can set up structures concerning the use of space -particularly shared space such as halls or specialist areas.

Communication networks relate to staff meetings, curriculum working parties, record keeping, liaison meetings, community links and so on.

Structures for staff and children mean the setting up of class groups, allocation of teachers to classes, teaching teams, departments, use of specialist and support staff such as ancillaries, peripatetic teachers and special needs staff.

Those of us who act as leaders (and that will almost certainly be all of us at one time or another) are involved in:

- providing structures
- maintaining structures
- re-designing structures
- adapting structures.

2. *Leaders Need to be Considerate*

Being considerate is a necessary quality of leadership but consideration is not a simple once-and-for-all quality. Being considerate means that we understand the views and attitudes of those with whom we have to work.

If we accept that people are different then the consideration we show them needs to be different. For example, if someone wants to be involved in decision-making, it may not be considerate to tell them exactly what to do. If someone is by nature hierarchical, asking them to take part in the process of each and every decision may be counter-productive.

By considering each individual and trying to understand their perspectives *and* by considering each situation we stand a good chance of improving motivation and commitment to the work and life of the school.

As leaders we also need an understanding of individual circumstances. People can be affected by bereavement, illness, family crises and so on. At such times it's not a good idea to ask a teacher to help you run three nights' rehearsals for the school play!

Whatever leadership role you have, it is quite usual for that role to be observed and commented on by colleagues. If you show consideration, fairness and understanding it will be noticed.

3. Leaders Affect the Way Decisions are Made

'Centralised' and 'de-centralised' decision making depends very much on the way a leader chooses to delegate or structure the process.

You may choose to lead in a centralised or de-centralised way as a result of:

- your own personality
- the needs of the particular situation.

When you examine your own leadership style try and make sure that you don't delude yourself into thinking you've made a decision based on the second when really it's the first! Centralised or de-centralised styles of leadership do have a lot to do with who you are but they must also have something to do with the demands of each particular situation.

4. Leaders Provide an Example

In every facet of school life—in teaching, in policy-making, in pastoral work—leaders set an example. Depending on the point of view of those working with you, the example you set may be a positive or negative one. Over time and through a whole series of issues and decisions a balanced judgement may be forthcoming. No one is going to be viewed positively all the time; in the end, it's the consensus opinion that counts.

Setting an example is complex. It can involve a whole host of personal qualities as well as professional ones. So energy, delegation, trust, consideration, personal organisation, dealing with differences, handling disputes, sense of humour, and temperament can all play a part!

5. Leaders Work in Particular Contexts

As leaders affect schools, so schools affect leaders. To be head of a small, rural school in a purpose-built, modern building with supportive parents and energetic staff is different from being head of a large, inner-city school in a dilapidated, vandalised building with disaffected parents and a staff whose morale is depressed.

But there is more to context than the buildings and the parents. Other contextual factors include:

- the way priorities are decided
- the private and professional relationships among the staff

- the resources available to the school
- the level of staff development
- the effectiveness of the headteacher
- the level of support from the LEA.

The context affects the work of all leaders in schools. From time to time leaders need to assess how their *present* context is affecting their work as well as how *they* are affecting the context.

6. Leaders Provide Their Organisation with a Mission

Mission means establishing a sense of direction, a feeling of going somewhere, of aiming at something. Mission does not imply a military exactness nor a religious fervour. Rather, it is commonly agreed that leaders have a vision of how they would like to see the school working, and use this vision or mission to stimulate other teachers, parents, children and governors.

LEADERSHIP-2

One consequence of a leader's work and responsibility is to remain self-critical. If leadership is concerned with six key elements it is also necessary for the leader to keep these dimensions under review.

The following questions are aimed at headteachers as leaders. They might also serve to suggest similar questions for deputy heads and curriculum leaders.

Questions for Headteachers to Ask Themselves

It may also be helpful for headteachers to keep a detailed diary for a given period, say a fortnight, and then to ask themselves the following questions:

1. *Time*

a) How often did I
- — go into classes on one day
- — greet children and parents at the beginning or end of the school day.
- — work with children?

b) What time did I give to meeting staff individually and in groups?

c) i) How much time did I spend out of school:
- — at County Hall/Town Hall etc.
- — at divisional meetings
- — at other schools
- — at conferences or in service courses
- — elsewhere?

ii) Was this time:
- — necessary
- — useful to the school or LEA?

d) How much time did I spend on administration and meetings in and out of school hours?

e) How much time did I give to visitors including parents, governors, inspectors and LEA officers?

f) Do I need to try to change the time distribution revealed by answers to the above questions?

2. *Objectives and Organisation*

a) What do I see as the priorities for the school in the next term/year/five years?

b) Do I know to what extent my view is shared by others?

c) What constraints exist?

d) Are any organisational changes desirable or necessary?

e) Which areas of the curriculum need attention and who can give this attention?

f) How do I ensure that resources are distributed in a balanced way to sustain current priorities and support new developments?

3. Internal Relations

a) How available am I—formally and informally?

b) i) What steps do I take to ensure that the staff feel that I am interested in their professional development, advancement and personal welfare? (ii) When, for example, did I last speak to:

ii) Was this time:

— a part-time teacher

— a cleaner

— a member of the non-teaching staff

— a new teacher?

c) i) How satisfied am I that postholders are able to influence their colleagues in the area for which they have responsibility?

ii) How could their influence be extended?

d) How accurate is my awareness of the load carried by different individual teachers:

— throughout the working day

— in voluntary activities

— in helping children and colleagues?

e) How accurate is my awareness of the load carried by non-teaching staff?

4. *External Relations*

a) What is the first impact of the school on visitors?

b) Do I know what impression is given to telephone callers?

c) Have I satisfied myself that parents from all ethnic groups know to whom they can turn for help and that it will be forthcoming?

d) Are relationships with governors positive and fruitful? Do I keep them fully informed about developments in the school?

e) Have I sufficient knowledge of the LEA administrative structure and inspectors to ensure the school is properly supported?

f) Do I make good use of the Education Welfare Service and the Schools' Psychological Service?

g) Do I make good professional and personal relationships with:

- — local primary school headteachers
- — nearby secondary school headteachers
- — principals of local colleges of further and higher education?

h) Do I know, and am I known by:

- — local community leaders
- — police and welfare agencies
- — local shopkeepers
- — neighbours of the school?

i) Do parents feel at ease with me? How do I know?

5. General

a) Do I listen without interrupting when people are talking to me about what is important to them, however pressed I am for time?

b) Am I ready to learn from other people and other institutions?

c) Do I praise and thank people whenever they deserve it?

d) Do I know myself well enough to be able to make important decisions or judgements when I am under stress?

e) Do staff and children know what I feel strongly about in matters of curriculum, organisation and personal relationships?

f) In spite of everything, do I still find being a headteacher exciting?

6. The Future

a) Are we clear about what we have been trying to do? How far are we meeting those intentions?

b) What are the priorities for action:

— next term

— in the coming year?

c) Who will initiate this action?

d) Do we need any outside support and advice? If so, what?

Ironically, leadership is not always defined by doing things. It is just as important to *be* someone and for the perception of what you are to be shared by those you are responsible for leading. If those you are leading don't carry around with them a perception of your capacity to lead as well as a perception of your willingness just to act then it is unlikely that your leadership will be as effective as it could be.

The ways in which such perceptions of leaders are created is difficult to define. One of the benefits of 'management by walking about' is that it enables those who depend on your leadership to see you engaging in informal as well as formal leadership, of allowing your own views, attitudes and aspirations to emerge in day-to-day life. It gives everyone a chance to see that the practice matches with the theory.

Finally, your effective leadership of others is defined as much in *their* perceptions of your leadership as it is in your own. The questions in this chapter are important in helping you consider the effectiveness of your leadership. Early on in the book we talked of the huge importance of understanding the range of perceptions carried by those around us. Try to make sure that the answers you give to these questions are not simply your own but include the honest responses of others, too. No good leader should become *a* victim of their own imagination!

HEADTEACHERS AND CHILDREN

That the role of headteacher in a school is changing is not open to doubt. Headteachers in primary schools are responsible for an increasing number of administrative and management tasks; the contents of a book such as this indicate how much has changed in recent years.

The influence of a headteacher on a school is a powerful one, constantly referred to in descriptions of good or bad schools. That influence extends to the curriculum offered to children, the organisational systems, the public reputation, inter-staff relationships and much more.

It also extends to the children in a more direct way; while a class teacher is often the central adult in each child's school day, the headteacher can exert powerful influences for good or ill upon many children.

Many headteachers enjoy contact with children and wish to retain some of their previous role as class teachers where possible. The dilemma for many is that increased administration and management reduce the amount of time available for working with and being available to children. What options are open to headteachers who want to continue this part of their job for as long as possible?

1. Class Teaching

Some headteachers in smaller primary schools have either a full-time or part-time responsibility for a class as a part of their job. For others, teaching classes for a limited period of time during their week, either as a timetabled activity or as an emergency stopgap is both alluring and frustrating. The advantages are:

- it guarantees the headteacher a reasonable amount of non-interference
- it allows some contact with children
- it enables some sort of teaching practice to be maintained.

The disadvantages are:

- the short time span doesn't allow headteachers to work with a class in the way they would like

- it is difficult to get to know many children
- working with one class often means that there isn't time to work with others
- lack of time for preparation.

2. Visiting Classrooms

Most headteachers visit classrooms informally and many use classroom visits as a way of analysing the strengths and weaknesses of a part of the organisation. The advantages of regular, informal or semi-formal visits to classrooms by headteachers are:

- it enables all children to see the headteacher each week
- it enables the headteacher to value positive work by children within the class setting
- it enables the headteacher and children to work together within the normal organisation of the class
- it enables the headteacher to communicate important messages about teaching and learning within the flow of a normal day.

The disadvantages are:

- such visits can become so quick and insignificant that many children hardly notice they have happened
- the headteacher concentrates on talking to the teacher or examining poor plumbing
- the headteacher makes comments to children which are not based on a deep understanding of particular circumstances.

3 . Working with Individual Children

Many headteachers work with individual children in or outside a classroom or within the headteacher's office. Most of these children are either very able or unable. The advantages are:

- good relationships can be built up with a few children
- specific extra help can be given to children who might not otherwise receive it.

The disadvantages are:

- relatively few children are seen each week
- it is time-consuming as a way of involving the headteacher with children
- it may be better for such children to be seen in groups rather than individually
- other children can perceive the visits as favouritism.

4. Receiving Visits from Children

It is not uncommon for some headteachers to operate an open-door policy which allows children to visit them (or to be 'sent' by teachers) at will. The advantages are:

- the headteacher often sees children who have made particular advances or who have behaved or performed disappointingly
- given the right circumstances, the visits can be motivational for children
- the headteacher provides another opportunity for children to talk confidentially about problems or difficulties.

The disadvantages are:

- sometimes it is inappropriate to see children, who may be disappointed. A specified time during the week for this sort of visit might help
- the open-door can be manipulated by some children
- it is time-consuming
- headteachers do not always see a full range of children (in terms of abilities, development or motivation).

5. Lunch and Mid-Morning Breaks

Headteachers often share the playground and other rotas with colleagues on the staff. The advantages are:

- the headteacher is able to see a large number of children
- the children are seen in another non-class context by the headteacher
- the headteacher can talk informally to many children
- the headteacher can help to use his/ her position to reinforce good relationships.

The disadvantage is:

- the headteacher might not always be able to guarantee regular rota-time.

6. Clubs and Extra-Curricular Activities

Clubs and extra-curricular activities provide a good way of getting to know some children in greater depth. Apart from the specific focus of the activity this is often the reason class teachers find them appealing (although, of course, pressures of time and the debate about teachers' professionalism have curtailed many extra-curricular activities). The advantages which apply to class teachers also apply to headteachers. At the present time, though, many headteachers find it difficult to commit themselves to a regular extra-curricular involvement with children.

7. Walking About

There is a well-respected theory of management called 'management by walking about'. For headteachers thinking about their involvement with children, it means taking every opportunity, however slight, to work with children somewhere in the school, formally or informally. The advantage is:

- it enables the headteacher to develop a high profile amongst children.

The disadvantages are:

- the randomness doesn't guarantee that the headteacher works with or meets different children
- at various times during the term the opportunities for walkabout may be more limited than others.

Like most things in this book, no one approach is likely to be wholly satisfactory and headteachers will have to choose a number of approaches which compensate for each other and which fit in with the general context of the school.

Notwithstanding the increased administrative and managerial load of headteachers we remain committed to the view that a headteacher who is isolated is no longer one in any understandable use of the term. Contact with children is not only fundamentally important to many headteachers as individuals but it should also remain a necessary part of the job, until such time as schools are run by managing directors.

13

Collegial Schools

Since the 1978 Primary Survey by HM Inspectors, teachers have been urged to ensure that the curriculum is coordinated, continuous and coherent. To achieve this staff have been encouraged to take on curriculum coordinating roles. At the same time the school-as-an-organisation should enable healthy communication, consultation and collaboration. Consequently there are two interdependent and simultaneous management tasks. When both tasks are effectively managed and accomplished it is claimed that the school will not only develop but also become a *collegial school*.

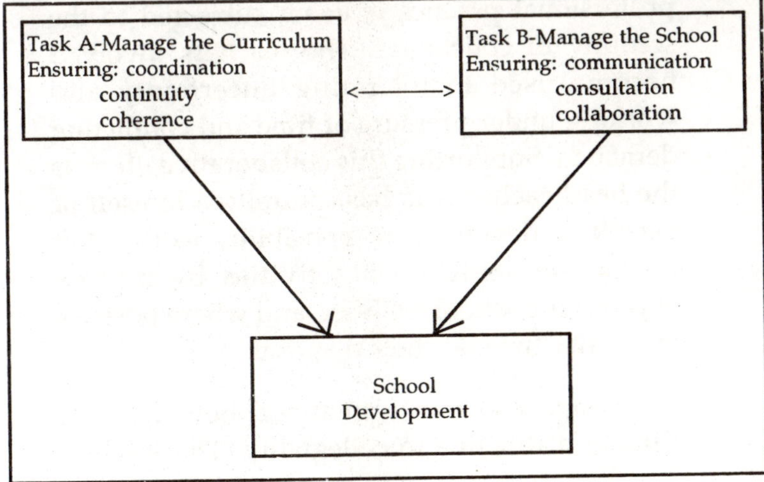

> The contemporary image of good practice has been promoted by the Inspectorate since 1978 ... It is of the 'collegial' primary school, predicated on the two values of *teacher collaboration* and *subject expertise* ... The image itself... *shows* small working groups of teachers reporting back recommendations for school-wide change to the collectivity of the whole staff meeting for decision-taking. These groups are led and organised by the curriculum postholders, who draw upon expertise from outside school as well as upon their own professional knowledge, in order to enable the staff to develop the curriculum as authoritatively as possible. Occasionally the postholder works alongside class teachers to illustrate ideas in practice, and to become aware of progress throughout the school. The skills involved in these processes are not only academic; considerable sensitivity, personal enthusiasm and charm are required in order to maintain good working relationships in schools where professional practice is being subjected to the scrutiny of colleagues. The teachers involved become used to tolerating uncertainty and working under pressure of time and conflicting demands. Supporting this collaborative effort is the headteacher who has committed himself or herself to devolving responsibility to the staff group; servicing their activities by putting appropriate school facilities, and where possible his or her time, at their disposal.
>
> The image also shows an atmosphere, ethos or climate distinctive to collegiality. The teachers

exist in a school in which constructive and critical scrutiny of each other's practice and ideas is the normal expectation. There is a continuing commitment to professional development through in-service activities both within the school and outside it. Although the teachers are not insensitive to the implications of such involvement for their own career prospects, the major focus of in-service training is the whole school, and there is an open understanding that teachers will feed back into school implications they see for their colleagues of off-site in-service courses. The ethos is not created simply by encouraging teachers to feel solidarity with one another, but by deliberate strategies that make role expectations explicit to all staff, and by the head's involvement in school-based development in practical and supportive ways that do not undermine the authority of teachers with special expertise. The overt commitment to evaluate their initiative collectively accustoms the teachers to giving accounts to each other of the reasons and justifications for particular approaches to the curriculum, and so helps them to anticipate representing their subject or subject area to people outside the school ... The school thus becomes collectively accountable for its curriculum. The teachers committed to collegiality see the atmosphere in the school as the element most critical to its maintenance, and derive strong personal and professional satisfactions from their involvement in, and contribution to, its continuance. They see the creation and maintenance of such an atmosphere as the

> responsibility not just of the headteacher, but of the whole staff group. Collegiality will survive the departure of the head.
>
> (Campbell, 1985, pp. 152-53)

> In each school the head and staff have agreed aims relating to the academic work and the children's personal and social development. A shared sense of purpose was most evident ... the schools had curricular guidelines ... and these had been written after staff discussions at meetings led by one teacher or a small group of teachers able to offer informed advice on the particular aspect of the curriculum.... A number of the schools were exploring ways of deploying the staff so that more effective use was made of their abilities and curricular strengths. Their aim was to ensure in all classes that the responsibility for coordinating the work of the class would remain with the class teacher ... (whilst at the same time) some teachers in these schools were acting effectively as consultants by helping to plan the work and prepare teaching materials ... In this way the schools were making positive efforts to strike the delicate balance which is involved in making the best use of the curricular expertise of a primary school as a combined teaching unit.
>
> (HM Inspectors, 1987, pp. 31-32)

Collegial schools need a number of key ingredients:

- a general and widespread
- agreement on aims and purposes

- a headteacher willing to devolve much decision-making to the staff group
- specialist expertise whereby teachers, in turn, can act as adviser and advised
- reasonably harmonious
- relationships so that discussion and differences can be handled without acrimony and alienation
- a school culture which supports professional and social collaboration.

Where one or more of these ingredients is lacking a school may not be ready for collegiality.

Some advantages of collegial schools are as follows:

- more people make more of the decisions; consequently staff feel more involved and more committed to making the decisions work
- people feel they know more (rather than less) about what is going on; the best practice of each teacher can spread and influence the work of others
- opportunities for teacher development can be increased
- teachers feel less isolated and more supported
- the headteacher's role is enhanced and enriched through the contributions of others.

Some of the disadvantages of collegial schools are:

- headteachers often feel they still need to hold the right of veto over staff decisions
- meetings can be very time-consuming

- small schools may not have sufficient expertise to cater for the whole curriculum
- generating staff cohesion in respect of aims, practice and philosophy can take a long time.

Collegiality is also useful because it demonstrates how primary school management is intertwined with curriculum management and development. Maybe whether a school is collegial or not is relatively unimportant compared to the fundamental question, 'How is the school and curriculum managed so *that everyone* feels involved, challenged and developed?'

COLLABORATION AND CONSENSUS

Notions of collegiality and effective school management require high levels of staff collaboration, but collaboration neither guarantees consensus nor is it necessarily a 'good thing'. We have highlighted four points which need to be considered when staff collaborate and when consensus is sought.

1. Collaboration Takes Time

Collaboration is not simply a matter of putting staff together and hoping they will 'get on with it'. Recent work into primary school staff relationships suggests that in order for staff to work together there needs to be a culture of collaboration; that is, a culture in the school which facilitates openness, and a sense of security. This culture takes time to develop.

Also, staff collaboration implicitly means working together in groups and Handy (1981) has shown that groups take time to develop:

Groups mature and develop. Like individuals they have a fairly clearly defined growth cycle. This has been categorised as having four successive stages:

1. Forming. The group is not yet a group but a set of individuals. This stage is characterised by talk about the purpose of the group. The definition and' the title of the group, its composition, leadership pattern, and life span. At this stage, too, each individual tends to want to establish his personal identity within the group, make some individual impression.

2. Storming. Most groups go through a conflict stage when the preliminary, and often false, consensus on purposes, on leadership and other roles, on norms of work and behaviour, is challenged and re-established. At this stage a lot of personal agendas are revealed and a certain amount of interpersonal hostility is generated. If successfully handled this period of storming leads to a new and more realistic setting of objectives, procedures and norms. This stage is particularly important for testing the norms of trust in the group.

3. Conning. The group needs to establish norms and practices: when and how it should work, how it should take decisions, what type of behaviour, what level of work, what degree of openness, trust and confidence is appropriate. At this stage there will be a lot of tentative experimentation by individuals to test the

> temperature of the group and to measure the appropriate level of commitment.
>
> **4. Performing.** Only when the three previous stages have been successfully completed will the group, be at full maturity and be able to be fully and sensibly productive. Some kind of performance will be achieved at all stages of development but it is likely to be impeded by the other processes of growth and by individual agendas. In many periodic committees the leadership issue, or the objective and purpose of the group, are recurring topics that crop up in every meeting in some form or other, seriously hindering the true work of the group.
>
> (Handy, 1981, pp. 160-161)

Clearly, collaboration involves a lengthy process of development. It is not a way of operating which, from the outset, is necessarily 'productive' or 'efficient'.

2. Collaboration Relies Upon Effective Group Work

'Productivity' and 'efficiency' can be greatly enhanced by groups being well managed and led. Some of the ways of managing groups are outlined in the section covering meetings. One way of beginning to improve group dynamics is to attempt to rate how effective groups are in one's own school or workplace. There are two obvious ways forward.

First, one might canvas staff opinion about meetings. This should be done face-to-face and informally. It is not difficult to suggest some of the questions to address:

- Do our meetings go on too long?

- Is our cycle or pattern of meetings appropriate (for example, weekly, monthly)?
- Is the group size appropriate?
- How might we improve our meetings?
- Do we say what we really think?

Secondly, one could use a systematic approach (see the chart opposite).

3. Differences Need to be Faced

Consensus does not occur because staff collaborate. Talking collectively about what you do and would like to do means that differences (in aims, methods and approach) will be identified. Collaboration can lead to conflict just as easily as consensus. As Handy's stages of group development show, it is important that differences are worked through and worked out. Whilst not always comfortable, done well it is usually constructive.

If differences are not worked out they don't go away, they go underground—creating more long-term difficulties than will ever occur in the working-out stage.

One way of avoiding the negative excesses of both concealed differences and unfettered frankness is to ensure that the social and informal aspects of school life are well tended. For example, the state of the staffroom matters. Comfortable chairs, decent coffee- and tea-making facilities, a sense of order and attention do contribute not only to making the room pleasant but also to staff feeling they actually want to spend time in there and thus with each other. No one wants to stay long in a room which is untidy, where the coffee cups are chipped and where the furniture is uncomfortable. It may seem trivial to spotlight such things as food, drink and chairs but research shows that these things are actually very important. These are practical ways of improving the climate in which staff collaborates. Moreover, the more staff talk about their personal lives, the easier it often is to talk about professional concerns (see Nias, Southworth & Yeoman, 1989).

4. Consensus or Consent?

Let us suppose, then, that the staff as a group are:

- well formed and mature, at Handy's performing stage
- formally and informally cohesive, spending time with each other
- well led, being effectively managed and economical with time
- sharing and airing differences in a constructive, creative way
- working in a school where there is a culture of collaboration.

Even in such schools (and some do exist! see Nias et al. 1989) *consensus* is not always present. Consensus means full agreement, something close to unanimity. We have stressed throughout the book that unanimity amongst teachers is going to be impossible; a staffroom comprises different human beings concerned at different personal and professional levels about a range of uncertain educational and non-educational issues.

Rating group effectiveness

	poor		*good*
A: Goals	confused; diverse; conflicting; indifferent; tittle interest	1 2 3 4 5 6 7 8 9 10	clear to all; shared by all: all care about the goals; feel involved
B: Participation	few dominate; some passive; some not listened to; several talk at one? or interrupt	1 2 3 4 5 6 7 8 9 10	all get in; all are really listened to
C: Feelings	unexpected; ignored or criticised	1 2 3 4 5 6 7 8 9 10	freely expressed; emphatic responses
D: Diagnosis of group problems	jump directly to remedial proposals; treat symptoms rather than basic causes	1 2 3 4 5 6 7 8 9 10	when problems arise the situation is carefully diagnosed before action is proposed; remedies attack basic causes
E: Leadership	group needs for leadership not met. group depends too much on single person or on a few persons	1 2 3 4 5 6 7 8 9 10	as needs for leadership arise various members meet them ('distributed leadership'); anyone feels free to volunteer as they see a group need
F: Decisions	needed decisions don't get made; decision made by part of group; others uncommitted	1 2 3 4 5 6 7 8 9 10	consensus sought and tested; deviates appreciated and used to improve decision; decisions when made are fully supported

G: Trust

poor	1 2 3 4 5 6 7 8 9 10	*good*
members distrust one another; are polite, careful, closed, guarded; they listen superficially but inwardly reject what others say; are afraid to criticise or to be criticised		members trust one another; they reveal to group what they would be reluctant to expose to others; they respect and use the responses they get; they can freely express negative reactions without fearing reprisal

H: Creativity and growth

poor	1 2 3 4 5 6 7 8 9 10	*good*
members and group in a rut; operate routinely; persons stereotyped and rigid in in their roles; no progress		group flexible; seeks new and better ways; individuals changing and growing; creative; individually supported

From Schein, *Process Consultation, 1969.*

To wait for consensus in such a situation could mean waiting forever; we might never make any changes at all. What is needed is consent. The cohesion we aim for in a school should be aimed at developing the willingness to go along with a proposal, to give it a good try as openly as possible. Management, remember, is often concerned with being 'as good as possible' rather than ideally perfect.

Work towards consensus but accept consent. Consensus is idealism; consent is realism.

THE DEVELOPMENT CYCLE

Whilst the phrase 'school development' sounds simple, it in fact labels a complex set of activities involving many key processes (see Holly & South worth, 1989):

- leadership
- self-evaluation
- teaching and learning
- curriculum development
- INSET
- management development
- school culture and climate
- school development plans

Another way of thinking about school development is to conceive of it as *learning*. A developing school is a *learning school;* it is a school which learns by looking inward and by encouraging others, usually outside the school, to help. Yet, this learning needs to occur at different levels:

- the children's learning
- teacher development, i.e. their individual learning
- staff development, the learning of the staff as a group
- the school, all who constitute 'the school'
- the headteacher, his/her learning.

It is possible for learning at all of these levels to occur simultaneously.

The inside line represents an individual's learning, the outside line represents the school's development. The two need to track' each other, first because there can be no school development without individual teacher development, and second because there can be no school development unless the teacher's individual development is coordinated with the school's development plans.

However, although it is useful to conceive of development in terms of levels, tracks and key processes, we also need to remember the complexity. Complexity occurs because of two things:

- *scale:* developing a school involves many aspects of a school, as the notions of level and key processes show
- *interrelationships:* development is not only to do with ensuring that learning occurs at different levels or that a series of individual processes are performed well; development needs *all* of these levels and processes to interrelate so that they interpenetrate and mutually reinforce each other.

Hence development begins to look like this diagram:

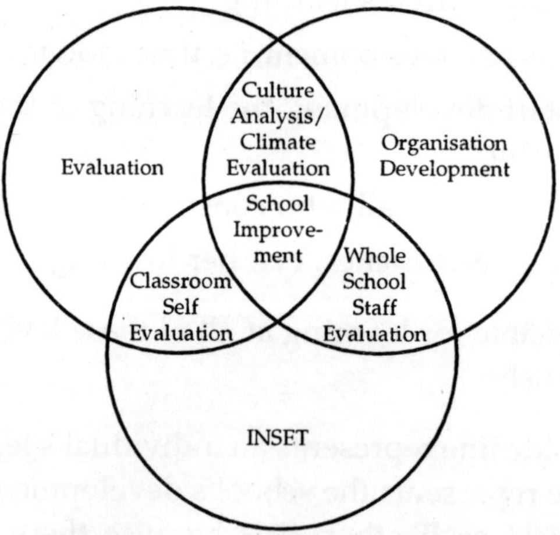

Fig. 13.1. The Developing School

This diagram groups the key processes into three major but overlapping areas: *evaluation, INSET* and *organisation development.*

Evaluation is concerned with reviewing, monitoring, questioning, problem-seeking activities which teachers and others need to undertake to begin to learn about

- the school's culture
- the school's climate
- teaching and learning
- classrooms
- teacher development

Organisation development occurs when answers are sought to some of the problems revealed through evaluation. Hence the school as an organisation might seek to improve the culture, the climate, staff development and curriculum plans. Consequently organisation development includes

- curriculum development
- management development
- leadership
- development plans
- teacher appraisal

INSET concerns all the practical activities, workshops, courses, discussions and reflections which facilitate teacher, headteacher and staff development.

The diagram also demonstrates that school improvement only occurs when all of these processes are arranged in such a way that they not only interrelate but interpenetrate. They support and construct the conditions which will nourish development of the school. By inference the diagram suggests that while it is possible for all of these activities to be taking place in schools (and we would say that they do take place), it is not only the presence of the processes that matters; it is that they are also managed and coordinated in order that the *configuration of these processes* enables the school as a unit to develop.

PRINCIPLES OF CHANGE

Everything in this book is relevant to the change process. The following principles have been selected because they are the major issues to focus on. We have chosen to highlight six principles.

Principles 1: Assess the Situation; Identify the Change

The key questions are:

- How are we doing?
- Where are we?
- Where do we want to be?
- How do we get there?

Asking these questions individually and collectively can unlock many perspectives (see pp. 23-31), generate calls for change and, crucially, provide a mandate for change. Assessing and identifying change needs to boost motivation:

- staff needs to perceive the need for change and feel a responsibility for implementing and sharing in change
- cooperation of staff needs to be gained; a sense of consent (see pp. 63-65) is needed
- communications need to be two-way and on-going
- there is a need for those involved to see benefits for themselves as well as for the school.

(adapted from Day, Johnston &Whitaker,1985)

Principle 2: Expect and Accept Resistance

Despite every effort being made to enlist support for the change and for staff to be motivated to make changes one must always expect resistance.

Resistance can come in many forms, not all of them being hostile; inertia, passivity and tokenism are just three kinds of 'resistance'. Another is 'innovation without change'.

> Organisations are dynamically conservative: that is to say, they fight like mad to remain the same. Only when an organisation cannot repel, ignore, contain or transform the threat, it responds to it. But the characteristic is that of least change: nominal or token change.
>
> (Schon, 1971, Reith Lecture)

Principle 3: Change Must be Managed

Although change can be unplanned and accidental, for whole school change to occur it must be managed. 'It is a prime management task to plan, support and monitor the innovation process, but not necessarily to initiate it.' (Day, Johnston & Whitaker, 1985, p. 109).

The management of change is rather too often seen as the sole task of headteachers; we would dissent from this. Headteachers have a role to play in planning, supporting and monitoring change. They can also initiate change. But they should also involve others and enable others to initiate change. Otherwise, the first principle becomes, over time, progressively more difficult.

Managing change is really a series of procedures:

Procedures in the Management of Change

1. Assess the situation (people, resources, constraints). *For* example, you may approach or be approached informally by individuals, or 'hear' a need voiced during a staff meeting, or initiate a staff meeting yourself.
2. Identify an area of concern (general or specific). The realisation that there is a need for change may come through listening to staff and being aware of their thoughts, needs and relationships. If not, the ground has to be prepared for change. This will include planning how and when to implement change.
3. Communicate the concern informally to:
   (a) Headteacher/deputy headteacher.
   (b) Staff colleagues.
   (c) Other involved people e.g. parents/ancillaries.

4. Meet formally with colleagues to: (a) Identify the specifics of the problem(s). (b) Clarify issues. (c) Generate discussion of new ideas. (d) Decide on group aims and specific strategies: consensus-seeking; joint formulation of valid alternative strategies, leading to establishment of priorities and agreed deadlines. (e) Decide on ways of monitoring the implementation of the plan.	Negotiation of meanings
5. Implementation of the plan (with back-up provided, e.g. time, resources). 6. Revision of plan in the light of experience (a recognition that the logic of planning and the logic of action may not match). 7. Reflective appraisal of the effectiveness and new planning if appropriate.	Flexibility as a critenon of action

8. Consolidation of new pattern/plan.
9. Long-term evaluation.

Principle 4: Leadership is Crucial

At times of change leadership is much more visible than at times of stability. Whoever leads the change needs to be aware that their role is crucial to the success of the innovation.

The leader needs to

- act as manager of the change and follow steps one to nine.
- provide adequate levels of support -both psychological and material
- offer (or be able to draw on) practical help
- keep the implementation plan going and on schedule
- apply pressure if complacency, inertia or avoidance begin to surface
- recognise small, incremental changes as the building blocks of major change and praise and advertise these changes to those who have made them and to all other involved parties.

Principle 5: Relationships Change

Changing things changes things! We must expect

- people to experience frustration, worry, doubt, perplexity, confusion, uncertainty, achievement, success, clarity
- relationships to alter as different colleagues individually experience different feelings.
- to deal with colleagues' feelings

The leader must be prepared to respond to these,

although not always. While support is essential it has also been argued that in order for change to be successfully implemented there is a need for pressure (M Fullan 'Change Processes and Strategies at the Local Level' *The Elementary School Journal* 1985, Vol. 85, No. 3, pp. 391-421). What one wants to avoid is both too much pressure (that is, stress) and too little (that is, no need to change!)

Principle 6: Change Small and Modest

Too often change is perceived as sweeping, wholesale and overwhelming. Far too much curriculum change has been seen as grandiose and spectacular. As such, what has been overlooked is the fact that most people only make long journeys in short steps: that major change is really the by-product of lots of little changes.

In order for any change to be successful it needs to be broken down into smaller, component parts which are more modest, more manageable and *doable.*

> . . . innovations have nothing to do with some grand design. They have to do with a thousand tiny things done a little bit better.
>
> (Peters and Austin, 1985, p. 201)

IMPLEMENTATION

Over the last 20 years staff in school have become used to formally meeting together and talking. Staff meetings, working parties, conferences and workshops have multiplied as staff have listed their aims, undertaken school self-evaluation and reviews and made plans to change things.

However, a principal characteristic of an effective school is that staff do not only consult and collaborate when planning, they also go on to do something in the light of their deliberations and plans. In short, *talking is not enough: things need to happen.*

How Do We Make Our Plans Happen?

Making our plans happen is a matter of implementation. So what are the factors which affect implementation? Michael Fullan (1982) has conducted some valuable work in this area and he suggests the following:

A ***Characteristics of the Change***

1. Need and relevance of the change
2. Clarity
3. Complexity
4. Quality and practicality of the programme

B ***Characteristics at LEA Level***

5. The history of innovative attempts
6. The adoption process
7. Support and involvement
8. Staff development (in-service)
9. Evaluation
10. Community involvement

C ***Characteristics at the School Level***

11. The headteacher
12. Teacher-teacher relations
13. Teacher characteristics orientations

D. ***Characteristics external to the local system***

14. Role of Government (eg DES)
15. External assistance

Fullan devotes more space to discussing these than we can. However, we will focus on the ones which appear to impinge directly on school-based change.

Need

Unless staff recognise and appreciate the need for the change, implementation will be severely hampered.

Clarity

Clarity about what teachers should do differently should be developed. All too often teachers are not clear as to what the change means in practice.

In agreeing to make classroom changes teachers need to know what the change will look like in classroom terms. Unless this is understood staff have no real means of knowing whether they have successfully introduced the change or not!

Complexity

Many changes involve lots of smaller or supporting changes. Parental involvement in classrooms means: training for parents; prior explanations of curriculum intentions, approaches and processes; follow-up tasks to see how the parents feel; arrangements at playtimes for parents to enjoy the comforts of the staffroom; discussions about confidentiality etc.

Any change should 'be examined in regard to the difficulty, skill required, and extent of alterations in beliefs, teaching strategies and use of materials' (Fullan, 1982, p. 58)

Quality and Practicality of the Programme

When the change involves the introduction of a new scheme (for example, science materials, reading schemes, maths materials, art activities, etc.) the materials should be

- provided in good time so that staff are familiar with them

- available in sufficient quantities
- of such a quality that they survive the rigours of use with children and are credible to staff.

Obvious as it may seem, lots of changes have foundered because of such basic problems.

Support and Involvement

LEA support and involvement can be a major boost to implementation. The interest and advice of LEA staff can be a stimulus and confers status on the change.

Staff Development

With the advent of the LEA training grant scheme this characteristic could also be school based. Nevertheless, if change is seen as a learning experience for the adults involved, then staff development will be necessary. Anticipating both the nature of staff development and its timing and sequencing will be vital to the success of the change.

The Headteacher

The headteacher strongly influences the likelihood of change. Projects actively supported by the headteacher are likely to do well. Headteachers and staff need to plan how the headteacher will be actively involved.

Headteachers need to: join in; help out; offer praise; support at times of setback; release staff; ask questions such as "How are we doing?" and so on.

It is important to note that it is what headteachers *do* that matters, not what they say they will do!

Teacher-Teacher Relations

Peer support and learning is important. Isolated teachers

with no access to colleagues cannot find out from others how to do the change, nor can they talk about the change. Collegiality, trust, open communication, advice, help and morale all affect implementation.

Teacher Characteristics and Orientations

When staff feel and believe they make a difference to children's performance, changes are more likely to work well. When staff have low expectations of children and/or of the change, these tend to be self-fulfilling prophecies.

Plan Implementaiton; Implement the Plan

In the light of these characteristics and context-specific variables, staff should work at how to implement the change.

The plan should:

- be thorough and careful
- be realistic, especially about time schedules
- include reviews

and then the plan should be put into operation. Once the plan has started, implementation then needs: persistence, energy, a sense of success and direction, and a feeling of getting there. The person leading the change needs to be *visible,* working with their 'sleeves rolled up', touring, talking, making practical adjustments, listening and leading on-the-job reports. Implementation needs energy and is hard work: but when done well it is very rewarding.

COORDINATION

Primary class teaching is a difficult and demanding job. Teachers have to

- cater for individual needs
- ensure that class work coheres
- respond to external initiatives
- manage, plan and evaluate the day-to-day work of a class
- be aware of and respond to public perceptions and pressures

among many other things. It is hardly surprising that primary teachers are not omnicompetent and not experts in each area of their professional lives. Given the sheer scale of the task, occasional difficulties are more likely to be natural rather than a sign of incompetence.

Because difficulty is natural, coordinators are needed to offer particular help in designated curriculum or organisational areas. We like the word coordinator. As the House of Commons Select Committee on Primary Education (para 9,11) said in 1986:

> 'Coordinator' ... cannot be confused with 'specialist' in the secondary schools sense. It suggests that the person carrying out the role has a positive role to play and does not wait to be asked, as a consultant might. It implies that one works with others rather than on them.

What Should Coordinators Do?

As we have already said, it is too much to expect every teacher to keep up with changes in knowledge and methodology in every field. Each would be helped by having a colleague nearby to turn to for information and help from time to time, and especially so if the roles of adviser and advised could be exchanged on other occasions, i.e. that there was no question of hierarchy.

We envisage that the colleagues giving help should do so in two main ways: by taking the lead in the formulation of a scheme of work; and by helping teachers individually to translate the scheme into classroom practice either through discussion or by helping in the teaching of the children. Much the most frequent method would be discussion. Direct teaching might often take place with the class teacher present, not least so that the class teacher can manage on his or her own next time. But sometimes it might be better to teach the children away from their own teacher because that is easier for the coordinator to manage, or because to do so makes it possible to avoid distraction, or because the class teacher could use the time to do something else. If the teaching is done separately, the class teacher should be responsible for ensuring that the work done fits with the rest of the child's programmes. Linkage with the rest of the programme is what matters, not where the teaching takes place. Children near the end of the primary stage are more likely to need access to additional teachers than those near the beginning.

All of these arrangements occur in primary schools and some have done so for many years....

Exchanges between Class Teachers

As we saw in schools, specialist teaching for music and physical education are often arranged by the simple practice of teachers exchanging classes. The critical factor is whether the 'other' teacher can take the music or the PE; what the non-musician or the unfit teachers can do is regarded as less important. They do whatever they can that fits into the time available.

The specialist's class is obviously likely to suffer, particularly if the specialist is required to take every other class in the school, which may amount to more than a quarter of a week for music in an eight class school. This practice cannot be regarded as satisfactory, though it may be unavoidable if every teacher has responsibility for a class. Remedial teaching, work with enrichment groups and the teaching of English as a second language depend on the availability of a teacher not in charge of a class, working either part time or full time. Provisions for these groups or for other children with special educational needs were, we were told, likely to be threatened if the education budget is cut.

The least developed practice is the one that so many witnesses argued for: the coordinator working alongside the class teacher. This practice also requires more teachers than there are registration classes. We accept the arguments that have been put to us for extending the practice and for four reasons: first, it provides an opportunity for in-service training of the class teacher; second, it offers the opportunity to concentrate available teaching skill on the group of children who for the time being require it; third and fourth, because the coordinator will acquire knowledge of what is happening in other

> classes than his/her own, it should be easier to develop continuity from class to class and to adopt the programme more nearly to the needs of the children and the capacities of the staff.
>
> (House of Commons Select Committee Report, 1986, paras 9.20-9.29)

In short, if class teachers are the weft of curriculum management, coordinators are the warp. Together they weave the fabric of a coherent curriculum (see Holly and Southworth, 1989).

Implications of Coordinators

Having sketched the outlines of coordination, it is necessary to note some implications of such an approach. We can see at least four:

1. Coordination is a key task in curriculum management. As such it relies upon teacher collaboration (see pp. 63-65) and may help develop a collegial school.
2. Coordination while aiding the creation of a coherent curriculum will not, by itself, develop a whole school. For whole schools to occur there is a need for further coordination. A key question arises in respect *of who coordinates the coordinators? We* think deputy heads could play a significant part in answering this question.
3. The role of the headteacher is also crucial. There are numerous implications for headteachers in respect of curriculum coordination and the coordinator's role:

- How much authority and responsibility will the head-teacher delegate?
- How much support will the headteacher offer coordinators?
- Critically, how much relief will the headteacher offer coordinators in order for them to visit colleagues?
- How much external support (e.g. advisory teachers) INSET time and GRIST funds will the headteacher channel towards coordinators?
- Will the headteacher enable coordinators to *lead* (meetings, workshops, INSET activities)?

4. How will schools utilise time to maximise the work of coordinators? LMS, GRIST (the LEA training grant scheme), INSET days, ancillary help, secretarial support, non-contact time, and development plans should all be husbanded and synchronised so that small amounts of time are used to their best effect. Although primary schools do not have lavish staffing levels and thus time is always at a premium, there is no excuse for wasting the precious and very limited amounts that are available.

PRIMARY SCHOOLS AND THE NATIONAL CURRICULUM

The advent of a National Curriculum in 1988-9 heralded many changes. The National Curriculum introduced

- a different way of talking about the curriculum since a new 'language' was devised

- new ways of assessing children, and an emphasis on assessment at certain ages
- a different role for central government and new relationships between schools, the LEA, the DES.

Each of these changes has triggered a number of consequences which are briefly outlined in the next three sections.

A New Language

A whole new set of terms was created by the National Curriculum Council (NCC) and the Schools Examination and Assessment Council (SEAC). While teachers were made aware of this language, schools will also have to help others, such as ancillary staff, supply teachers, parents and governors, to become aware of the terms.

New Ways of Assessing Children

Much could be highlighted here but it seems likely that schools will need to look carefully at how they

- informally and formally assess children
- monitor and record children's progress
- deal with children who enter and/or leave during the school year (especially Travellers' children, and children whose parents are in the armed services).'

Different Relationships Between Schools, the LEA and Central Government

Although LEAs will continue to play a role in the curriculum, schools have rapidly adjusted to the recent arrival of the NCC and SEAC and have begun to become accustomed to the policy statements and advice that these two agencies offer. It is likely that the NCC and SEAC will continue to contact schools directly, informing them of examples of good practice, resources, ways of timetabling and so on. Each school needs to take advantage of this advice while also utilising the help and support of the LEA.

In addition to these consequences there are six others which need to be given serious consideration.

1. Translating and Implementing the National Curriculum in Classrooms

Teachers and headteachers in England and Wales (since a National Curriculum does not affect Scotland at the present time) will have to ensure that the advice of the National Curriculum subject working parties, as finally agreed and recommended by the Secretaries of State, is put into practice. This means

- appraising existing practice to recognise what is already happening in each individual school and whether this practice is in line with the recommendations of successive working parties
- making adjustments, where necessary, to bring practice into congruence with the recommendations of the NCC
- *translating* the recommendations so as to take into account the needs of individual children and the school's individual circumstances.

This applies to the core and foundation subjects plus Religious Education.

2. Time

Each school will need, over the coming years, to monitor

how time is devoted to the core and foundation subjects. Where schools work in a cross-curricular, thematic and/or integrated way, schools will need to audit the proportions of time devoted to curricular areas.

Although time accounting will not involve the logging of minutes, individual schools will need to work out

- how to apportion time to curricular activities
- whether timetables are appropriate and to what degree of specificity
- over what periods time should be audited—weekly, fortnightly, monthly, half-termly, termly?

3. *New Roles*

The National Curriculum affects teachers' work to such an extent that headteachers, deputies, and coordinators should spend time thinking about their respective responsibilities. Here are just a few questions which staff ought to address and resolve:

- who will coordinate the school's development plan?
- who will offer advice on implementing subject working party reports?
- who will keep parents and governors informed and involved?
- who will organise school-based in-service work?
- who will lead staff discussions, evaluations, and reviews?
- who will record the school's policies and practices following discussion and decision?
- who will monitor translation and implementation of the NCC's advice?

4. Communication

At times of change communication is vital. Moreover communications should flow in all directions. Each school needs

- to keep alert to information coming from the NCC, SEAC, DES and LEA
- to build a staff library of pertinent leaflets, booklets, materials, videos, policy decisions
- to foster and encourage staff to use the materials and update them
- to ensure that governors are kept informed and involved
- to provide information for parents
- through INSET clusters, pyramids and meetings, to remain alert to what other schools are doing.

5. Children with Special Educational Needs

Each school needs to distinguish how each child with identified special needs should be supported. Also, what allowance, if any, needs to be made in respect of each child's programme of study? In the light of these two questions headteachers will also need to consider how the parents of children with special needs will be kept informed and involved.

6. Children Whose first Language is not English

These children could be disadvantaged by some aspects of the National Curriculum, particularly during key stage one (but not entirely so). How will schools and LEAs respond to this particular challenge?

A strong emphasis in these points is how each individual school will deal with each of these matters. This is because the National Curriculum affects each and every school, and each school must, to some degree, find its own solutions. Yet, so saying, schools should not feel isolated by this emphasis. Each school should also avail itself of the advice of the LEAs, and their support agencies. Furthermore, much will be learned from schools working together and sharing ideas, responses and solutions. While each school might be responding to the findings of the technology working group, it should not mean that each school is simultaneously reinventing the National Curriculum wheel!

14

Special Educational Needs

Definition

The 1981 Education Act tells us:

> A child has special educational needs if he has a learning difficulty which calls for special educational provision to be made for him ... and a child has a learning difficulty if ... he has a significantly greater difficulty in learning than the majority of children of his age.

Who Falls into the Category?

The Warnock Report talked about 20 per cent of pupils coming into the special needs category at any one time. Obviously such definitive statements must be treated cautiously (as the Warnock Report pointed out) but it does highlight the broad nature of special educational needs.

If one in five children may need special educational provision during the course of their school career, we must create at least adequate provision to prevent the problems of this large number of pupils being 'compounded by continuing experiences of failure'.

So the answer to the question is *anyone.* For the majority of children the help will be temporary and they will receive support relevant to their particular need and then return to mainstream teaching.

For some—Warnock suggested about two per cent—continuing special needs provision will be needed, possibly throughout their school life. For these children the procedure of *statementing* was introduced and is now a familiar part of the management of special educational needs (see below for a detailed explanation).

But before we can begin to try and solve the problems we must identify the child's needs.

Needs Identification

Behind the processes used for identification lie *four basic principles:*

1. The approach to identification is essentially optimistic in the sense that where pupils do not learn, there is assumed to be a flaw in what's being offered, not necessarily in the child.
2. A need can only be identified in terms of outcome. Processes of identification must be formative (including a strategy for future action) as well as summative.
3. The process of identification must take place as early as possible.
4. Identification and appraisal must be a continuous affair, 'so that the child is seen as a changing person for whom there is a continuous monitoring system'.

The following procedures offer a strategy for the identification of a pupil with special needs.

(a) Close liaison with other staff who have taught the child.

REFERRAL PROCEDURE

Each school should have its own procedure for referring children so the one set out here is only a model for your consideration. It's based on a large primary school where there is a special area provision which means that children from quite a wide area can be statemented to attend the school and receive specialist help from special needs teachers.

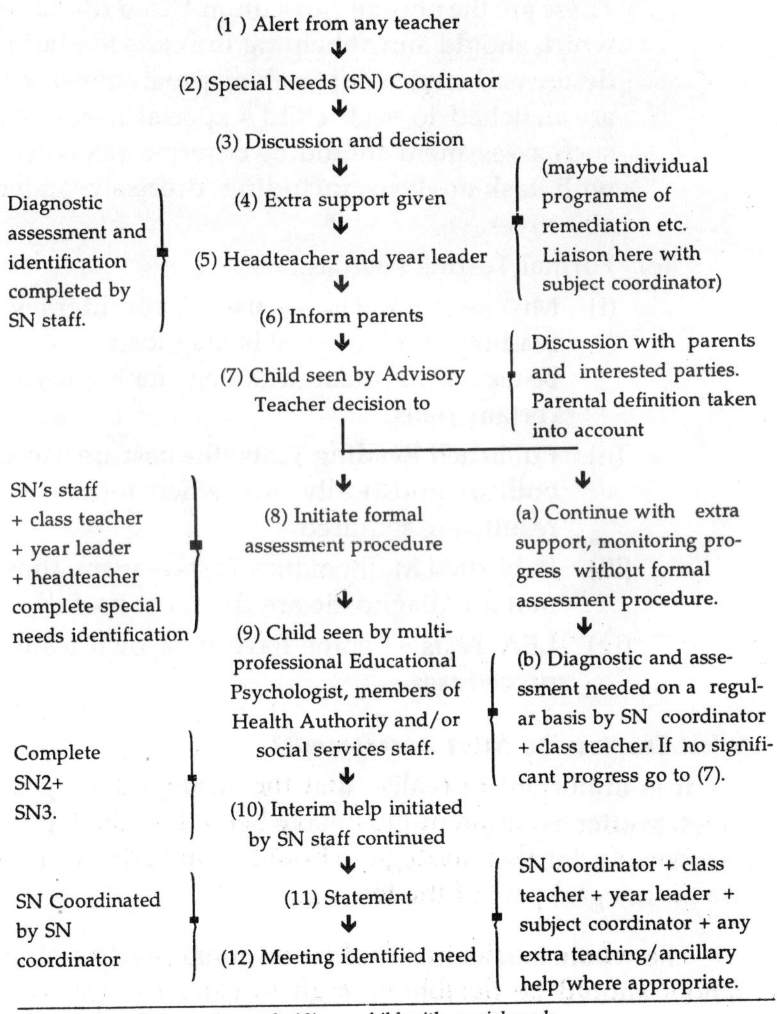

A procedure *for assessing and aiding a child with special needs*

(b) Advice from class teachers. Using the class teacher's professional judgement, and informal testing.

(c) Standardised group tests-a screening procedure to be used as a safety net.

(d) Assessment materials used by the class teachers. These are the normal curriculum-based resources which should aim at helping the class teacher to design and implement teaching programmes that are matched to each child's special needs. All such assessment should be criterion-referenced with task-analysis including precisely stated objectives.

(e) Formal Testing such as:

 (i) Miscue Analysis — useful for literacy/reading problems as it is diagnostic and can be used to formulate a strategy for improving certain skills.

 (ii) Published Reading Tests -the best are useful both diagnostically and when formal test results are required.

 (iii) Published Mathematics Tests—again, those that are diagnostic are the most useful.

 (iv) LEA Tests — some have their own testing procedures.

What Do You Do After Assessment?

It is important to realise that the strategies for good practice after assessment must have been described in the assessment. Further strategies should be included as they are an integral part of the testing.

The whole curriculum and educational practice of the school should be flexible enough to cater to individual needs. However, there are three basic procedures which need to be modified and adapted to suit individual needs.

1. If the evaluation of the child's progress indicates they are falling behind their peers in basic academic skills, for example areas of literacy and numeracy, in order to bridge the gap learning should be accelerated. A variety of problem-solving strategies and general skills and concepts should be taught and used in different contexts and situations. This may be done by short-term withdrawal related to the class-year curriculum plus support and extension work in the classroom.
2. The child should be placed 'on the curriculum', identifying skills already learnt and mastered, and so realising skills which still need to be taught. Again the logistics of the teaching should be as above.
3. There should be selection of suitable teaching methods and materials and the correct and appropriate classroom environment must be available for the particular child.

It should be noted that the organisation and teaching strategies for any ancillary help should be coordinated by the special needs staff in collaboration with the class teacher.

What about Record Keeping?

1. The records and monitoring of progress will be a continuous process throughout the child's school life.
2. The 'records' of children with special educational needs must be kept where both special needs staff and class teachers have access as they will both be contributors to the records.

3. Children with special needs should not have separate records but will require additional information to be added to the standard school record. This information is to be basically the monitoring and mastering of different skills. It will also include the results of any of the formal, informal, and group tests used.
4. Whether or not National Curriculum Attainment targets are appropriate will depend on the child's statement. It is possible for pupils to be exempted on the grounds of special educational needs but this has to be reviewed every six months.
5. Use of checklists and test results to be included in records—but it is useful to remember the limitations of locating pupils on a predetermined ranked checklist of skills. Also, as with any can do/can't do testing, the context-dependent nature of the child's performance must be taken into account when examining results.
6. The video camera is an invaluable tool in record-keeping, particularly as a record of behavioural objectives.

Who is Responsible?

'*All teachers* are teachers of children with special needs.'

(Warnock Committee Report)

From this we take it that primary responsibility for the pupils is in the hands of the class teacher. As shown on the referral flow chart the next stage is the *special needs coordinator* whose role includes the following:

1. To provide information and dissemination of any information about special needs children to all staff and to other outside agencies involved,

for example parents, support agencies.

2. To provide materials and resources for special needs children throughout the school.
3. To coordinate the curriculum for individual work and general curriculum work with special needs in mind.
4. To coordinate and modify curriculum and curriculum design methodology and teaching materials.
5. To organise school-based in-service work.
6. To liaise with schools, outside agencies, families, etc.
7. To integrate the special needs children into the full life of the school and to provide support and teaching to ensure this comes about.

Also, the *headteacher* has a crucial role in managing special educational needs—particularly in the smaller primary school. It should not be forgotten that an effective special needs policy benefits *all* children in the school. The concern and adequate resourcing provided by the headteacher can make a vital contribution to the success of special educational needs policy in any school.

In the final analysis it is the *governors* who have the ultimate responsibility — this is clearly set out in the 1981 Act. Invariably this is exercised through the headteacher but it is worth remembering that governors should be kept closely informed of special needs policy and the procedures necessary for statementing.

How Do Special Needs Fit into the Curriculum as a Whole?

The following principles are worthy of serious consideration regarding the curriculum and special needs:

1. *Collaboration* towards achieving shared goals. When designing the curriculum, collaboration between special needs staff, subject coordinators and class teachers is essential.
2. The sharing of a *common purpose* between adult and child in curriculum terms usually enables the child to become a much more competent communicator.
3. The *curriculum* for special needs *is the same* as for the rest of the school not a 'watered-down' version It should be flexible enough so that it may be adapted or emphasised in areas but essentially it remains a curriculum with real purpose and context.
4. The curriculum is so designed that its real *purpose is obvious to the child* as well as the teacher and it deploys the child's existing strategies as well as introducing new ones.
5. The curriculum is designed so that it deals with conceptual difficulties children encounter. The curriculum for the special needs child should not just try to 'bridge the gap' in certain basic skill areas but should try to *deal with fundamental conceptual difficulties.*

Underpinning all of this is the essential child/parent/teacher relationship. This, combined with other support from outside agencies such as educational psychologists, makes special needs management difficult but very rewarding when we get it right!

LEA SUPPORT AGENCIES

Although individual LEAs will place different emphases upon their support agencies in terms of staff and scale of operation, all LEAs offer some kind of support personnel who focus on

- special educational needs
- disruptive pupils
- welfare
- health
- curriculum development
- buildings and maintenance
- non-teaching staff
- school meals
- in-service education and training
- staffing
- early years education
- libraries
- galleries and museums

This list is not exhaustive since the listing of support personnel relies upon some definition of support. We have chosen to take a relatively wide definition at this point because it is important to alert staff and governors of schools to the *range* of support which should be available to them.

So the headteacher and other staff might be involved with

- schools' medical services
- schools' psychological service
- educational welfare officer
- advisory teachers/teams
- teachers' professional development/ curriculum development centres, wardens
- advisers/inspectors

- meals supervisors
- schools' library service
- caretaking and cleaning supervisors
- officers of the LBA's architects' department
- play group/nursery advisers.

You may find it useful to make your own list of support agents.

The first issue which arises from LEA support agencies is one of communication. Staff in school need to develop and sustain positive links with each and all of these agents and with others. It is possible to depict this as a diagram.

The main purpose of this diagram is to illustrate the size of the communication task. However, before looking further at size, the diagram also shows the changing nature of support work. Although only published in 1982, this diagram is already out of date. Absent from it are educational support grant teams, that is teams of (usually) seconded teachers who offer support in specific curricular or organisational areas. You might like to compare this diagram with your own.

The size of communicating with all these tasks implies that more than one person should be involved. We would prefer, for example, to see both headtéacher and deputy head in the centre spot. We would also suggest that many of these agencies deal direct with designated staff. Although custom and practice (and courtesy) dictates that anyone entering a school informs the headteacher of their presence, the scale of such greetings can be dysfunctional (at times) for the headteacher and/or secretary! Once the headteacher and visiting agent have met and become known to each other it is not always necessary for them to keep meeting.

MODEL OF RELATIONSHIPS FOR THE PRIMARY HEAD NB. Similar models could be constructed for other members of staff.

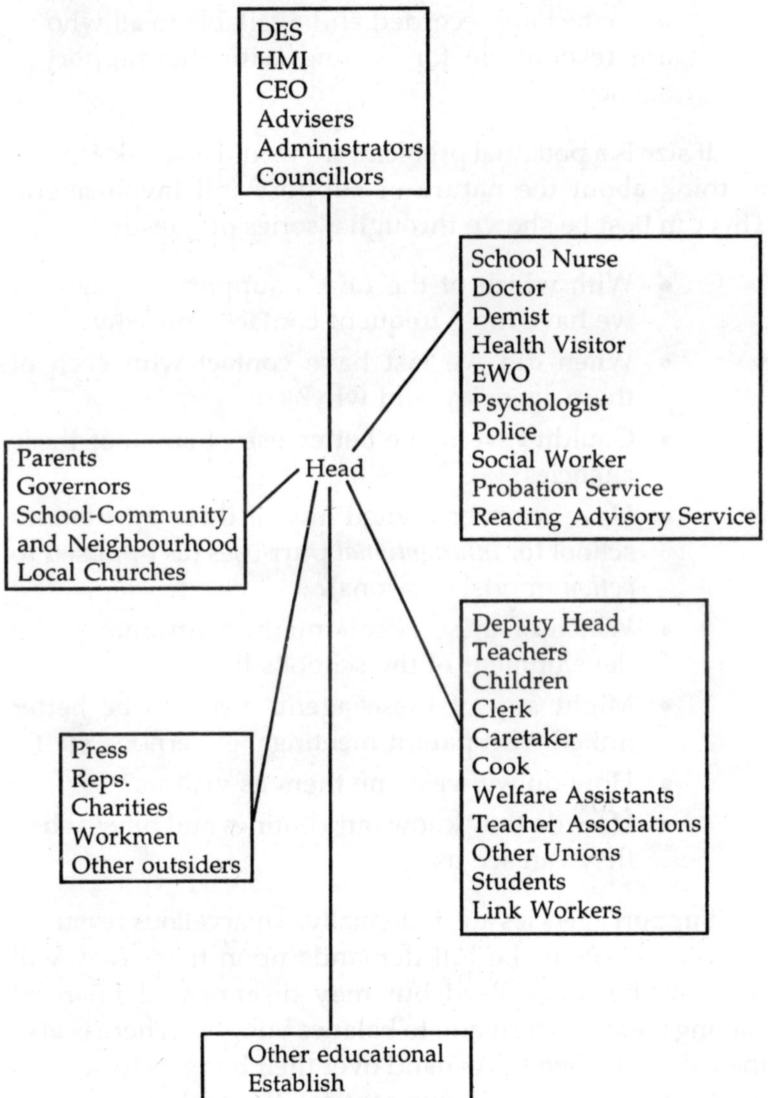

(from Profile '82 Salford LEA. 1982)

> Managing communications can be made easier and more effective if names, 'phone numbers (including extensions) and best times and days of contact are recorded and available to all who are responsible for liaising with the support agency.

If size is a potential problem, we would also ask schools to think about the nature of support and involvement. This can best be shown through a series of questions:____

- With which of the LEA's support agencies do we have most frequent contact, and why?
- When did we last have contact with each of these agencies, and why?
- Couldn't we make better use of some of these agencies?
- Have we ever invited any of these agents into school for *informational* purposes (as opposed to *action* or crisis reasons)?
- Which of these agents might contribute to the development of the school's life?
- Might any of these agents need to be better linked with parent meetings, governors, staff?
- How do we welcome them as visitors?
- How do they know our routines and times when they can see us?

Support agencies are, potentially, a marvellous resource. Unless schools make full demands upon them they will not only be under-used but may disappear if financial 'savings' have to be made to balance budgets. There is also the risk that when LEAs hand over their budgets to schools (and retain only seven per cent for themselves) support agencies may disappear or that schools will have to `buy into' them.

Supporting Curriculum Development

Another way of thinking about LEA support agencies is to regard them as offering direct support for curricular activities and innovations.

During the 1980s many LEAs have expanded their advisory and support teams in respect of early years, multicultural education, science, technology, arts and humanities, and computer's. Where such teams or individuals exist they can be a tremendous resource to schools — particularly smaller schools.

Sometimes these teams will come and work in the school, alongside teachers, for a period of time. Sometimes they can be used for in-service days, workshops and conferences, as well as attending curriculum staff meetings where they might offer advice or information. Used in any of these ways they can prove a valuable supplement to a school's development programme.

DOCUMENTATION

The 1980 Education Act obliged schools to publish information about their curriculum, organisation, discipline and examination results (although the latter was intended only for secondary schools). Of course many schools were already doing much of this before the Act made it mandatory. Nevertheless, the Act gave a new impetus to information and documentation and many schools reviewed, revised and redesigned their approach.

As this extract from Sallis (1988) shows, the rationale for the Act was consumerist rather than aiming to develop partnerships between home and school:

> **Information for Parents**
>
> Apart from the rights given to parents in the

1980 Act itself to information affecting their choice of schools and to consultation about proposed changes in local schools, parents were given important new rights to information from individual schools by regulations (4) made in 1981 under Section 8 of the Act. Individual schools are required to publish specified details about their staff, organisation, curriculum, rules and sanctions, and, in the case of secondary schools, examination results.

I would be the first to complain that these requirements have a strongly consumerist flavour, and are related more or less directly to the support of choice, rather than to the concept of parents in partnership with schools. For instance, schools are not required to tell parents what arrangements they made to involve them in the school, inform them of their children's progress, enlist their help. They are not required to tell them whether there is a parents' association or give them the names of their parent representatives on the governing body—just the chairman. This seems extraordinary when the information rights form part of the same legal package that gives parents for the first time statutory representation on governing boards. The strong implication is that parents need to know more about schools in order to *compare* them, not so that they may through their understanding play a more supportive role in their own. It is precisely this element of comparison of schools which made many people so fearful of the requirement to publish examination results.

The motivation underlying this whole process

> of opening up to public scrutiny what the schools offer and how they perform is undoubtedly that of the market place. Yet I cannot accept that it has been a bad development, so far as it goes, or that we should try to reverse it. What we must try to do instead is to move forward to better and more complete information services, join up the dots, flesh out the bones. No one in a public service should be allowed to withhold information about its performance from those who have a legitimate interest, and the fact that the information, because it is incomplete, may be used to make misleading judgements is not a reason for denying people the means to make those judgements, but rather an urgent reason to assist them to make better and more rounded judgements. It is essentially the same issue as I raised . . . about the bad press schools get. There is no means of suppressing criticism based on misinformation. One can only build up knowledge and experience to counteract it. To do violence to Gresham's Law once more, I do believe that good information drives out bad.
>
> J. Sallis, 1988, pp. 30-31

Information for Partnership

Where schools want to provide information which enables parents to feel part of the school then these schools need

- to provide information about the life and work of the school—and not just the school's rules and preferences
- to provide specific information about the curriculum—what children do and why
- to organise opportunities to see the school at

work as well as opportunities to see the work of one's own children

- to strive to find out what the parents want to know, as well as tell the parents what the school thinks is appropriate

Sample page from a school's Humanities document, available to parents

How the Teacher Can Make Use of the Key Concepts

TOPIC: *'Our Community Past and Present'*

Objectives:	Intellectual skills 1, 2, 3 Social skills 1, 3.
Key concepts:	Power, Values and Beliefs Similarity/Difference Continuity/Change
Key questions:	The topic will raise key questions for both teachers and children. There is a close relationship between these key questions, the objectives and the key concepts

Key Questions for teachers	*Key Questions for children*	*Skills*
POWER		
Who makes decisions?	Where does the money come from?	
How do they make them?	Why do we have to come to school?	Intellectual Skill 1
	Why do we have to have rules?	Social Skill 3
VALUES AND BELIEFS		
What values guide the residents?	How do we live in our community?	Intellectual Skill 1
	Why do we live in this way?	
	Why do people decide to live where they do?	Social Skill 3

- to ensure that the information for parents is jargon-free but not patronising
- to ensure that information about the school is, if necessary, translated into the language of the children's homes
- to provide information on the ways in which parents could help or encourage their children (being mindful of the two previous points)
- to provide information about how parents might participate in the life and work of the school.

These eight points are not exhaustive.

It is all very well listing principles, but how does a school put them into operation? Here are a few suggestions based on wide experience of helping schools create imaginative packs of documents for parents.

- Look at how other schools organise and publish information about themselves.
- Do not just think about booklets. Also use regular newsheets, newsletters, children's work and magazines.
- Why not encourage governors (especially parent governors) to write a termly newsletter?
- Parents' meetings, open evenings, curriculum workshops, open afternoons, etc. are valuable occasions.
- Induction events are essential—but try to provide creche facilities.
- Do not just think paper or face-to-face information: many schools make use of slide photograph sequences to show aspects of the school's work; many schools have made videos of themselves; many schools have sets of

photographs (the school's photographer will often oblige) showing children at work.

- Curricular documents should be available to parents — especially the National Curriculum Council documents.
- Headteachers should foster and facilitate the involvement of other staff in many of the above. Governors, too, should play their part.
- Parent governors and visiting governors might like to contribute to or write a news-sheet.
- Word processing now means that rewriting/updating information from year to year should be easier.

Perhaps more than anything schools should remember a maxim of Joan Sallis's that "an ounce of access is worth a pound of information".

MANAGEMENT AND THE LAW

The Head's Legal Guide (Croner Publications Ltd) contains about 1000 pages concerning the law in relation to education; it is an invaluable reference work which is updated at frequent intervals and we recommend it to you.

Our section here is not detailed—what we do hope to do is set out the broad legal framework within which schools must operate and highlight areas where further research could be useful.

Acts of Parliament

The regulation of the British education system is set out in a number of Acts of Parliament. Some of these apply only to Scotland, some to England and Wales and some to Northern Ireland. In general, the legal framework in Scotland is different in a number of significant ways. The Acts which affect education are listed below in chronological order:

- Education Act 1944
- National Health Service Act 1946
- Education Act 1948
- Education (Miscellaneous Provisions) Act 1953
- Education Act 1959
- Education Act 1962
- The Local Government Act 1963
- Education Act 1964
- Education Act 1968
- Local Government Act 1972
- Local Government (Scotland) Act 1973
- Education Act 1975
- Sex Discrimination Act 1975
- Education Act 1976
- Education (School-leaving Dates) Act 1976
- Race Relations Act 1976
- Education (Northern Ireland) Act 1978
- Education Act 1979
- Education (Scotland) Act 1980
- Education Act 1980
- Education Act 1981
- Local Government (Miscellaneous Provisions) Act 1982
- Local Government Act 1985
- Education (No. 2) Act 1986
- Teachers' Pay and Conditions Act 1987
- Education Reform Act 1988

As if this was not enough there are also a number of *statutory instruments* which carry the force of law!

The legal basis for the educational system in England and Wales is the 1944 Act which has been amended over the years by a whole series of acts and *statutory instruments*. New provisions have also been brought into effect by some of the new acts. Scotland and Northern Ireland have had their own legislation.

Government Circulars

Although all the acts mentioned above have a legal bearing on the management of schools, we can cheerfully take much of what they say for granted. For example, the age of transfer for pupils is defined by law but most headteachers don't need to refer to an Act of Parliament to find out what it is for their school. Most of the legal framework stemming from the 1944 Act is familiar. Where new and complex legislation has been introduced the major sources of definitive information are *government circulars*.

These are issued by the Department of Education and Science, the Welsh Office or the Scottish Education Office and give clarification and guidance on legislation. Many of these circulars require a response from LEAs and so there can be a further stage where new information is given as a result of the LEA response.

Department of Education and Science

Circular No. 3/89
20 January 1989

Elizabeth House
York Road
London SE 1 7PH

To: Local Education Authorities
The Chief Executives of
Inner London Boroughs and
the Remembrancer
Heads and Governing Bodies
of Maintained Schools
Teacher Training Institutions
Diocesan Bodies
Other Bodies

The Education Reform Act 1988: Religious Education and Collective Worship

Contents

Annexes

Scotland

The Scottish educational system is regulated by the Scottish Education Service (SED) under the control of the Secretary of State for Scotland. The Education (Scotland) Act 1980 is the act which set up the legislative framework although a new education act for Scotland is likely. The day-today running of schools is administered by 12 education authorities usually known as EAs.

Northern Ireland

Northern Ireland has its own Department of Education which oversees all aspects of the province's education except for universities. There are also five area education and library boards which work at the local level.

Wales

Apart from the teaching of Welsh the legal framework for Wales is almost identical to that of England. The biggest difference is that the minister responsible is the Secretary of State for Wales rather than the Secretary of State for Education and Science. There is a separate Education Department in the Welsh Office with special responsibilities.

Education Reform Act 1988

This is the most significant piece of legislation to affect education since the 1944 Act. Reference is made to this act in other parts of this book, for example in The School and its Governors pp. 215-219, and as the Act warrants a book on its own we simply list the main areas which affect schools' management' fuller details are contained in other sections of the book.

Major Areas Affected by the Education Act 1988

- The Curriculum—the setting up of a National Curriculum
- Religious Education and worship
- Pupil Admissions—a policy of open enrolment

- Local Management of Schools—in particular the shifting of financial and budgetary control from LEAs to schools
- Grant Maintained Schools — the 'opting out' of LEA control by a school and transfer of funding to central government.

The Education Act 1988 is having, and will continue to have, a profound effect on the legal aspects of educational management—how far-reaching the change will be in terms of curriculum delivery and the attainment of individual pupils remains to be seen.

The 1981 Education Act brought about a radical change in the ways in which schools deal with special educational needs. The most crucial change was the introduction of *statementing* which set down a legally defined procedure for identifying and resourcing individual pupil's special educational need.

EVALUATION-1

Evaluation is not a single, simple activity. It can take many forms and occur for several reasons and purposes. For example, evaluation can be conducted at different levels (individual, team or department, school, school clusters, LEA). It can be internal to the school (for example, conducted only by the staff) or external (carried out by people outside the school such as LEA inspectors or consultants) or some mixture of the two (for example staff and consultant; staff and governors). Lastly, evaluation can focus on different things — from the 'whole' school to some highly specific part of school (for example what do four year olds do in the reception class?). In this unit we will consider evaluation as internal to the school: what has been called self-review or *school self-evaluation.*

> When a school is reflecting upon and assessing its own work then it is engaging in self-review or self-evaluation. The underlying purpose of such activity invariably is to improve the teaching and learning process in the school. A self-review can have many positive outcomes and may result not only in changes and improvements in the curriculum or organisation of the school but also in the professional development of the staff.
>
> (McMahon et al., 1984)

Many LEAs have produced guidelines for self evaluation (in 1981 40 per cent of LEAs had produced guidelines) but such documents tended to have some disadvantages:

> The majority of the British guideline papers and documents for teachers about school self-review consist of lengthy checklists of questions, many of them value-laden, about the organisation and curriculum of the school. These checklists can be very daunting, not only because of their length but also because they seem to assume that a review should cover every aspect of the school. Few, if any, suggestions are included about how the review process might be tackled.
>
> (ibid.)

Taking up this last question, evaluation is not just about *what* we shall evaluate, it is also about *how.* To *do* evaluation you need to be able to know both *what* to and *how* to evaluate. Hence McMahon et al. (1984) sought to achieve both in order to develop the school (see School Development Plans pp. 143-148):

> **The GRIDS Method**
>
> The materials in this handbook are designed to

help teachers review and develop their curriculum and organisation. The title 'GRIDS' or 'guidelines for review and internal development in schools' has been carefully chosen. First, the materials are guidelines: they contain structured step-by-step advice about how to conduct a school review and development exercise; schools are not expected to follow these suggestions slavishly but rather to adapt and amend them as required. Second, the focus is on review leading to development for improvement and not on something that stops short at the review stage. Third, the word internal indicates that the review is not for external accountability purposes. Finally, the word school emphasises that the GRIDS process is directed at the whole school rather than at individual teachers or small groups.

The ideas in the title are reinforced and extended in the list of key principles that underpin the materials and which are central to the GRIDS method. These are that:

(a) the aim is to achieve internal school development and not to produce a report for formal accountability purposes;
(b) the main purpose is to move beyond the review stage into development for school improvement;
(c) the staff of the school should be consulted and involved in the review and development process as much as possible;
(d) decisions about what happens to any information or reports produced should rest with the teachers and others concerned;
(e) the head and teachers should decide whether and how to involve the other groups in the

school, e.g. pupils, parents, advisers, governors;

(f) outsiders (for example, external consultants) should be invited to provide help and advice when this seems appropriate;

(g) the demands made on key resources like time, money and skilled personnel should be realistic and feasible for schools and LEAs.

(ibid.)

In order to enable an evaluation to take place the GRIDS team, mapped out five stages of review and development. These are set out in the diagram on page 219.

GRIDS is now a well-tried and tested approach; it is also sufficiently widely available for schools to obtain and utilise (for example, it can be found in university and colleges of higher education libraries, teachers' and curriculum development centres, LEA resource centres, LEA adviser/ inspectorial teams). We believe that, despite some problems, the five stages of review and development still offer a useful model.

EVALUATION—2: DOING EVALUATION

If the GRIDS approach suggested in Evaluation -1 still offers a useful approach, this is not to preclude other approaches. Peter Holly was a member of the GRIDS team, and he has taken some of the ideas further. For one thing he has simplified the evaluation process into five basic, but fundamental questions:

- What do we need to look at?
- Where are we now?
- Where do we want to be?
- How do we get there?
- How are we doing?

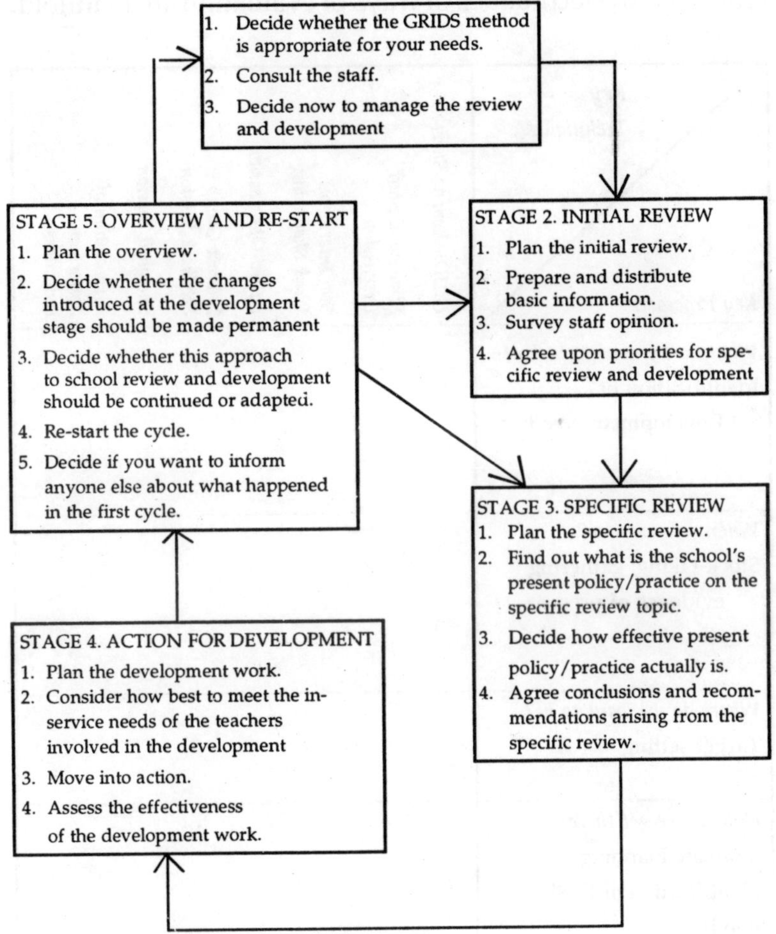

These are simple but *powerful* questions.

Furthermore, he has also arranged them alongside possible techniques which could be selected for each question. The result is a matrix (see above).

This matrix shows that evaluation is a blend of processes and techniques. GRIDS and Holly's five questions are useful ways of structuring the process of evaluation. However, the techniques of ways of evaluation are manifold.

Key Techniques / *Key Processes*	*GRIDS Review Sheet*	*Structured Staff Discussion*	*Staf Interviews Work Shadowing*	*Paired Observation*	*Interest Group Feedback Session*	*Snowball Session*	*Formulation of Performance Indicators*
What do we need to look at? Identification of Development Needs							
Where are we now? Stock-taking; gathering evidence of present situation							
Where do we want to be? Target-setting							
How do we get there? Strategic Planning; identification of INSET needs							

Examples of Evaluation Techniques and Activities

Evaluations will focus on many things. For example, staff might individually, in pairs or trios talk about and report on:

The quality of interpersonal relationships How well do members of the school relate to each other? Do they mix informally? Is cooperation a factor of the school?

Cohesiveness To what extent is there agreement on the aims of the school and of the methods to be used in achieving them? Do all members understand the roles they are to perform in order to help achieve these aims?

Levels of morale Are members of the school happy to be there, or are there factors which produce restlessness and discontent?

Decision-making patterns How are decisions arrived at? Does everyone understand the nature of the process? Does everyone have as much involvement as they want? Are some vital decisions not taken?

Leadership styles How does the head perform that role? Is there consistency in the style of leadership adopted? Who are the informal leaders in the staffroom? Do individuals have an opportunity to exercise leadership qualities? Are the children encouraged to show initiative?

Levels of commitment Are all the members of the school fully committed to it? Do some teachers feel a conflict between their loyalty to the school and their career aspirations? Is the school adequately supported by the parents? Do the parents feel that the school is adequately meeting their requirements?

Motivational features How are members of the school motivated? Is it by intrinsic or extrinsic means? Are these recognised, understood and appreciated?

(Rodger & Richardson, 1985, pp. 49-50)

Another area of investigation might be to observe how much time was actually spent on curricular tasks in the classroom. It has been shown by research (Mortimore et al., 1988) that in effective schools maximum amounts of time in classrooms are spent on task; or expressed another way as much time as possible is given over to teaching and learning rather than to administration (for example registers, messages, interruptions, classroom organisation). How might teachers investigate use of time? Here is one suggestion:

PRACTICAL ACTIVITY

Aim: To record the time available for curricular activity.

Method: The time available for curricular activities is the time remaining in each teaching/learning session, once it has properly started, excluding interruptions and up to tidying-up' time. All that is necessary here is to use a notebook and a watch to record the actual time available for activities throughout a school-day.

Follow-up: Assuming that a fairly representative day has been chosen, it may provide a salutary experience to multiply the total for the day by the total number of school-days in the year, excluding holidays, 'occasional days' and election days if the school will be closed, etc. Similarly, it may prove interesting to analyse the proportion of time spent on each area of the curriculum.

(Pollard & Ann, 1988, p. 108)

Lastly, how might a school manage the introduction of parents working in classrooms? Here is one way:

PRACTICAL ACTIVITY

Aim: To prepare for having parents or ancillary assistants working in the classroom.

Method: A pro forma, such as the one below, could be used to prepare for a session with parental involvement, to monitor it and to get the parents' feedback.

Initial discussion with parent about involvement ☐

Parent's feeling about involvement . . . .

Parent's strengths . . . .

Interests . . . .

Availability . . . .

Any possible problems . . . .

Educational activities and objectives for sessions

1 . . . .

2 . . . .

3 . . . .

Best contribution for parent . . . .

Specific discussion about parent's contribution with parent ☐

The aim, and parent's degree of responsibility, is agreed ☐

Comments . . . .

The sessions in action ☐

Comments on how it went . . . .

Follow-up discussion with parent ☐

Notes on feedback . . . .

Follow-up: It is unlikely that this activity would be carried out for every session involving parents, but it is very valuable when starting off a new partnership for classroom work with a parent. It is also useful on an occasional basis to heighten awareness and to check that benefits are being maximised.

(Pollard & Tann, 1988, p.14.18

These are examples — but what they infer is that there is a wealth of material available to schools to adopt. Self-evaluation does not mean *doing everything oneself,* there are lots of ways of making both the task more realistic and the process more effective. We would encourage schools to look at, even obtain for their staff libraries some or all of the following.

Suggested Further Reading

P J Holly & G W Southworth, *The Developing School* (Falmer Press, Lewes, 1989)

A McMahon, R Bolam, R Abbot & P Holly, *Guidelines for Review and Internal Development in Schools: Primary School Handbook* Schools Council Programme 1: Purpose and Planning in Schools (Longman/ Schools Council, York, 1984)

A Pollard & S Tann, *Reflective Teaching in the Primary School: A handbook for the classroom* (Cassell, London, 1988)

I Rodger & J Richardson, *Self evaluation for Primary Schools* (Hodder & Stoughton, London, 1985)

ISSUE INTO PRACTICE

ANALYSING THE ORGANISATION

THE BENEFITS AND CONSTRAINTS

Primary schools are particularly busy places. If those who work in them are not involved in producing curriculum policies then they are responding to the demands of the National Curriculum; if they are not thinking about what resources they need and can afford, they are concerned about where to store those they already have; if they are not working with children in classrooms then they are dealing with them during lunch breaks; if they are not setting up a stall at the annual jumble sale then they are concerned with reporting financial management to governors; if they are not desperately trying to find a new member of staff two weeks before the Christmas break then they are trying to decide how best to help a colleague with personal or professional difficulties.

And none of this, of course, takes into account the lavatory which won't work, the leaking roof, the broken window, the new parents who have just walked in the door, the established parents concerned that their child's reading is not good enough, the visit from the education committee, the INSET session after school or the two children who have bloodied each other's noses ten minutes ago in the playground.

It is only too easy to see why recommendations to sit still or slow down, to think about and analyse the classroom or school in which we are working should be met occasionally with hoots of derision. "When have I time?" seems an only too reasonable response.

'Seeming to be reasonable' doesn't make it right, though, and all our personal and organisational experience suggests that an overview of where we are, an understanding of our situation and that of those around us and an inventory of our strengths and weaknesses can bring benefits which help to reduce rather than increase the pressures upon us.

Analysing our classroom and school isn't time wasted; it is time well spent.

The Benefits

1. We have a Clearer View of What is Happening

Much of this book tries to explain the complexity of schools. Because schools are complex the truth is that it is unlikely that anyone will fully understand the range of views held by staff, children and parents about one school or classroom or totally comprehend all of the strengths and weaknesses which exist within it. Not being able to understand everything fully is no excuse, though, for not trying to understand at all. We need to have a clear view of the shape of the wood as well as an intimate knowledge of every single tree it contains.

2. We have a Better Chance of Taking Appropriate Action

There are a variety of responses we can make to any situation, including doing nothing at all. Whether we always choose the most appropriate is doubtful and some fine tuning of our decisions is usually required. Understanding the organisation we work in is more likely, however, to help us resist making inappropriate responses to situations which occur.

3 We Develop a Set of Reference Points for Future Judgements

Most of our judgements are relative ones; they depend

upon comparison with other judgements we hold about similar activities, people, situations. Increasingly staffs of schools are being asked to report on what they are doing, why they are doing it and how it is going. Without a reference point developed through analysis these questions are almost impossible to answer; with such reference points they become much easier. Analysing classrooms and schools is a fundamental part of running an effective organisation. What we choose to analyse given the limited time that is available is equally important and we will suggest certain key features of schooling and one or two ways in which the analysis can be carried out in the next few pages.

Before we get there, though, there are also constraints upon analysis about which we need to be aware.

The Constraints

1. Our Own Personal Perspectives

Perhaps we need to analyse these first; they will certainly form an important part of everything which goes on around us. If, for example, our principal aim is to create a 'happy school' we may be unaware of, or unwilling to analyse, the academic performance of the children we teach. (The opposite is, of course, also true!)

If we don't know much about modern primary science practice it is going to be difficult for us to analyse the strengths and weaknesses of our colleagues in that area of the curriculum.

Equally, our own perspectives will affect the judgement of what we see. Research of any kind works in two ways:

- researchers have points of view which they use as evidence to confirm or deny (but usually confirm!)

- researchers gather evidence as neutrally as possible and then develop a theory from it.

Both are problematic. The first often ignores much useful evidence so that the researcher can say "This school is just like/completely different from my last school". The second presents difficulties for the researcher in interpreting evidence without allowing it to be coloured by personal views.

The second method is more helpful in organisational analysis, if you can manage it. During the period of your analysis, keep a check on which approach you are taking and how your own perspectives are affecting the judgements you make.

2. Time

Despite the fact that "when have I the time?" is not an excuse for failing to analyse our organisation, it is still true that there is only a limited amount of time available. If we don't use that time effectively by choosing appropriate areas for analysis and appropriate methods then we are hardly likely to reap the benefits of the time we put in.

3. Choice of Focus

Precisely because schools are so complex there is an almost limitless range of possibilities for analysis, but some are clearly more appropriate than others. A class teacher concerned about the social relationships of the children in her class shouldn't perhaps spend too much time analysing the colour of everyone's socks;.a headteacher could perhaps do a little better when going into classrooms than checking on the quality of the skirting boards. Our choice of focus will affect the quality of our overview which will, in turn, affect the quality of our actions.

4. Methods of Analysis

Choosing an appropriate focus doesn't guarantee useful information. We need to think carefully about the methods we use to gather the information too, both in terms of the quality of information they will provide and the time they will take. (The trade-off between these two is one we all have to get used to.)

5. The Confidence of Others

Because schools are people-dealing places much of the information we will need in our analysis of our school or classroom will have to come personally from those involved in it. Few of us are willing to disclose information to those whom we don't trust or to those who will misuse it.

If our colleagues, parents, governors and children haven't been able to develop confidence in us then we shouldn't be surprised if they are unwilling to reveal attitudes, opinions or practices which are very personal to them. Nor should we be surprised when, consequently, the analysis we make is critically flawed.

WHAT TO ANALYSE

We mentioned in the previous pages that the very complexity of schools presents us with a bewildering array of possible areas for analysis. All of them can be interesting and many of them will be important. Within the time available, though, priorities have to be made. Some of those priorities will occur as a result of local demands made upon schools and some as a result of the individual interests of those making the analyses.

There are areas of analysis, though, which seem to us to have importance to almost everyone working in schools. Some of them are obvious, although that won't stop us from at least mentioning them. One or two others may be less obvious but are still, in our view, very important. On these three pages we itemise what these areas might be.

1. The Curriculum

(a) The Usefulness of School Policies

- How clear are they?
- How do they help colleagues' classroom practice?
- How up-to-date are they?
- How are they communicated to different audiences?
- How many colleagues were involved in their production?
- How have newer colleagues been introduced to them?
- How many curriculum areas do they cover?

(b) Classroom Action

- How much does classroom action reflect the policy statements?
- How does each classroom atmosphere add to or detract from children's opportunities to work to their best ability?
- How much do the relationships in the class between teacher/ children and children/children contribute towards non-academic growth in children?
- Are the classrooms organised effectively?
- Are children allowed a reasonable degree of independence?

(c) Teachers' Planning

- How much of the work which takes place in classrooms is planned?
- How do the plans help teachers implement what they want to do rather than describe it?

- How much do the plans take into account not only objectives but also activities, resources, relevance, time and some idea of finished work?
- How much do the plans build upon that which has gone before?
- What procedures are there for plans to be shared between teachers throughout the school?

2. The Children

(a) Attitudes

- To what extent are children understanding of each other?
- What level of care do they show towards their environment?
- Do their attitudes reflect an interest in their work, a bored acceptance or an obvious rejection?
- How confident do they seem when facing newcomers in the school?
- How do the children behave when unsupervised?

(b) Classroom Performance

- Does the work given to children in each class seem to be pitched at appropriate levels?
- Are there grounds for concern about the apparent performance of some children?
- Does the general level of performance seem reasonably appropriate for the ability of the children?
- Are the informal judgements made by teaching staff appropriate or inappropriate?
- Are the formal tests used in the school appropriate? Do the results of those tests give cause for concern?

3. The Parents, Governors and Community

(a) Attitude

- Does the feedback from the parents, governors and community seem generally supportive or antagonistic? (Supportive does not rule out critical!)
- Have parents, governors and other members of the community any opportunity to gather real evidence for their opinions and views?
- Are there cliques within each group which appear to present an apparently majority view?
- How much evidence has been gathered by you in order to arrive at these views?
- Are there particular people within or activities of the school towards which these groups hold particular views?

(b) Involvement

- Do those parents, governors and others who wish it have an opportunity to be involved in the life of the school?
- How much information does the school provide to parents and others?
- Is this information appropriate?
- Is it presented appropriately?
- Are there established procedures throughout the school for those parents and others working in classrooms or with children?

4. Administration

(a) Areas

- Are there systems in operation for the administration of:

  Admissions to and departures from school

Financial matters
Appointing staff
Stock ordering and control
Producing reports
Dealing with parents and visitors
Sickness and absence
School visits and journeys
Handling local authority and
DES material?

(b) Administrative Staff

- Have the administrative staff been given duties beyond their abilities?
- Has so much been 'delegated' that they are doing the jobs of others?
- Do they know what it is they are supposed to do?
- Have they the opportunity to provide input and give feedback?
- Do they work cooperatively on behalf of the school or antagonistically against it?
- Do they work in a pleasantly conducive environment?
- Do they present an acceptable first impression of the school?

5. The Teachers

(a) Knowledge and Understanding

- Do the staff understand what is being asked of them at a local and national level?
- What individual difficulties can be identified within the staff group?
- What use is made of school or centre-based INSET by staff?

- Are professional magazines and journals used in the school (other than to look for new jobs)?
- Does informal professional debate take place?

(b) Relationships and Influence

- How professionally do staff handle each other?
- Are there particular friendship groups on the staff?
- Do these groups work positively or negatively for the school?
- Are there individuals with particularly clear positive or negative power in the school?
- Are some staff more hierarchical than others?
- Do some colleagues appear to feel isolated in any way from the rest of the staff?

There are others, too. Even our list of very important areas runs the risk of appearing to be endless. (We would, for example, want to give the same consideration to an analysis of the caretaking, cleaning and school meals staff as we have done to all the others who work in our schools and we would also want to find some way of analysing ourselves in our own roles.)

You may reasonably have a different view of your immediate priorities; that is all well and good. What we should share in common is our understanding of the importance of both analysis and prioritising.

ANALYSIS IN PRACTICE

Analysing is an active verb. Everything we have spoken about until now has been preparation for the doing of it; important, but preparation nonetheless.

Let's examine some factors which help to make analysis effective:

1. Focus Down

Before you begin gaining evidence be sure you are clear what you are gaining evidence about and why. You won't be able to analyse all of the issues at the same time even though some may conveniently overlap. Knowing what you are looking at and why will help to determine the strategies you use, who or what you use them upon, which evidence can be temporarily discarded and which is likely to be immediately useful.

2. Gaining Evidence

There are a whole range of formal and informal strategies for gathering evidence about schools. Some of them are very sophisticated and require the specific understandings of trained researchers. This shouldn't prevent you from considering them. Sometimes the introduction of external researchers or consultants into a school can reveal things which would not otherwise have come to light.

Many of them are less sophisticated and can be carried out within the normal life of the school. The problem with less sophisticated approaches, such as talking conversationally with colleagues, children or parents, is that we have to be aware of the interpretations all the parties are placing on the conversation. Generally, the less sophisticated the analytical technique the more evidence is required to support any conclusions which might be drawn from it.

Strategies which might be used include:

Formal Strategies

(a) standardised tests
(b) questionnaires
(c) annual exams
(d) record cards

(e) written profiles
(f) comparisons involving national or local statistics
(g) inventories

Informal Strategies

(a) observation of
  (i) lessons and class activities
  (ii) parental responses
  (iii) staffroom atmosphere
  (iv) children around the school
  (v) governor involvement
  (vi) administrative staff

(b) talking with (individually and grouped)
  (i) parents
  (ii) teachers
  (iii) children
  (iv) governors
  (v) ancillary staff

(c) comparing with
  (i) other schools
  (ii) other points of view
  (iii) previous experiences
  (iv) HMI reports

(d) general impressions of as much as possible

(e) using
  (i) outside consultants
  (ii) inspectors

Each of these strategies has its strengths and weaknesses; each is more or less appropriate in a given setting. It is important that we choose strategies which are best suited to the information we are trying to find out.

Comparing the reading ages of three different class groups of children is not best done by discussing with each child their views about the test they have just taken. A well-designed chart, a pencil and a little statistical understanding will see you through.

On the other hand, finding out about children's attitudes to reading will not be successfully achieved by handing each of them a piece of paper on which is written 'Do you like reading? Answer YES/NO'.

Analysing your school or classroom should, for the most part, be a shared activity. Sharing the analysis

- relieves the load;
- can help to create a group identity;
- challenges individual interpretations of the evidence;
- enables a range of strategies to be used more easily.

3. Has Enough Evidence been Obtained?

You will never know whether you have all the evidence it is possible to gather but you should be aware when you might not have enough. Rushing to judgement is very tempting; the time constraints and sheer volume of work in schools can cause those making the analysis to shorten the evidence gathering period to such an extent that any decisions resulting from it are counter-productive.

This doesn't mean that you should go on gathering evidence interminably. You have to decide when to stop. However, determining parental reaction to the school (or an aspect of it) is unlikely to be successful if all you have done is stand at the gate and talk to three parents. Determining the interest and understanding of your colleagues towards the teaching of history will be similarly doomed if you only ask "Do you think we ought to teach it?"

Think about the amount of evidence you have obtained, its quality and the breadth of strategies you have used. Extra care is required because you haven't the time to behave as full-time researchers.

4. Recording Your Evidence

The process of gathering evidence and formulating decisions is both a circular and a cumulative one. It is circular because you will gather evidence and form temporary decisions which are subsequently affected by the next batch of evidence. It is cumulative because the evidence, and the decisions, keep on growing.

Even where the analysis has been well-focused it will be difficult to retain everything you have seen or heard. (Formal analysis is less of a problem since there will be written evidence available.)

The evidence you have gained is vital. You will use it not only to make decisions about the direction of the school but also to support and defend those decisions, too.

Where possible, keep notes of important evidence you gather, particularly that which refers to remarks made in conversation, to things seen in and around school and so on. Jot down summaries every two or three days. Then, if your decisions are challenged by parents, colleagues or governors, for example, you will have some of the support you need.

5. Does the Evidence You have Gained Enable You to Make a Decision?

There are two important decisions which result from an analysis of your school or classroom:

- What is it like?
- What action needs to be taken?

In the first instance you should be concerned with answering only the first of those questions. Deciding about action is important but only when you have a clear idea of why action needs to be taken. In analysing your organisation you are trying, first, to describe it as accurately as possible.

The 'decision' you need to take first, then, is "Are we able to describe our organisation?" and not "What are we going to do?". Sometimes, the answer to that question will be negative. You will have to decide to carry on gaining more information.

When you feel you can describe the organisation with reasonable accuracy test the description you have made. By making it with others it has a greater chance of accuracy. Nevertheless, test it against the evidence you have accumulated and against some of those to whom it refers. Your analysis of your school or classroom is going to underpin almost every significant action you take in the future.

15

Staff

STAFF SELECTION

Selection is really a *process*. Selection is much more than advert, application, interview and decision. It should be a *systematic process* which seeks two goals:

- to attract candidates suitable to do the job
- to achieve a match between person and post which eliminates, or reduces as far as possible, the risk of mismatch in the eyes of either party.

Thus, selection is not just about the head teachers and governors wanting candidate K to do the job, it is also about candidate K wanting to do the job on offer. *Selection is a two-way process.*

Selection involves thinking about four questions:

- Do you know what you want?
- How do you get the right person in front of you?
- How do you recognise the right person when you see them?
- How do you know you have got it right?

(from Barry & Tye, 1972)

1. Do You Know What You Want?

This question needs to be asked before any action is taken. The selectors need with some precision to *decide the nature of the vacancy.* To decide the nature of the vacancy there is a need to:

- assess the present situation
- look at the opportunities this post may afford
- ask the person who is leaving to write down all the jobs they do
- talk with staff
- talk with governors
- look at the school's development plan.

In the light of this kind of diagnosis of need the headteacher and others should then *define the post.* To begin with, you need a job description, even though the final working version will be negotiated between you and the successful candidate. You cannot select without knowing something about the job on offer, thus the writing of a job description is central to the whole process. From the job description flows the advert and supplementary details.

Asking the question, "Do we know what we want?" means:

- describing the job to be done
- describing the situation where the job will be (for example, school context, policies)
- specifying the person to do it.

Specifying the person sounds mechanical and dehuman. Yet, unless we know the professional qualities we are looking for, how can we appoint? In truth, most people *do* know but are not prepared to tell others. This can mean:

- it is difficult for applicants and candidates to work out how they are being judged
- it is difficult for the selection panel to work together. Unless the panel know and agree what they are looking for they could each be looking for very different people!

In thinking about the person we need to focus purely on *professional* issues. Let's look at the following example.

In seeking a teacher to accept an Incentive Allowance B post for Language Development in a medium sized 5-11 primary school we would look, perhaps, for a person who:

i) possesses a clear philosophy and interest in the teaching of language skills and arts throughout the primary years;
ii) is able to design and revise school policies and programmes of study in consultation with the headteacher, deputy head, teaching colleagues and ancillary staff;
iii) has a working knowledge of the requirements of the National Curriculum and Schools Examination and Assessment Council programmes;
iv) is experienced in curriculum implementation;
v) is able to offer help and advice to colleagues;
vi) is willing to inform and advise governors and parents.

Hence, the desirable *qualities* might be:

- to involve others in the language work of the school (for example, staff, parents, governors)
- to be able to consult

- to be able to secure the maximum cooperation of others
- to be aware of developments beyond the school
- to be able to write policies and reports
- to read relevant reports, documents.

"Do you know what you want?" is the fundamental question, and knowing the answer (as far as possible) provides the key to unlocking answers to the other three questions and to enabling the full and enriching involvements of all other parties to the selection.

2. How Do You Get the Right Person in Front of You?

Here we need to think about:

- the advert
- the job particulars
- any specific questions/issues we might want applicants to write about
- preliminary visits of applicants
- references
- shortlisting

Increasingly, applicants are being guided to address and write about specific issues in their application. This is useful, but do ensure that the issues you ask them to address are pertinent to your particular school and the vacancy.

Visits are useful for the applicants to get 'the feel of the school'.

References are needed but they can be misleading. It is easier to write a reference when the referee:

- knows about the post on offer

- is guided to write about specific issues
- knows whether the reference is open or confidential
- knows how long they've got before the deadline.

Short listing should involve *all* who will be at the interview (and perhaps some who will not). The criteria for selection (for example, the job description and person specifics) should be set out for everyone to apply to all the evidence before them.

Candidates should be short listed according to the criteria for selection.

3. How Do You Recognise the Right Person When You See Them?

Here, we are thinking about short listed candidates, the final four, five or six who will be interviewed.

The successful candidate should be recognised by:

- being invited to visit the school and meet the selectors
- being interviewed 'informally' by the headteacher and/or chairperson of governors and perhaps one or two other selectors
- being interviewed formally by the panel of selectors.

However, each of these approaches should serve only to provide more information about the candidate.

Then, in the light of *all* the information, for example:

- letter of application
- application form
- references

- data from visit
- data from informal interviews
- data from panel interview

a selection is made on the basis of the best match between person and post.

The criteria established in answer to the first question should provide the basis for the selection and thus be the means by which a group of selectors recognise the person they perceive to be the most suitable.

4. How Do You Know You have Got it Right?

In truth it will be some time before you can answer this. Selection is really a matter of making a prediction, and only when the person is actually in post, settled in, and doing the full range of tasks described in the job details can you really say whether they are the right person for the post or not.

INTERVIEWING

The formal selection interview is a well-established, traditional part of the selection process. Unfortunately it is all too often regarded as the only part of the process. Staff selection should entail far more than a single 30 minute interview. Indeed, the interview is only one part of the selection process and in many ways it should be the least important.

The panel interview is notoriously unreliable. All too often selectors:

- make hasty and subjective judgements
- fail to ask appropriate questions
- take small pieces of evidence and expand them to create negative impressions of a candidate

- spend too long thinking about the next question and fail to listen to the answer
- have not studied in depth the documentation on each candidate.

We undoubtedly need to make an interview as good as we can. This means we need *to plan, and prepare.*

Planning Means

- reading each candidate's papers
- analysing the evidence
- thinking about what else we wish to know
- determining the areas we will focus on and pursue in our questions.

Preparing Means

- choosing the interview room with care
- thinking about appropriate furniture and layout
- providing a timetable for candidates so they know when they will be interviewed
- ensuring candidates wait in a suitable room
- providing selectors with summary sheets on each candidate (but also having sufficient full copies on each candidate to hand)
- letting candidates know if they need to stay afterwards or not
- giving each candidate a list of names and titles of each selector on the panel.

Such preparation is little more than courtesy.

Interviewing Rests on

- planning the entrance and settling in of the candidate
- controlling the interview so that the candidate is telling you things you need to know

- letting the candidate speak for the greater portion of the time (they ought to talk for around 70% of the time)
- listening actively
- asking appropriate questions
- avoiding stress methods
- avoiding showing the candidates they are wrong—the panel should remain neutral.

That being so, at the heart of the process lie *questions.*

Asking Questions

Asking questions is not as easy as it sounds. A good question is straightforward and shows the candidate what they are to talk about in their answer.

Open Questions

The conventional view is that one should ask open questions but not too open! For instance, "Tell me about yourself" is too open, but "Tell me about your classroom this week" is better balanced—the candidate has a subject to talk about but is not confined to talk about a specific detail which might be irrelevant or inappropriate.

Closed Questions

They should be used sparingly but they can be used to check some facts, for example, "Have you taught in open plan schools?"

Questions to Avoid!

1. Mazy questions such as:

> "What are your views on handwriting? Should it be taught or caught? When and how should it be taught and do you favour a single style for every child or a more pluralistic approach?

Importantly, what about handwriting and the slow learner and children with special educational needs?"

2. Leading questions such as:

   "You will want to continue as the previous postholder did, in supervising the environmental area?"

3. Questions which show a judgement such as:

   "I'm sure you'll agree with us that the National Curriculum has been a useful development?"

4. Fantasy questions such as:

   "Let's imagine you've got the job. It is the first day of term, the head's just 'phoned to say she's had a car crash, the heating isn't working and the building is cold, the cook's unable to prepare a lunchtime meal, it's snowing and two staff think the school should close, another believes in trying to stay open and the caretaker's just broken his leg. What would you do?"

Listening

Listening is not easy but it is absolutely vital if an interview is to be effective. Good listeners work out, in advance, the main questions they intend to ask each candidate. They resist imposing their own views on what the candidate is saying. They listen to the nuances of meaning the words emphasised, the hesitations and inconsistencies in answers. They talk as little as possible, concentrate as much as possible and show the candidate, by nods and eye contact, that they are interested in what is being said. They have the patience to allow the candidate to complete the answers and they can tolerate silence. They are also sympathetic to candidates who struggle to articulate an answer by allowing them time to gather their thoughts. Listening can be made more productive if the questioners use what they have heard to ask *supplementary questions.*

If fairly open questions are used as a starter then they should be followed up with a series of supplementaries so that you probe candidates, and pursue things they have said. That way you will find out about the candidates' attitudes, understandings, and experience.

Keep Some Brief Notes

If you are interviewing several candidates it is hard to remember what each has said. Therefore, after each candidate has left the room spend two or three minutes writing down your impression of them—both strengths and weaknesses.

Obviously, these ideas are merely introductory. Interviewing is a great skill. If you want to improve your skill as an interviewer we recommend you look at:

C Roberts, *The Interview Game and How It's Played* (BBC Publications, London,1985)

J Gratue *Successful Interviewing* (Penguin Books, Business & Management Seminar, London, 1988)

STAFF DEVELOPMENT

It is widely accepted that both school and curriculum development rely upon staff development. Unless teachers develop—either in terms of improved skills or new skills—nothing will really develop.

Staff development means the development of everyone on the school's staff: it is an all-embracing term—no member of staff should be excluded from developing. Secretaries need 'developing' in order to enhance the school's communications and image. Ancillary staff should be included since they have important conversations with children. Headteachers need developing as managers, as leading professionals and as enablers. Teachers need to develop in order to keep abreast of new developments in knowledge and in research.

Staff development can occur in many ways, for example through:

- award bearing courses at universities and colleges
- non-award bearing courses at universities, colleges, teachers' centres
- conferences
- professional association and union activities
- local support/interest groups
- visits to other schools
- school-based workshops and activities
- experience of working in a number and range of schools
- teachers learning from colleagues in school
- increasing awareness through discussion and reading
- critical friendships, paired observations, peer appraisal.

Not all of these need to be planned, since a lot of staff development can occur informally and almost casually. Nor are any of these listed examples mutually exclusive; many teachers, over the course of a year, are involved in a number of these activities, sometimes occurring simultaneously or overlapping.

It can be seen from this introduction that staff development:

- does not mean only *career* development
- is not only for the lethargic and weak
- is for everyone including the able and 'gifted' members of staff
- includes appraisal as one component part
- can be a by-product of other developmental processes
- is not achieved simply by attending courses.

Individuals or Institutions?

One important feature of staff development is the need to strike a balance between developing individuals and the institution in which they work. Until recently many teachers attended in-service events and activities, and acquired numerous skills and insights. Yet all too often these skills were gained opportunistically, randomly acquired and/or served the interests and needs of the individual teachers, as this in-service record suggests:

Northstone Education Authority
Schools' In-Service Record; Academic Year199 -199
School: St. Nowhere School

Activity	*No. of staff involved*	*Length*
Investigational Maths Workshop	1	1 day
Pottery for Beginners	1	6 evening sessions
Parental Involvement in Reading	2	10 evening sessions
Evaluating Computer Software	1	3 evening sessions
Deputy Heads Management Course	1	2 days (weekend)

Classroom Observation conference	2	1 day (Saturday)
Diploma in Geographical Education for 6 terms	1	1 evening per week
Special Needs in the Ordinary Classroom	2	3 day conference

Now such a record of in-service could be both useful and creditable. But suppose that no school-based in-service activities took place and that throughout this particular year the school was seeking to develop its work in science? Plainly, insufficient in-service time, of the kind recorded here, would have been devoted to supporting the *school's* emphasis on science. In short, the issue of individual/ institutional development is not one of either/or, rather it is one of *synchronisation.* Unless staff are involved, in some way or other, in teacher developmental activities which correspond to the school's emphases, then the development of both the curriculum and the teacher is likely to be inhibited simply because the two are not coordinated or even congruent.

This view is supported by several research investigations into curriculum change and into teacher development. However, let us also make it clear what we are not saying. We are not saying there is no room for individual teachers to pursue their individual needs, interests or aspirations. We are simply saying that the individual's and the institution's development should be linked and school development plans are one way in which they can be linked and coordinated.

In-Service Days

The introduction of in-service days also facilitates school-based development. Now all the staff can meet together, during the daytime, and focus on some particular issue of concern. What will be important for schools—especially those with stable staff groups—is to record how, over a two or three year period, the in-service days are adding to the school's development. In-service days might need to be conceived as offering a spiral curriculum of school development. This is stressed because just as St. Nowhere's staff were devoting too much time to individual interests, so too might in-service days become an unconnected series of 'one-offs'.

The introduction of teacher appraisal will obviously contribute to the diagnosis of individual teachers' needs. In-service arrangements will need to respond to whatever the appraisal highlights. Moreover, appraisal should reveal things about the school as an organisation. Some of the 'weaknesses' of teachers may turn out to be 'weaknesses' in the school. In-service, and staff development schemes will need to be alert to this.

One powerful method of developing staff is for each teacher to act as host to all other staff. Thus the staff will assemble in their colleague's classroom and the host teacher might then:

- why the classroom is organised as it is
- explain the reasons for and purposes of the displays
- focus on a particular curriculum area/activity
- talk about the work of the class in general.

These are only suggestions and lots more could be generated. Variations on this might be to visit pairs of classrooms, or departments or teams.

Visits to other schools is another idea.

Use trigger questions or sentence stems to develop discussion. Day, Johnston & Whitaker (1985) have many examples, as do Pollard & Tann (1988). Schools might also find Patrick Easen's book *Making School-centred INSET Work* (1985) useful.

The staffroom should have a staff library. Perhaps part of the INSET funds could be given over to this. The library might contain:

- weekly—the *Times Educational Supplement*
- monthly—a selection of professional journals
- termly—a new book or two. These could be practical or more theoretical.

Where schools do have a staff library (or shelf.) the materials should be utilised from time to time. Articles and extracts might be seen as topics for formal staff discussion.

Each teacher should keep a record of their in-service work and contributions to school-based INSET activities. The headteacher should draw upon the records when coordinating the school's development plan. The school's INSET coordinator should also have access to them. The headteacher should make use of them when writing a teacher's reference.

THE PROBATIONARY YEAR

> For new teachers, the first months in a school have too often in the past been more of a test of survival than a time of professional growth and development. What can be done to smooth their path into the profession so that their early experience can be a secure foundation on which they can build their teaching careers?
>
> *Making Induction Work,* DES, HMSO, 1978

> "No one has said anything to me since I arrived and no one has been into my classroom. I'm really floundering and don't know what to do."

> "My headteacher has been really good. Every time I come into school he says 'Hello' and he always says 'Goodbye' in the evening. He's very nice."

The pattern of local authority provision for probationer teachers across the country is very patchy. Some probationers receive very little input, others a hastily thrown-together few sessions, others well-planned meetings after school and some—a lucky some—a full induction programme including numerous day-releases throughout the year. Probationers have said

> "I get regular visits but nothing much seems to happen afterwards. No one discusses them with me or gives me any advice."

> "As soon as I arrived at the school I was given lots of information and a full programme of what was going to happen. They have stuck to it, as well. It's been good."

The induction of probationer teachers into the profession ought to be a right which they come to expect rather than a luxury they hope to receive. However good the local authority's central induction programme is, each school has a key role in introducing new colleagues into the profession.

Why the school-based induction of new teachers should be so patchy is not clear. It may be, although unlikely, that induction hasn't been identified as a priority by many schools.

Whatever the reasons, successful induction programmes have revealed some interesting similarities.

The Components of Successful Induction

1. A Supportive Atmosphere

Such atmospheres are common in most good schools. Where probationers had particularly good induction years, though, the staff had made a professional commitment to be as available as the probationer needed them to be. The support wasn't defined by luck or any one individual's personal qualities.

2. A 'Professional Friend'

A professional friend is one who takes on the role of guaranteeing personal and professional support throughout the induction year. That support is usually confidential between the 'friend' and the probationer.

An important feature of the success of the professional friend is that they are not chosen because of any hierarchical position in the school. Indeed, the use of someone in a senior position can often cut, across the beneficial confidentiality. Given that someone with experience is required, good 'friends' are chosen to meet the needs of each probationer; probationers are not asked to fit in with the school's designated and permanent friend'.

3. Good Documentation

Probationers like to feel they are a part of the school as soon as possible and documentation which helps them to learn about and fit into routines quickly is welcomed. Staff handbooks usually fulfil this role admirably.

Schools which are well documented with good policies, parents' booklets, staff handbooks, newsletters and so on can confuse probationers by issuing them all at one time. There is a need for both the planned introduction to the full range of documentation a school possesses and also some digest versions of policy and other important documents which provide probationers with a flavour of what is happening.

4. Identification of Key Areas

It is impossible for a probationer to focus on everything during their first year and difficult for them, without help, to know what to focus on. Identifying key areas within which to work with probationers seems to help. Areas of importance include:

- *Planning:* what to plan, ways of going about it, the problems of over-planning, breadth, relevance, firsthand experience
- *Classroom, organisation:* how to physically organise classrooms to contribute to the good working conditions
- *Classroom management:* how children are spoken to, giving them independence, dealing with queries, staying one step ahead
- *Display:* a variety of effective and efficient ways of displaying children's work
- *Assessment:* formal methods used by the school and the strengths and weaknesses of informal methods used by teachers
- *Record-keeping:* the records kept as part of the school's own system and those which might be usefully kept by teachers in addition
- *School organisation:* how the school works, channels of communication, using the structure effectively, finding out what is there
- *LEA organisation:* putting the school in the broader context of the LEA, its decision-making processes and its demands.

5. *Visits to Other Classes and Other Schools*

Most probationers understandably want to concentrate on their own classrooms in their first few months in school. Once reference points of what it is like to be a class teacher have been established, then planned visits to other classes within their own school and subsequent visits to other schools can be very useful.

6. *A Structure for the Year*

Even the most experienced teacher would be unable to take all of this on board simultaneously. Schools need to identify a structure which introduces all of the elements gradually and appropriately throughout the year. For one school the structure looked like this:

> *Autumn term* Planning, classroom organisation and classroom management
> *Spring term* As above but concentrating on display, assessment, record-keeping and in-school visits to other classes
> *Summer term* As above but concentrating on school and LEA organisation plus release time to other schools.

7. *Regular Visits to the Probationer's Classroom*

If probationers are to be advised throughout their induction year then such advice needs to be based on the probationer's own practice. Probationers should be visited each week, if possible, by someone who works alongside the probationer rather than sits back and 'inspects'.

8. *Opportunities for Discussion*

Most discussion in schools takes place informally. Probationers need more than that, particularly as they may not be confident enough to take part in informal discussions at the beginning of their time in school. One school

- guaranteed a follow-up meeting to every visit to the probationer's classroom. Where possible, this took place on the same day as the visit, provided feedback and gave the probationer opportunity to raise any immediate points
- organised fortnightly after-school meetings between the probationer and the headteacher or deputy head at which the probationer could raise any matters of concern. These meetings were put into the school diary at the beginning of the school year.

MOTIVATING STAFF

Headteachers, deputy heads, curriculum coordinators, departmental coordinators, and others all perform leadership tasks. Being a leader is all very well and good, but how does one motivate staff?

Well, first, it is important to rephrase the question. It is clear from the research into motivation that if someone tries to 'motivate' others then that person is slightly 'off-key'. Rather, work should be approached and organised in such a way that the work itself will be sufficiently motivating. Therefore, planning and organising the work is a basic task in itself. Do staff want to teach their allocated classes, in their chosen spaces and with their nominated levels of ancillary help? Motivation and de-motivation have their roots in such questions. Rather than ask "how do I motivate you", which in any case implies you need to be motivated, it is better and necessary to review the prevailing working conditions and climate, and see if things might be organised differently.

Motivation is not really external; it is generated by our own 'internal' needs. Our needs cause us to act as we do. There seems to be widespread agreement that there are four needs common to us all, although they occur in different strengths and alter at different times. Hence each person will have a unique 'profile of needs'.

Needs Common to us All

Day, Johnston & Whitaker (1985, p. 98) identify the following common needs:

1. *Affiliation:* the need for a sense of belonging. Do all staff feel that they belong in the school and are regarded as part of the team? The headteacher's skills as a communicator are of great importance in meeting this need.

2. *Achievement:* the need for a sense of 'getting somewhere in what is done. Do the staff feel that they are achieving things in the tasks they undertake? An ability to ensure that roles and responsibilities are clearly defined and understood will help people meet this need.

3. *Appreciation:* the need for a sense of being appreciated for the efforts one makes. This relates very closely to achievement—are the staff shown appreciation for both effort and achievement? People thrive on praise and it is probably one of the highest motivational factors — when did the headteacher last offer praise to someone on the staff? Has the headteacher praised all the teachers during the last term?

4. *Influence:* the need for a sense of having some influence over what happens within the work setting. The ability of the headteacher to delegate effectively has considerable bearing on this issue. Staff do not wish or expect to have complete control over everything that happens in school but there are specific areas where they are able to use their expertise and have some influence. Teachers are most highly motivated when they feel that they can contribute significantly to the shape of the curriculum.

Given these four common needs it is not difficult to compile lists of 'things to do' and 'things not to do' when considering the motivation of staff. Day, Johnston & Whitaker (1985) have done such a task when running in-service courses on primary school management. They suggest the following considerations.

First, teachers are most likely to be well motivated in regard to changes when:

- they are involved in the formulation of the new approaches
- there is a feeling of solidarity's/community among the staff
- there is a demonstrable need for change
- staff are confident of their own abilities to deal with an activity
- skills for dealing with an activity have been fostered within teachers, or will clearly be developed in the future
- the headteacher recognises the extra time/effort put in by staff
- the headteacher provides positive support and involvement
- the teacher feels generally secure within the school
- there is a sense that what is being done is also laying a foundation for future success
- as a venture, it is easy to join in at any time
- clear educational and social goals are obvious
- there are regular discussions for the interchange of ideas, information and experience
- the previous experience of staff in comparable situations is utilised

- there is an open and friendly atmosphere generally within the school
- teachers are sure of support if difficulty is experienced
- the staff have confidence in the headteacher based upon their credibility and reputation for success
- the staff concerned have specific and clearly defined responsibilities
- a provision of time in 'working hours' is made
- the senior staff are actively involved in the work.

Teachers are least likely to be well motivated when:

- they are simply told that they must. . .
- they are put into a threatened position
- the activity is not well planned
- it is felt by teachers that the plan is a 'gimmick' promoted by a senior member of staff to further their own ends
- the teachers feel that the plan is being carried out merely to satisfy higher authority
- a lot of hard work is involved without any apparent or obvious results
- initial moves are badly organised, with consequent initial negative feedback
- the teachers feel alienated from the school or from whoever is responsible for the plan
- the headteacher assumes the role of the 'expert', and there is a lack of opportunity for teachers to develop, or to exercise responsibility
- there is group pressure from colleagues to 'opt out'.

The practical steps that a headteacher might take to increase the likelihood of the staff being well motivated include:

- facilitating early initial discussion within the staff
- keeping overall control of the programme
- developing staff, especially their skills, understanding and self-confidence
- making available as much time as possible (and letting it be seen that they are doing so)
- leading by example
- involving all staff and not just teachers
- providing aid, back-up and support, especially when there are particular difficulties
- utilising the skills and expertise of particular staff
- making a very careful appraisal of the status quo, prior to committing the school to change
- encouraging staff to suggest developments and modifications once the change process is under way
- building up a system of steady, reliable support for teachers who are attempting to innovate in their own work
- building upon success and not failure
- delegating carefully; and delegating authority as well as responsibility
- appreciating work already done, however trivial; not alienating those who are committed to the system which the headteacher may wish to change
- not personalising opposition — keeping it on a professional level.

Work in America also suggests that when leaders provide a purposeful context for teachers increased motivation occurs. Some of the practical ways of setting such a context are:

- leaders avoid, or keep to the absolute minimum, interruptions to the teaching
- teachers are involved in curricular decisions
- staff meetings are useful to teachers since they are targeted at teachers' concerns, are result orientated, stick to the agenda and end on time
- in-service activities match teachers' and the schools' needs
- time is set aside for teachers to exchange ideas
- teachers learn from one another by observing one another's strengths
- leaders display sincere interest in teachers' work
- staff receive ongoing recognition and support.

This last point is significant. Although the list tends to talk about teachers, there is a clear need to consider *all* staff. Ancillaries, secretaries, peripatetic, supply and welfare staff should all be given due recognition, interest and support. After all, one thing must be absolutely clear, ancillary workers can hardly be in the job for the money! What is it that motivates them? And what else might be done to make their work more interesting and motivating?

Perhaps the greatest aid to motivation is simply talking to people about their work, their aspirations and desires to do a good job: *and then doing something alongside them to help*.

JOB DESCRIPTIONS

Job descriptions can be very useful tools in the management

of a school. For the headteacher, good job descriptions:

- provide a quick check that important areas of the school's development are being covered
- enable evidence of this to be presented to other interested parties such as the LEA and governing bodies
- help to ensure that appraisal procedures relate to previously agreed, and therefore more neutral, agendas.

For the 'owner' (including the headteacher) they:

- establish the boundaries of responsibility over a given period of time
- provide a way of defining work done when applying elsewhere
- give confidence that appraisal procedures should not cover unexpected areas.

Job descriptions also have negative features, too. They can:

- create mistrust—'Are you saying that you don't trust me to do anything without having it written down?'
- create demarcation disputes—'We agreed that I was responsible for mathematics in this school. I don't want her to have anything to do with it.'
- create friction—'It's his job. It says so here. Why hasn't he sorted it out then?
- create distress — 'I know we need someone to look after science but I'm the last person she should have chosen. Fancy not even asking me if I minded. I just can't do it!'

Negotiating and maintaining job descriptions need to be carried out with sensitivity.

The apparent definitive quality of job descriptions can also lead to other misunderstandings about what they can and cannot do.

Job descriptions describe what should be done; they describe a series of activities. What they cannot do is describe how those activities are to be carried out. In schools and other organisations, *how* the post-holder carries out the job is as important as the nature of the job itself.

> "I know that Arthur has the post of responsibility for maths in this school and I know that I am supposed to go and see him if I am in any difficulties, but I just can't. He's so horrible. I don't know what it is but he is so superior. Every time I talk to him I feel as though I'm not his colleague but bis worst pupil.
>
> What do I do if I have problems with my maths teaching? I go next door and talk to Liz. I know she has the responsibility for PE but she is so much more understanding. I get so much from her."
>
> The fact that Gill has responsibility for the art and craft stock doesn't mean that the only time I should be able to go into the cupboard is when she says so—on a Tuesday lunchtime."

Giving someone a job description, therefore, doesn't also confer the ability to carry out the tasks the job description contains.

Devising, Negotiating, Allocating and Accepting Job Descriptions: Some Golden Rules

1. The tasks need to be within the capabilities of the person.

There is little point in presenting people with a list of tasks they cannot do. This is more likely to create tension and breakdown than positive feelings. There is nothing wrong, though, including in a job description the need for preparation, as in the following:

'During the year I will prepare for the introduction of problem-solving into the school by developing it in my own classroom, attending relevant INSET and building up appropriate introductory resources.'

2. The tasks need to be as precisely defined as possible

The introduction of appraisal procedures, greater involvement of governing bodies and more rigorous interviewing procedures all mean that the frequency of judgements upon teachers is becoming greater.

One way of helping both the judge and the judged to meet this situation more equably is to reduce the ambiguity of job descriptions as much as possible. A sentence which reads 'I am responsible for improving resources in PE this year' is open to all sorts of interpretations and misunderstandings. Changed to 'I am responsible for introducing new resources which enable hand-eye coordination to be developed in the first three years' is much better.

3. Job descriptions should be negotiated, not given

Job descriptions which are given rather than negotiated have two major failings.

First, they can only be given on the assumption that the person defining them understands everything there is to know about the organisation. This is unlikely.

Second, most of us work better when we have a sense of ownership of our work. Job descriptions which are given cannot create as strong a sense of ownership as job descriptions in which the recipient has been a creator, too.

Given those two factors and a degree of confidence it seems reasonable, where possible, to ask the recipients to write their own job descriptions and negotiate around those.

4. Job descriptions should be dynamic rather than passive

The tasks in a job description should help to move the school forward in one direction or another. Job descriptions should, therefore, follow on from analysis of where the school is and, if possible, the creation of a school development plan. At the beginning of each negotiation the key sentence is not 'What can I do?' but 'What needs to be done?'

5. Job descriptions should be time specific

It is well known that not everything gets done in the time allocated for it, but it is also often true that if deadlines are not created little gets done at all. If both the school and the 'owner' of the job description are to benefit from what it contains, some time scale is vital.

Often this means that a job description will be re-negotiated each year. It can mean, though, that different activities within the job description can be allocated different deadlines of a term, a few weeks or, occasionally, more than one year.

DELEGATION

Nobody can do it all—and those of us who think we can simply make our schools run less effectively. There is just too much to know, too much to understand and too much to do for one person to even pretend they can manage everything.

Hence the need to share or delegate the work we do. Sharing can be carried out between any two or more people but delegation is different. Delegation involves the concepts of hierarchy, power, authority and responsibility.

The person delegating is invariably in a position of power. Delegation involves giving over some of that power to someone else. Delegating the *power* to make things happen doesn't mean, though, that we also delegate the *responsibility;* that stays with whoever is able to delegate.

> "In a large school such as the one we work in—it's a Group 7 primary school—the new INSET arrangements obviously take up a considerable amount of time and I just didn't feel as though I had enough time to do it properly.
>
> When we were sorting out our job descriptions for the year I asked Peter if he would take on the job of arranging our INSET and looking after the INSET budget—and he's made a really good job of it.
>
> Every so often he and I get together and he tells me everything that has happened—partly so that I know what is going on, partly just to check that I think we are heading in the right direction and partly to give Peter the confidence that everything is going well. It's only right that if we should mess it up I should be responsible."

In this school the headteacher has delegated reasonably. She has trusted Peter to cany out the task effectively, rarely interferes in the day-to-day work and yet keeps herself sufficiently involved to be able to take full responsibility should anything go wrong.

Almost everyone in the school will be involved in delegation at some time or another either by having tasks delegated to them or by delegating to others. At whatever level within the school delegation takes place, it is important to remember that the responsibility for the task stays with the person doing the delegating.

Trust and Control

The two elements always at the centre of delegation are *trust* and *control.*

Control remains in the hands of those delegating through the responsibility which they retain, but to delegate effectively those in possession of power must have *trust* in the person to whom they are delegating. Trust is usually based upon previous experience; we earn trust as a result of the sum total of our past joint experiences—that is why it is, quite rightly, so difficult to delegate immediately to a new colleague.

Trust, though, is two-way and those to whom we are delegating must have trust in us if they are to carry out the tasks they are set with commitment and enthusiasm. A number of factors can affect the levels of trust given to the person in positions of power. It is reasonable, for example, that:

- the delegated tasks are matched to willing individuals
- the tasks are matched to individuals capable of doing them
- the tasks are appropriate to an individual's perceived role in the school
- once delegated, the day-to-day ownership of the tasks is given to those most closely involved
- the tasks should be seen as useful to the school

- the act of delegation is seen as team-building rather than team-destroying
- the task should be clearly defined and the amount of day-to-day control for it clearly established.

> "We were worried about the little amount of parental consultation that seemed to take place in our school compared to other experiences we had all had, so the headteacher asked me to chair a working party to see what could be done.
>
> As a deputy, this was one job I really wanted to do and so I brought together some colleagues from across the school. After a couple of months of visiting other schools and discussions with everyone about what was reasonable we produced a policy for the full staff to consider.
>
> At the staff meeting there were obviously some disagreements about our final recommendations — including one or two from the headteacher, I think—but after some discussion our recommendations were accepted.
>
> The headteacher was really good, actually. He had seen our recommendations before they went to the staffing and told us that they were so much along the right lines that he wasn't going to make any fuss about the one or two bits he disagreed with. He was very supportive throughout."

This school seemed to get this particular piece of delegation about right. The task was seen to be important, the person delegated to the task was keen to be involved and had, as far as we can tell, status in the school. She was allowed to organise things in her own way although the headteacher was constantly informed and was able to accept the final recommendations even though they weren't exactly as he might have wished. The deputy and her team, quite rightly, felt as though they had done a good job.

Matching the task to the person is one of the key skills in delegation. To do this it is necessary to have a clear view in your own mind as to exactly what the task is and of the particular qualities and attitudes of those to whom it might be delegated.

Delegation is very much a part of staff development. Selecting the right person to carry out a particular job should be as important as which jobs are given out. Your colleagues, or the children in your class, will have different skills and needs; appropriate delegation can help them to build on existing skills, develop new ones and improve their strengths.

Carefully thought out delegation can have a profound effect upon the self-concept of those to whom we delegate. We have all taught children for whom the delegation of a particular task has been a turning point in their lives; our colleagues are not that much different.

One of us remembers only too well the feeling of being a probationer, struggling to keep a head above water and not too sure about the success of much that we were doing. The moment of being asked to take responsibility for the entrance hall display - "because you have done some smashing things in your classroom" -seems like only yesterday. It was a moment which defined a professional status which was able to grow from that point onward. Without that simple—and appropriate—act of delegation who knows what sort of career might have followed?

The Negative Power of Delegation

As with most of the concepts in this book, delegation has its negative side.

> "We had a litter problem at school. I'm not suggesting we didn't—but it was mainly caused by the children being sold snacks to eat at playtime to raise money for the school fund and not enough bins to throw their rubbish into.
>
> We were discussing it at a staff meeting one day when the headteacher suddenly asked me to do something about it. I was so taken aback I hadn't time to say no and anyway, I didn't want to cause a scene in the staff meeting.
>
> When I finally got round to it, it was obvious what the problem was but when I discussed it with the headteacher he said he wasn't going to stop the tuck shop because we needed the money, we weren't going to spend any on new bins and the children couldn't come into school at playtime to throw their rubbish into a classroom bin because it was one of the rules.
>
> The whole thing was a farce and a waste of time. We still haven't sorted out the problem and the other day Mrs . . . blamed me for not doing anything about it. It's really made me fed up."

Delegation helps to create atmospheres. It can be a vital and positive force in a school or it can be negative and deadening.

MANAGING MEETINGS—1

In primary schools meetings take place all the time. Whenever two or more staff get together they are having a meeting. The fact that most of these meetings are informal, may be concerned with personal or professional matters, and are often *ad hoc* and of short duration should not prevent us from calling them meetings. Nor should their informal nature make us underestimate their value. Informal meetings play a vital part in the smooth running of the school's network of communications and they contribute to the life and work of the school.

Informal meetings, though, are only one approach to developing and sustaining healthy communications. Regardless of their size, primary schools also need formal meetings. The current buzz words of HMI, LEA advisers, management pundits and many schools are:

- collaboration
- consistency
- continuity

All of these words imply that teachers need to work together. All of these words rely upon effective communication during meetings.

It is no surprise then that virtually every primary school has regular and frequent staff meetings. Many schools also have other kinds of meetings; working parties, year team meetings, departmental meetings, case conferences, and planning meetings for particular events (concerts, visits, sports events, festivals, etc.). Yet having a meeting may not, in itself, be enough. We have all been in staff meetings which were a waste of time, went on for too long, devoted too little time to the important business, and which we did not really need to attend in the first place!

In recent years primary teachers have increasingly noted that there is a lack of time to cater for all the demands they face. Meetings are both important ways of helping teachers work together and a way of using up precious time which could be allocated to any number of other pressing tasks (preparation, marking, planning). Meetings may be necessary but it is not sufficient simply to have meetings; what is needed are effective and efficient meetings.

Organising Meetings

If a meeting is to be worthwhile, some thought should be given to its preparation. The questions in the flow chart opposite are designed to help avoid some of the common pitfalls of meetings, such as staff not knowing where the meeting was to take place, whether or not a teacher should or could attend, the aim of the meeting, and so on. Problems like these occur more often than you might expect, and are avoidable.

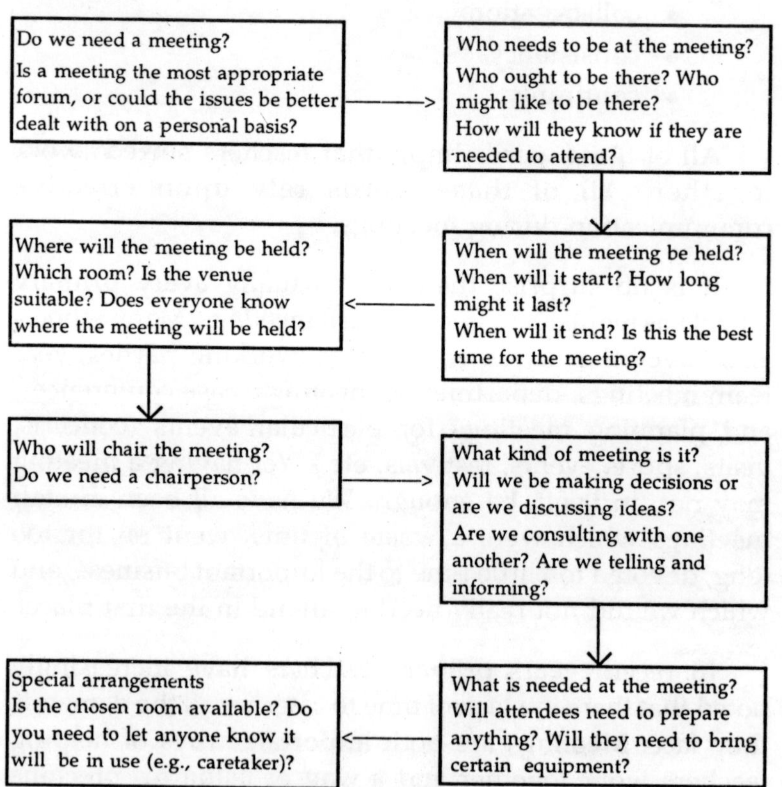

The questions might also trigger fresh approaches. For example, perhaps the caretaker and/or ancillary staff should attend certain meetings. Maybe the parent governors' views would inform certain decisions. Perhaps some meetings could take place at times other than before and after school, or during a lunchtime? Decisions taken when staff are rested, relaxed and in comfortable surroundings and not interrupted may be more effective.

Many schools proceed from one meeting to another out of habit and custom. These questions should stimulate you to reflect on practices which may need revising.

Agendas

Questions about how to organise a meeting are largely to do with the context of the meeting. The next thing to organise is the content, which is where use of an agenda can prove valuable.

It is worth considering defining some agenda items in detail to avoid any confusions over what is to be discussed. An agenda should be circulated to all those expected to attend. In addition, it may sometimes be useful to display a copy in a prominent place so that all members of staff have access to it.

Priorities

From looking at the advantages and disadvantages of approaches to creating agendas a number of points emerge:

- Priorities for the meeting's agenda should be identified by someone. What is included/excluded? What is urgent/can wait?
- How much time should be allocated to some items? It is wasteful to spend 40 minutes on the colour of tissue paper for party hats and five minutes on a new paired approach to reading!

- Staff do need to feel involved, consulted and listened to. If they do not then their participation in the meeting may be reduced.

Too Much?

Agendas that are too long are frustrating and inefficient. It may be more useful to have two meetings instead of one. Many staff now use one meeting, often each week, to deal with 'housekeeping' matters — things that require little discussion and are invariably concerned with giving information (lost property, list of visitors, tidiness around school, changes in arrangements).

Another option is to suggest that certain items are present under any other business (AOB). This usually works well. However, in large schools there can be another whole meeting's worth of items under AOB and if the meeting has already been lengthy it can go 'an item too far' for some members!

Remember!

If you want your meetings to be successful there's more to it than putting a group of people together and starting them talking. Agenda creation is one element that will contribute to the effective and efficient management of meetings.

MANAGING MEETINGS—2

The Role of the Chairperson

The changes initiated in the latter part of the 1980s have increased the number of meetings held in school. You've probably noticed it already. Staff need to look at the implications of the National Curriculum, to discuss the findings of the subject working groups and may have to reconsider their approaches to evaluation and assessment.

Moreover, many of these meetings will be in addition to most schools' existing programmes of staff meetings as there will still be a need to consider such things as resources, timetables, budgets and day-to-day 'housekeeping' matters.

Unfortunately, the time available for all of these meetings remains constant, therefore more meetings have to be packed into the same amounts of time. Consequently, the need for efficient meetings is all the more important. One way in which meetings can be improved is by having an effective chairperson.

Who Should be the Chairperson?

In primary schools, the headteacher commonly chairs meetings. This can have advantages, but there is a danger that too much control rests with one person. For example, such an arrangement usually means that the chair does most of the talking.

Chairing is not the privilege of position and meetings in school should not be chaired by just the headteacher and/or deputy. Everyone on the staff should have the chance to chair meetings. This also has advantages when staff are not chairing in that they are likely to have a clearer understanding of the difficulties involved, and are more likely to perform better in meetings generally.

Preparation

The chairperson needs to be well prepared. This includes knowing who is coming to the meeting, and ensuring that an agenda has been circulated to all concerned. The chairperson should decide whether minutes should be taken or not. Copies of minutes of any previous meeting and other relevant notes and papers should be prepared in advance and circulated with the agenda.

The setting for the meeting should be given some thought. If possible, chairs of similar height should be arranged in a circle so that all members of the meeting can see each other and feel included. Tables may be needed, but if so all members should sit around them, rather than just one or two individuals sitting magisterially behind one.

If someone is to make an individual presentation or lead the discussion on some particular agenda item, then that person should be consulted prior to the meeting to check how long is needed or is available.

Preparation is thus fairly obvious and a matter of common sense, yet in the hurly-burly of school life it can easily be forgotten. Preparation by the chairperson will not necessarily ensure a smooth meeting, but it should increase the meeting's chances of being effective.

What Kind of Meeting?

One of the most important pieces of preparation is to determine what kind of meeting or discussion will take place. This is not a matter of deciding whether the meeting will be friendly or hostile—unfortunately, not even the chairperson can predetermine that! Rather, it is to know whether the whole meeting, or certain agenda items, can be categorised as:

Informational concerned with the giving out of news and information.

Consultative finding out what those present think and feel about some specific matter.

Decision-making making decisions either by the collective meeting or by an individual who is party to the meeting.

Whether it is on an item-by-item or a meeting-by-meeting basis, everyone needs to know the function of the meeting or discussion. The chairperson should preface each discussion by clarifying its objectives.

Starting the Meeting

The chairperson should not be late, and should take steps to avoid being called away or interrupted by something outside the meeting's focus. The meeting should start on time. Do not wait for someone who is late — a person who is five minutes late keeps the whole group waiting five minutes per person and will waste a considerable amount of collective potential working time.

At the start the chairperson should make such introductions as are necessary, inform the group of the time the meeting is to end, explain the aims of the meeting or discussion and commence the work of the meeting without further ado. A few simple words, some preface to the first item and such 'rules' and procedures as are necessary should be all that is required. The meeting should not be delayed by a fussy or garrulous chairperson.

During the Meeting

The most obvious rule is *'keep to the agenda'*. This is sometimes easier said than done, but nevertheless the chairperson should try and keep the discussion relevant to the business in hand. If discussion begins to take an inappropriate direction then it is up to the chair to call the group's attention to serious diversions from the agenda.

The chairperson should be *vigilant about time* and warn the group if prearranged schedules are slipping. When time begins to run out the chairperson may need to rearrange the agenda or appeal to the group for guidance as to which items should be given priority.

Another function of the chairperson is to *help the group*

establish shared meanings. For example, if abbreviations, acronyms and jargon are used, the chair may need to intervene and check that everyone understands the terminology. Such checking is fairly straightforward. More difficult is the establishing of shared meanings at the end of a group discussion. Here the chair should try to summarise the discussion and reflect back to the group the positions taken up by the group or individuals. This is not easy but it is very important as otherwise individuals may leave the meeting unclear of what was said, meant or decided.

Of course, it is not always clear what has been said or decided! Talk is often contradictory, inconsistent or imprecise. It may be appropriate at times to ask the person taking the minutes to read back the relevant part, as ultimately this will be the record, and, as such, should be clear to everyone.

Throughout the meeting the chairperson should *constantly listen, and talk only a little,* but this should not be taken as sign of inactivity. It is up to the chair to show that they have heard, remembered and considered what others have said.

The chairperson should *ensure that everyone feels included in the meeting,* through eye-contact and invitations to individuals to speak or comment, and they should try to avoid creating favourites or enemies. On the whole, the chairperson should be relatively neutral since it is the chair's function to enable the group to work. However, if the chairperson has views central to some particular issue, then they may need to consider temporarily handing over to someone else.

Common Problems

Overtake People

The persistent talker usually adversely affects the

progress of the meeting. When it is clear that such a person has exhausted the goodwill or the concentration span of the group, then the chair should intervene. A few diplomatic words may be needed, or a direct question such as, "So you are against this proposal?" The overtalkative use up precious time, so they may need to be reminded of time (and thus controlled), "We've only 10 minutes left, please could we hear another view?"

Sometimes it is not the sheer volume of a single statement that takes the time, but the persistent pressing of opinions. The overtalkative may modify their behaviour if the chair fails to approve of or acknowledge their comments. When 'controlled', an 'offender' should be reinstated into the group otherwise relationship and communication problems may ensue.

Silence

When gaps occur in the conversation the chairperson could invite those who have not contributed to do so. Eye-contact with a silent member, whilst another is talking, may establish whether a contribution to the discussion is going to be forthcoming.

Sometimes an individual's silence may imply fatigue, anger, boredom, lack of interest or ill-health. Frequently in schools one is aware of such things, but some sensitivity will be needed when directly inviting the quiet members to speak. The chairperson should not insist on an individual contributing.

There are different sorts of silence, the reflective, the anxious, the puzzled, the confused, even the embarrassed silence. Occasionally silence can mean that there is nothing else to say. The chairperson should not always feel a need to fill each silence -sometimes a few moments reflection is very useful. However, letting a silence go on so long that it becomes awkward for anyone to break should be avoided.

Differences of Opinion

In most discussions differences will emerge. The chair should try to remain impartial and to see any differences as constructive. Quite often a contrary view stimulates greater thought and awareness, thereby contributing to more sensitive and informed decisions.

There may be outbursts of anger or hostility. Where they are directed at the chairperson, an appeal to the group will usually help to defuse the tension, for example "Is that how you all feel?" or, "Is that a fair summary of what we believe?"

If the anger is directed elsewhere, say outside the group, it may be prudent to encourage the ventilation of pent-up frustrations, fears and disappointments. When a decision has to be made it is easier for the chairperson to be leading a group the members of which agree and like each other. While consensus is a worthy aim in meetings, chairpersons might be better advised to seek consent. Not everyone need agree with the proposals, not all differences need to be resolved; consensus is a bonus rather than a necessity. Perhaps all that needs to be secured is the extent to which the group will go along with a decision.

If consent is limited or difficult to ascertain then it may be useful to defer a decision. Allowing more thinking time often means that people have a chance to get used to the idea.

Ending the Meeting

At the close of a meeting the chairperson should recap briefly what has happened, note decisions taken and points which need further action. Often one meeting leads to another, in which case the date, time, venue and purpose of any subsequent meeting should be mentioned and minuted.

Effective Chairperson—Effective Meetings?

You may feel that the picture presented here is of a chairperson who is some paragon of judicial restraint and diplomacy. That may be, but if the chairperson can contribute to people wanting to meet, looking forward to discussions and sharing different ideas and approaches, and if the chairperson conducts effective meetings, then the outcome is a healthier climate amongst staff, a greater sense of oneness and thereby the opportunity of working in a more effective school. Chairpersons contribute to effective meetings; effective meetings contribute to effective schools.

MANAGING MEETINGS—3

Minutes

Minutes can play a valuable role in the management of meetings.

Unfortunately they are often not used, and when they are they tend to be taken for granted and not used to advantage.

Why Take Minutes?

The first and most obvious reason is the need to record what happens in a meeting. This is particularly necessary when some staff do not or cannot attend all meetings, or when there are a lot of meetings in the school. Minutes help all members of staff to keep track of what is going on.

However, minutes can do two other things. First, they can act as an *aide-memoire.* A rapid read of the minutes of the last meeting should remind us who agreed to do something and when they agreed to have it done by. This is very useful if that person turns out to be you! An *action* column helps to highlight those who need to do something as a result of the decision made in the meeting.

Second, minutes should give a consensus of understanding. At the start of a meeting, members should agree the minutes of the previous meeting. In effect, what they are doing is saying:

- this is an accurate record of what happened
- this matches my understanding of what was decided.

Minutes are intended to ensure that those things which were agreed in the heat (or the cold) of a meeting are understood and accepted.

Keeping Minutes

Whoever keeps the minutes usually has a thankless task. It means:

- extra work
- being able to listen
- being able to write quickly and succinctly, and selecting and reordering the vital elements from what may have been a discursive and unstructured exchange of views
- often having to take a less directly involved role in the meeting.

It is not necessary for the same person to keep the minutes each time, but it is never a good idea for the chairperson to try to keep the minutes. Neither is it helpful if the minute-taker is someone who is likely to make a major contribution to that particular meeting. However, it is unlikely to be a popular job, so perhaps the most democratic solution is for everyone to take a turn.

Although the person who takes the minutes may be less directly involved in the meeting, it does not mean they should be passive or silent. At certain points, perhaps at the chairperson's invitation, it is a good idea for them to report back their impression of what has been said and decided. In so doing the minute-taker should not feel that their record is being tested for its integrity and accuracy, but to ensure that common understandings are being developed. Thus the process of keeping minutes can help create consent and avoid misunderstandings.

What Should be Included?

Minutes should recall facts:

- date, time, venue
- name of meeting
- who was present
- apologies.

They should include agenda items serving as headings, under which should be noted:

- main points raised in discussion
- decisions taken
- actions required, by whom and by what date
- future plans
- unresolved matters
- date, time and place of next meeting (if relevant).

Minutes should not record everything that is said, only the main points. However, deciding what the main points are can sometimes be difficult.

The minute-taker should concentrate on identifying the key points a speaker is making. In discussion it is reasonable and normal for speakers to illustrate their points with a variety of anecdotes, explanations and illustrations. It's quite normal, too, in many forms of writing. Minutes, though, are a specialised form of writing and should be as concise as possible.

One advantage of letting members take it in turn to minute meetings is that colleagues can learn from each other's approaches. They can also understand how long-winded speeches or lack of clarity can make the minute-taker's task more difficult and, more importantly, make the speaker's contribution to the meeting less effective.

After the Meeting

The person who minutes the meeting should be responsible for ensuring that the minutes are promptly circulated, approved and filed in the appropriate way.

The circulation of minutes is particularly important. If actions are required as a result of a meeting, minutes can be used as a prompt to the person who is responsible for taking that action. Minutes which arrive two weeks after the meeting has taken place may be an accurate and concise record, but may not be helpful in getting things done!

The attitudes of the people who receive your minutes often depend on the way in which those minutes are presented.

Informal meetings can often be represented by quick, handwritten, informal minutes. But the minutes of a meeting at which important decisions have been made should be presented in a way which reflects the status of what has taken place.

The prepared minutes should be shown to the chairperson prior to circulation. Again, this is not to judge the minute-taker's ability, but to agree the recorded impression of the meeting.

List might indicate full names, if there are newcomers on the staff

Clear heading, main details clearly shown

YEAR TUTORS' MEETING MINUTES

30th April, 12.15 PM

A.P.'s Office

Effective synopsis of discussion

Present: AP LC DJ BT LJ PS RD — Action

A. Meeting for Summer Term

The proposed groupings for meetings as set out in Anne's document were discussed.

Timing of the meetings were discussed, including the possibility or re-introducing some 8.30 am staff meetings for points of information only. LC suggested that we should try, as a temporary measure, to reduce the number of full staff meetings so that people would have more time to give to working parties.

Clear statement of agreement

Agrees: Attendance at meeting will be in directed time.

Re-introduction of 8.30 am staff meeting will be put to next full staff meeting on 7th May.

Newcomers might need further information

Dates and timings of working party meetings will be decided by those opting to join the groups.

B. Activity Week

Agreed

This will be in the week beginning 8th June. The usual option system will operate and planning and deciding on options will take place at year group meetings. Y.G. Tutors will co-ordinate the week. DJ will design an option form for consideration at our next meeting — DJ

Clear indication of responsibility

C. A.O.B.

RD asked that from 11th May to 15th May we avoid any activities which might causes distraction to Fourth Years as Higham Secondary has requested that we arrange for parents to be present when Fourth year pupils have their individual interviews with Higham School staff.

D. Date of Next Meeting

Tuesday 12th May at 12.15 pm

Unclear—this actually meant to say that children moving from primary to secondary should be available, and on normal timetable, when secondary staff visit the school.

Opposite there is an example of some minutes taken at a real meeting. We have added some comments to them which emphasise their strengths and weaknesses.

SCHOOL POLICIES

A'policy', according to *Chambers Concise Dictionary*, 1985, is a 'course of action'. By that definition schools are already full of policies, each of which responds to the hundreds of situations in which teachers, children, parents and others find themselves each day.

The weakness across the whole school is that many of these individually held policies can be contradictory and confusing, reducing the smooth running of the organisation and ensuring that children's education, as they move from class to class, is haphazard and unstructured.

School policies attempt to counter that weakness by creating agreed procedures, methods, approaches and decisions which enable a school to work as an integrated unit, moving and developing in more or less the same direction. School policies are not only about curriculum matters, although they are obviously important. A school might want to create policies about (among others):

- acceptable children's behaviour
- the involvement of parents
- community work
- staff duties

The existence of a policy doesn't mean that it will be followed identically by everyone in the school. One of the common threads running through this book is the inevitability of different perceptions within and about a school and, clearly, each individual will interpret a policy in a slightly different way. What it does mean is that those interpretations should be focused around similar procedures and outcomes.

Why are Policies Important?

1. Policies provide a measure of agreement

Schools are incredibly busy and demanding places. If they are to run as smoothly as possible then everyone who is connected with them needs to have a framework within which to work. Policies exist to provide this framework.

2. Policies help to provide continuity

Schools, like many other organisations, cannot function effectively without some measure of continuity. If each change of staff were to alter the broad direction in which a school is heading the likely result would be chaos. Policies ensure that the direction of a school, while not resistant to change and development, is also stable enough to withstand certain inevitable pressures.

3. Policies create security

At a time when the pace of educational change is great and the external pressures on teachers and schools so enormous, the existence of policies can help to create security for teachers. A policy document represents an accumulation of professional discussion and the translation of that discussion into recommendations for practical action. Policies explain what a school is doing and why. A good policy document should free teachers from having to make individual defences of their work and provide evidence to others — parents, inspectors, HMIs and so on—that decisions have been clearly thought out by the school.

4. Policies help to ease negotiations about practice

Personalising issues—feeling that a contrary point of view is a personal attack on ourselves—is counterproductive to professional development. Unfortunately, because education is essentially a human activity the opportunities for such personal and interpersonal offence are frequent.

If we are to be able to think through issues in a less personalised way we need a neutral starting point from which to begin discussions. School policies can help by creating such a neutral context. With them, the evaluation of practice can begin with questions such as "How does what you are doing fit in with our agreed policy?" rather than "I disagree with what you are doing."

What Should Policies Contain?

Certain features do seem to be important if policies are to be useful to schools.

First, policies need to provide examples of what should happen as a result of the policy being put into action. In other words, policies need to be practical.

All of us will have either seen or worked on school policies which, in the end, resemble nothing more than a text-book about a subject, often apparently written more for the career prospects of the writer than for the benefit of those who are supposed to use it.

If policies are to coordinate a school then they need to be used. It is unlikely in these busy times that teachers will even give policies a thought if they don't offer strategies which can be used in practice. So the first thing a policy must do is to answer the question "Will people who use it have a good idea of what they are supposed to do?"

Because many of us who read policies have a range of different abilities it is also important that such practical strategies should be understood by the least informed and able in the school rather than the most. This has implications for the process through which policies are produced.

Second, policies need to provide reasons why the strategies they contain have been recommended. In other words, it isn't enough for a policy to only contain practical strategies. If the policies are to create confidence and security amongst their users then they need to provide reasons for action as well as the action itself.

Third, policies need to be designed in such a way that those who have to use them can gain access to the information they need as quickly as possible. A policy presented as a series of densely written A4 pages is likely to be neglected. Once neglected, the advantages of school policies are lost, however much hard work has been put into the early stages.

How Should Policies be Produced?

Policies should benefit a school long after the process of their initial production has ended, but there is no doubt that we need to think carefully about that process if the policies are to be as effective as possible. The process of producing policies in a school has a personal and professional effect upon those involved and upon the outcome of the policy itself.

Just occasionally, we can understand that some schools might need hastily written and imposed policies for specific reasons.

In general though, school policies are more effective if as many as possible of those whom they will affect have had a part to play in their formulation. In involving the whole staff and others:

- a considerable amount of INSET work takes place
- the range of attitudes and abilities with which the policy has to deal is revealed more clearly

- a fuller range of expertise can be utilised than resides in one or two individuals
- the presentation and appearance of the policy can be criticised before 'publication'
- the 'ownership' (and, therefore, the effect) of the policy is likely to be greater.

Involving the whole staff is a phrase which sounds simple but which hides complexity. Those involved in producing policies need to understand that it takes time, patience, diplomacy and understanding. On the other hand, if policies are to be long-lasting and effective such involvement is essential.

One Final Point

Policies, however well prepared and useful, will not continue in a school unless they are supported. The production of a written policy document is only the beginning. Issues contained within each policy need to be regularly brought into focus, reviewed and discussed. Those responsible for school policies need to make them live rather than remain inert; those who take ultimate responsibility for the school need to ensure that an agreed policy is respected, worked towards and followed. Only then can we hope to maximise the advantages such policies bring.

SCHOOL DEVELOPMENTS PLAN—1

A school development plan is a policy statement which maps the school's intended and anticipated areas of development. This could be expressed in terms of curriculum:

- to introduce the proposals of the National Curriculum working party report on geography by summer term 1993 or in terms of organisational arrangements:

1 to review the way supply teachers are introduced to and supported in the school and the classroom.

A school development plan might embody both of these.

Primary schools need to plan on a broader rather than a narrower front. For example, if a school decided to develop only maths this year and science next year it could be many years before other areas of the curriculum were developed. Moreover, schools need to develop more than the curriculum, which is only one strand, however important, in the organisational life of the school.

The sheer scale of school development creates the need for priorities. Priorities will help staff make sense of the log-jam of issues needing or awaiting development. Thus, making priorities is one characteristic of school development plans. There are others:

- a belief that school development grows best from within
- the plan is a whole school plan
- the plan takes into account LEA and central government policies
- the plan is agreed with the school governors
- time schedules should be provided
- outside help should be identified
- the plan defines responsibilities
- the plan is a contract.

Below, we examine these points in more detail.

1. A belief that School Development Grows Best from Within

Although there is benefit to be gained from the kick in

the pants from outside an organisation, most *development* does grow from within. In good schools teachers work continuously and actively towards their own and their school's improvement. There are three obvious reasons for this. First, staff feel more in control and committed when relating to their own development. Second, spreading the talents of those who work together facilitates much staff development. Third, internal school development is always necessary. No scheme — national, *LEA* or local— can work unless each school and teacher is a part of that development.

2. The Plan is a Whole School Plan

All staff should be appropriately consulted and involved in devising the plan. The planning should provide a forum for staff to share and bring together the views of all members of the school's staff. As much as possible, the plan should also be the staffs collective view of how and where the school should be developing.

3. The Plan Takes into Account LEA and Central Government Policies

While development grows from within, teachers and schools work and exist within the context of national and local legislation such as policies for equal opportunities or special needs, Diocesan Agreed RE Syllabuses and the National Curriculum Council. Internal development does not mean ignoring such policies.

4 The Plan is Agreed with the School Governors

The 1986 and 1988 Education Acts make such a characteristic an imperative. Schools clearly need to consider:

- involving parent governors in the processes of planning
- involving the chairperson
- presenting and explaining the plan to governors

- securing the governors' support.

5. Time Schedules Should be Provided

Target dates should be agreed and noted on an action sheet. These might vary as in:

Action Sheet: Academic Year 1990 to 1991
Curricular Developments

1. Handwriting policy and scheme to be adopted and working in all classes by end of Autumn term.
2. Each class to undertake one educational visit within locality, each term for this year.
3. Technology Working Party Report to be discussed in Autumn term; our interpretation and resources analysed in Spring term; implementation to commence in Summer term and following academic year.

6. Outside Help Should be Identified

'Growing from within' means that the responsibility for developing the school comes from those who are associated with it. It doesn't mean that outsiders should never be involved.

7. The Plan Defines Responsibilities

Given that the plan is a whole school plan and that the staff are committed to making it work, it is reasonable for it to contain statements of individual responsibility which will enable the plan to happen. These statements of responsibility will be very close, if not identical, to job descriptions.

8. The Plan is a Contract

Agreement on the plan by the staff, governors and possibly the LEA effectively makes the plan a 'contract'. Having gone through the process of creating a school development plan it would be folly not to see it as 'morally' binding on all.

As new members of staff join a school they will need to be made aware of the school's plan and, crucially, be expected to accept it until such time as it is renewed, when the time for input occurs.

All of these characteristics are important. Each interlocks with the others to give the plan its strength. From these characteristics it can be seen that school development plans are:

- sensitive to issues both internal and external to the school. They should be a judicious blend of inside and outside interests and concerns
- a mix of wide ranging consultations and decisiveness. At some point consultation must pause and decisions be taken
- firm yet flexible. The plan must be sufficiently firmly established so that staff are committed to it and know that it really matters. Yet some flexibility is needed to take account of unexpected events. The plan must not be allowed to evaporate, but neither must it become unalterable.

School development plans will thus offer some clarity and certainty. At a time of change and uncertainly school development plans provide continuity and way of making sense of the existing and new demands being made of school. They provide help for everyone to:

- know what is to be done
- know why it is to be done
- know when it is to done
- know what help is available to do it.

16

School Development Plans

THE KEY ELEMENTS AND THE MAIN AREAS

There are three key areas to school development planning. They are:

- review
- action
- evaluation

Review

Before saying where we should go it is necessary to find out where we are. Hence some system of review, school self-evaluation and self-appraisal is needed. At this stage policy documents laid down by national government and local authorities are likely to be particularly important as they provide an opportunity for schools to find out how far their existing practices already reflect the proposals contained in existing documentation.

The review procedure will involve consultation with all interested parties including parents and governors. The results of the review are particularly important as they will be instrumental in determining the first action statements the school makes. Any temptation to rush into 'action' should be resisted until a consensus of agreement has been reached about the school's present position.

Action

'Action' is self-explanatory. The action part of a school development plan describes what the school is going to do within a particular area over a given time span. The use of the word 'action' also implies a commitment to getting it done.

For the 'action' to be more than words on a page, a number of conditions have to be fulfilled.

1. Priorities have to be Established

There is only so much a school, and particularly a small school, can achieve and attend to whilst simultaneously continuing with the day-to-day education of children.

2. The Priorities have to Respond to Perceived Needs

Priorities have a greater chance of being realised if those involved in delivering them can see the benefits which accrue. There is little point in embarking on a grand scheme to build a swimming pool for the school if teachers, parents and governors are aware that the book provision is both out-dated and of poor quality.

3. The Priorities Must be Achievable within the Time Span

A school development plan is not an opportunity for grandiose boasting. It is a way of representing honestly the school's strengths and weaknesses and what is to be done. Once priorities have been declared then it is only reasonable for teachers, parents, governors and others to expect them to be achieved. Achievement should be the aim.

It is also true that priorities which are unachievable will very quickly lose the support of those expected to achieve them.

Evaluation

Evaluation represents a very similar stage to 'review' with one important difference. In the review stage the school was judging itself against wholly external criteria; in the evaluation stage the school also judges itself against criteria—the action priorities—which were created in-house. The evaluation stage assesses the school's ability to devise effective action plans as much as it assesses the school's ability to achieve them.

The Six Key Areas

We can identify six key areas around which a school development plan might operate. They are the developing curriculum, the staff, the school constituency, resources, organisational systems, and the school climate.

The Developing Curriculum

'Curriculum' means here 'all the learning that is planned and guided by the school'. Divisions of this curriculum have always been open to debate although agreement is more likely as the National Curriculum becomes established.

The word 'developing' is important. No one would expect schools to *be* fully developed across all curriculum areas, but they might reasonably be expected to be responsive to changing ideas, perceptions, insights and demands so that their curriculum provision is continually developing.

The Staff

The quality of the whole staff in a school is of immense importance. All members of staff are capable of developing as people and as professionals. The notion of school development plans assumes that each will exhibit strengths and weaknesses relevant to their role which can be supported and developed.

The School Constituency

Schools are not insular places; they interact with and respond to a variety of outside influences. The way in which a school interacts with those influences and the confidence they return to the school will influence the effectiveness of children's learning.

Resources

Resources can mean those items which directly support curriculum action, such as tape recorders, books, paintbrushes and so on. It can also mean the buildings and the use to which they are put to enhance the way in which children are educated.

Organisational Systems

Schools need effective systems for a wide range of activities. Whichever systems are chosen will depend upon the context of each individual school, its size, the age range of its pupils, the nature of the buildings, the levels of support staff and so on. Ineffective systems are both time-wasting and confusing; school development plans should consider them carefully.

The Climate

'Climate' is much harder to describe but no less important than the other elements. 'Climate' is something felt, the essence of a school which binds everything else together. It is what you feel as soon as you walk in the door. The fact that it is hard to describe shouldn't preclude schools from considering it very carefully.

School development plans are at the organisational heart of this book.

Everything it contains affects in some way or another the actions which need to be developed and contained within a development plan.

School development plans are not an aspect of a school's life; they are the guiding force behind it.

IN-SERVICE EDUCATION AND TRAINING (INSET)

The purpose of INSET is to further develop teacher professionalism and so help the implementation of change. So INSET aims to serve both

- the individual's needs and wishes
- the school's needs

In addition INSET is viewed by central government and LEAs as an agent of change. It is within these three circles of interest that INSET is provided. When analysing and identifying needs this simple model is worth keeping in mind, as there will be occasions when the provision can fall within the area where all three circles intersect; this might help in drawing up priorities.

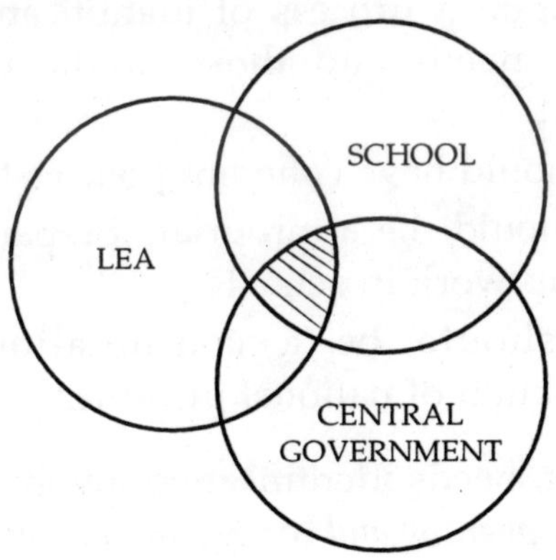

Fig. 16.1 Inset Circles of Interest

There are bound to be times when a tension exists between the individual's perception of their own needs, and those of the school, LEA or central government. A school may not wish to fund or use up allocated space to allow staff members to attend a course which appears to be for their benefit alone. On the other hand individuals may not see the need to take part in INSET activities on behalf of the school without apparent benefit to themselves. It is, therefore, vital to make sure that the process of identifying INSET needs is as effective as possible.

Identifying Needs

Identifying needs is central to the provision and support of INSET. How they are to be identified is often problematical—but there are strategies which can help.

A Framework for Policy Making

The Advisory Committee on the Supply and Education of Teachers (ACSET) made the following recommendations:

1. Every school should have a policy for INSET, based upon a process of identification of the school's needs and those of the individual teachers.
2. LEAs should have coherent policies for INSET.
3. There should be appropriate preparation and follow-up work in schools.
4. There should be a continuation of the identification of national priorities.

At its simplest, needs identification involves looking at *what is actually happening and comparing it to what we want to achieve.* It's also worth remembering that INSET also has the dimension *of what others want from us.*

Weindling (of The National Foundation for Educational Research) suggests the following stages as a method of determining needs:

1. Identification of the problem.
2. Collection of the data.
3. Needs analysis.
4. Specification of objectives based on the priority needs.
5. Development of strategies.
6. Implementation of the programme.
7. Evaluation of the programme.
8. Revision.

Number 1 above sets the tone for the exercise by taking a 'problem-solving' approach in which a definition of INSET requirements emerges as a response to problems the school or individual is likely to face rather than a straightforward external assessment of their needs.

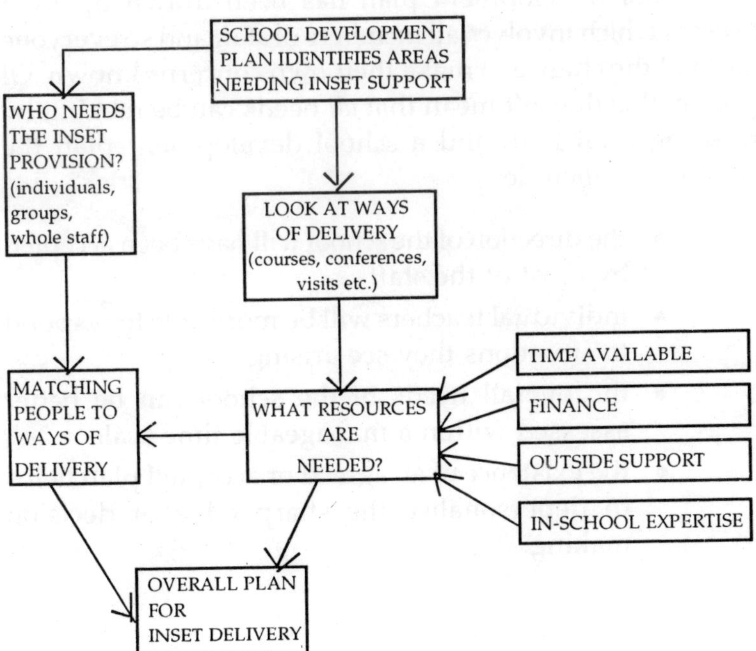

What we must do is move away from the "Jill's going on another maths course", which simply defines what is happening, to "does Jill need to go on another maths course?" and if so, why?

Hopefully the answers to such questions lie in the *school development plan.* This is a means by which the staff of a school contribute to identifying the major thrust of the school's activities over a given period. The plan covers a number of important areas in the life of a school and takes into account both the internal wishes of those who work in it and the external constraints imposed by parents, governors, LEAs and central government's policies.

A needs identification process, starting with a school development plan, might look like this:

There is a crucial assumption made here which is that the school development plan has been drawn up by a process which involves all members of staff and so everyone has had the chance to make their own concerns known. Of course, this doesn't mean that *all* needs can be met but by focusing INSET around a school development plan the advantages include:

- the direction of the school will have been accepted by most of the staff
- individual teachers will be more able to respond to situations they see arising
- the overall needs of the school can be better assessed within a manageable time scale
- the existence of an agreed or accepted plan helps to depersonalise the sharp edge of decision making.

Making INSET Work-a Brief Guide

Weighty tomes have been written about INSET; from many of these sources (some of which we list in the bibliography) it is possible to distil some key points:

- professional development is more effective when it is part of an overall plan
- 'one-offs' are not usually very useful although they are frequently used
- school-based courses are greatly helped by follow-up support
- teachers tend to prefer practical input rather than theory
- the aims of any INSET provision should be clear to all potential participants
- the best INSET providers listen to and act upon feedback
- there should be an interaction between the demands of school. LEA and central government
- whenever possible individuals should be able to define their own needs while accepting the necessity of overall planning.

Management's task in all this is to set up genuinely consultative processes to identify needs, decide on priorities, plan provision, acquire and allocate resources, set up and respond to evaluation.

Final Thought

In times of rapid change the important role of staff development/INSET becomes vital. Without doubt it is one of the key tasks in managing the primary school.

TIME MANAGEMENT

Time management is about planning your time effectively. If school development plans are a way of responding to the increasing complexity of school life, and term and lesson plans are a way of responding to the increasing complexity of classroom life, then time management is a way of responding to an increasing complexity at a personal level.

Time management, too, begins from the premise that the more complex a situation, the more important planning becomes as a means of dealing with it. Teachers and headteachers need to be:

- calm
- well-organised
- thoughtful about educational issues and arguments
- conscious of all aspects of their organisation
- influential
- open to outside influences and not totally school-bound.

A Headteacher's Day

08.00	Arrive at school Deal with mail, staff absences, phone messages
09.10	Assembly
09.30	Teach a class
10.30	Breaktime See a parent
10.50	Teach second class
12.00	Lunch duty
12.20	Staff meeting
13.00	Eat sandwich
13.15	Work on governors report
14.00	Go over School Development Plan for LEA
14.30	Phone LEA and deal with Development Plan School Finance. Support Services

15.15	See two new families coming to school
15.45	See concerned parent
16.15	See two members of staff
17.00	Arrive (late) at Headteacher's liaison meeting
17.45	Go home and read report on local management of schools for later meeting
18.30	Return to school
19.00	Governors' meeting
22.00	Leave school

It is impossible to conceive how, within the present context of teaching and headteaching, these attributes can be maintained without an effective time management plan.

Two Difficulties

Most people find time management difficult to think about for two reasons. Sit still for a moment and ask yourself the following questions.

1. Do You Appreciate the Need for Managing Your Time?

Often, time management is seen as something which someone else needs but not ourselves. Consider the list of attributes described above. If you cannot answer yes to all of them then you need some degree of time management help.

2. Do You Appreciate How Your Job has Changed?

Primary school teaching and headteaching have changed enormously over the past fifteen years and the pace of change and the levels of responsibility and complexity continue to increase.

> "I used to take a club every lunchtime at school and people used to say to me 'You are doing too much' but I really enjoyed it so I carried on. During the teacher action a couple of years ago I stopped doing lunchtime clubs as part of my protest and suddenly found that I was enjoying

my afternoon teaching so much more. I've gone back to running one lunchtime club a week now but it took the action to show me that I was using my time badly."

These changes mean that our approach to the job has to change, too. Unfortunately, some of us find that change harder to make than others. By refusing to assess how the job has altered we try and hang on to an outdated style of teaching or headteaching, with the result that we are always trying to fit a quart into a pint pot.

One of the realities of those changes is that some things may have to be discarded or given lower priorities. If the fundamental shifts in the job are not appreciated those changes will be almost impossible to make.

What Can be Done

In the first place, as with all planning, it is important to understand the situation now.

Think about the Most Important Functions of Your Job

What is your job about as we move into and through the 1990s? You will probably experience some conflict between what you would like it to be and what is being demanded of you but try and develop a list of priorities.

Think about How You Spend Your Time Now

For a week or so, write down a summary of what you did every half hour you were at work. How much of that time was concerned with the priorities of your job you thought about earlier? How often did you manage to build in longer than half an hour for any one task?

Think about Yourself

At what time of the day do you work best? Which aspects of your job are you really committed to? Which are you most enthusiastic about? How frustrated about time do you feel? Is lack of time having an effect upon you, your family, your social life and your friends? Does it matter to you?

Taking Action

Second, you need to take appropriate action. No one of the strategies we suggest below works for everybody, but they have all been proven in different situations to be more rather than less effective in helping people control their time.

Prioritise

Be ruthless in the tasks you choose to do. Jettison temporarily or permanently those which are not crucial to your job. Concentrate on the tasks which matter. There is significant research which suggests that 80% of our results come from concentrating on just 20% of our possible tasks. Identify that 20%! It may be the key to your success.

Delegate

Sounds simple, proves difficult. Many of us seem to want to hang on to everything, to be personally responsible, to have everything done to a level of expertise only we can master. We are also concerned that delegation means overloading someone else, even though one great attribute of delegation is that it also gives people experience. (Much of the worry new headteachers have when taking over their first school is attributable to the lack of responsibility previously delegated to them.) When you delegate:

- delegate authority but not responsibility—that remains yours
- delegate to others' strengths, not to their weaknesses
- don't overload the delegation

- delegate for results rather than method. Accept some ways of working different from your own.

Question

While you are getting used to managing your time, question every activity against your priority list. Don't let too much interfere with it.

Plan Time Blocks

Some very important tasks need a considerable amount of time. Writing your report to governors is even more important now; planning your talk to parents about the National Curriculum needs very careful preparation.

Plan well ahead for these situations; their success will have an important effect upon your school and your colleagues. Block off enough time in the diary to do them well. Don't try and find time at the last moment.

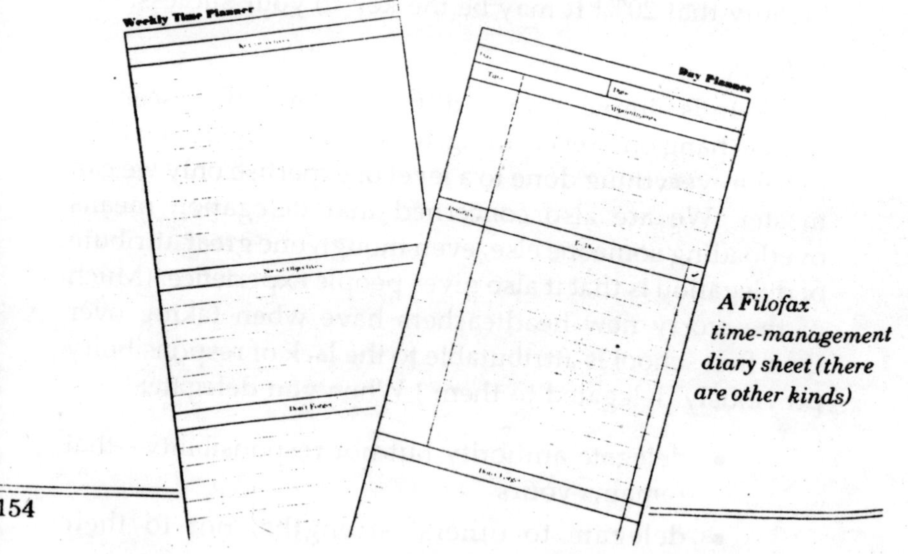

A Filofax time-management diary sheet (there are other kinds)

Fig. 16.2

Fit Tasks to Suit You

Some times of the day are better for you than others. Do the difficult, more thought-requiring tasks when you are alert. Save the mundane for another time. Try and create congruence between your personal state and the tasks you have to do.

Use Time Management Systems

Filofaxes, and their like, have become a yuppie joke but they were in use long before the middle eighties made them socially acceptable. Their long history and military and religious origins are due to the fact that they are a help. Use the many different pages which are available to help you prioritise your daily, weekly and monthly tasks. Writing it all down and being responsible to your writing does help. It is also wonderful to put a line through tasks achieved!

CHILDREN AND CLASSROOMS

ORGANISING THE CLASSROOM—1

Children and Teachers

Classroom organisation is one of the key management tasks of a teacher. Well-organised classes enable rather than hinder effective learning.

Classroom organisation should respond to the needs of the teacher and the class, to the work they have to do and to the peculiarities of resource provision and classroom or school design. Many attempts to display diagrams of effectively organised classrooms' fail because they don't take into account this personal and particular context. Everything you read on the next four pages has to be put into practice in situations only you know.

Whatever decisions are made about classroom organisation will have a major effect on the day-to-day running of the class, the freedom available to both teacher and child (but particularly the teacher) and the quality of the learning which takes place. In many ways the organisation of classrooms is a sure indicator of the degree to which the aims and objectives of a school are being implemented.

Looking at six school brochures at random, all of them contained statements such as:

> "We believe in the importance of developing independent learning"
>
> "We believe that our children should begin to take responsibility for themselves as soon as possible"
>
> "Practical work is important in our school"

The key to translating these beliefs into action is the effective classroom organisation of people and resources.

Children

Organising children in classrooms involves:

- basic day-to-day systems which cope with 'low-level' activities
- a format within which most learning can take place.

Basic Day-to-Day Systems

The section about 'Motivating Children' suggests that children enjoy calm and fair classrooms. One of the ways of creating such conditions is through establishing a series of acceptable and workable routines which everyone has to follow. They may include:

- what children should do (or can and cannot do) when they come into class first thing in the morning
- what has to happen at the end of each working session
- what the arrangements are for going to the toilet
- who is responsible for the distribution or care of classroom equipment
- what freedom children have to move around the classroom on their own
- what noise levels are acceptable.

The decisions you make about these and other areas need to take into account first, your aims. (It is difficult to justify the development of self-responsibility if a child is not allowed to sharpen a pencil unless given permission.)

Second, they need to take into account their effect upon the general atmosphere of the class and the children's ability to concentrate. (No one is going to concentrate if everyone wants to sharpen their pencil at the same time.)

Third, they need to take into account the needs of individual children. (Some children are just not capable of even sharpening a pencil without 'training'.)

Fourth, they need to take into account your teaching time. Systems are necessary but they should be self-operating. No one is paying a teacher to monitor systems which control the sharpening of pencils. The systems are supposed to free you of that.

A Format for Learning

Organising effective day-to-day systems and sticking to them will create more time and a better atmosphere in which teaching and learning can take place.

Those systems add to the learning situation; they don't define it. What does that is the general organisational pattern you choose for your class.

There are three basic models -whole class, individual or group. Which you choose should take into account the same four factors mentioned earlier. No one pattern of organisation will suit all learning situations or all children, and you have to be prepared to alter your basic framework when it is right to do so. Nevertheless, it is difficult for a class to work effectively with a constantly changing organisational pattern. A choice has to be made.

Assuming the kind of aims suggested above there are advantages and disadvantages to all three models:

- Whole class teaching

+ More direct teacher control
+ Allows for the teaching of common topics
— Teacher/child contact time low
— Practical work by children difficult
— Rates of child development vastly different
— Resource provision is high
— Teacher talking time tends to be high
— Children's involvement can be low.

- Individual teaching

+ Theoretically, the inverse of almost all of whole class teaching's disadvantages
— Repetition of teaching points throughout the class
— Time defeats good teacher/child contact
— Resources difficult to look after
— Organisation difficult

— Children tend to visit teacher when problems occur and not before
— All children need to be well-organised.

- Group teaching

\+ Class can be divided into ability or other groups
\+ Child/child support is possible
\+ Allows more discussion between teacher and children
\+ Resource organisation easier
\+ Easier to monitor progress
— Different rates of progress can still exist within ability groups
— Other groups need to be well-organised.

Remembering that none of these models is perfect and that all can be used appropriately in every classroom, there are strong arguments for group teaching being the basic model for most classrooms. The major criticism teachers make about both group teaching and individualised teaching is the need to make sure all other children are reasonably well-organised before the teacher can work uninterrupted with a child or a group of children for a reasonable amount of time.

This criticism is fair. It can only be answered by saying:

- the alternative (whole class teaching) is wholly inappropriate for mixed-ability classes or for an education which values practical work and first-hand experience
- other factors are important in maintaining order and enthusiasm in a class (see basic systems above and 'Motivating Children' pp. 182-184)
- good planning which provides well-chosen work can alleviate the difficulty.

The Teacher

Usually, teachers respond to the demands of children in the classroom so it seems difficult to imagine how teachers can 'organise' themselves.

In one sense the systems teachers operate with children also define their behaviour and the mix which is decided upon has to take into account a teacher's ability to put it into action. New headteachers who immediately announce that "We are all doing group teaching now" in schools where class teaching has been the norm for the past twenty years risk disaster. It is much better to work with and through people than against them.

The other key element in teacher organisation is the desk. If 'management by walking about' makes sense elsewhere it also makes sense in the classroom. Busy, active classrooms need teachers who are on the move — checking, reassuring, intervening. Teachers who operate their classrooms by remote control from their desk will either encounter inevitable behaviour problems amongst their children or fail to be a part of either the children's learning process or their lives.

Examine the part your desk plays in your classroom. Is it the central focus of the room? How often do you leave it?

ORGANISING THE CLASSROOM — 2

Resources

'Resources' here means everything in your classroom except the people — desks, chairs, tables, cupboards, equipment, books, etc.

The same four principles apply to resource organisation

which applied to people organisation. You need to take into account

- your educational aims
- the effect on the atmosphere of the class
- your needs and the needs of individual children
- your teaching time.

and, of course, the particular nature of the classroom and the resources you have. The suggestions on these pages take into account some of the basic issues, but they are not tablets of stone. Each teacher will have to interpret them in the light of their own situation.

Tables and Chairs

Tables (or desks) and chairs obviously take up most space in classrooms. Organising and arranging them carefully is vital. Don't be nervous of taking advice from other colleagues about this; some people have the knack of 'seeing' how furniture can best be arranged. Others, including the writer of these pages, always seem to have problems'.

To decide on group learning as the basic structure for your class means that your tables or desks will have to be organised in groups. The way in which tables are grouped will be defined by:

- the academic or social mix of your class
- the need for space
- the decrease in teacher/child interaction once groups become larger than six
- the needs of individual children
- the wish to create certain 'areas' in your class for, say, mathematics, science, language or art.

Most of these are self-explanatory but one or two reinforce the idea that no one single method of organisation will be wholly satisfactory. The social mix of your class may mean, for example, that for a time certain children should not work together however evenly they may be matched academically.

This doesn't mean that such children should be separated for ever. The aim should always be to work with those children in order that they should be able to work alongside each other; continuing opportunities should be given for them to succeed in doing so. The reality of classroom life tells us, though, that this isn't always possible.

Similarly, you may want to create one or two work areas in your class to which individual children can go as the need arises.

Space is another controlling influence. There is little point in having all the table arrangements you need academically if no one can move or, in doing so, they interfere with the working conditions of others.

Equipment

Even the worst-equipped classroom carries more equipment than anyone realises. Well-equipped classrooms often seem like warehouses.

Before considering the organisation of the equipment two questions should be asked:

- Has this room the basic equipment it needs?
- Do we need all of the equipment this room contains?

Definitions of 'basic equipment' can differ from teacher to teacher and school to school. It is a good idea to define as part of the internal school policy exactly what equipment should be in rooms used for teaching children of different ages. This enables each teacher to check what is required, makes stock-ordering simpler and "manages" away a potential source of conflict or aggravation between colleagues.

Many classrooms—even those which are short of agreed 'basic' equipment—are over-equipped with other resources. Many of those resources are justifiable within individual classrooms but some are not. Having an over-equipped classroom:

- makes the management of equipment more complex
- denies the use of some equipment by other colleagues
- often damages otherwise unused equipment
- causes over-ordering through unawareness of existing stock (and, therefore, wastes money)
- takes up valuable space.

The first step in managing equipment in the classroom is to look at what you have and discard everything which is unlikely to be useful in the forthcoming year.

What is left can be divided into two categories:

1. Usable by children.
2. Dangerous or unusable by children for other reasons (e.g. size).

As a basic principle everything which is usable by children should be arranged so that children can use it on demand. This means that such equipment needs to be:

- stored at child height
- clearly and understandably labelled
- easily able to be returned after use.

It is at this point that the organisation of people and the organisation of equipment meet. Most teachers accept the importance of developing independence and self-reliance in the children they teach. To do so means giving children the opportunity to practise. To do that means arranging the classroom so that children are able to carry out tasks independently of the teacher. To help them do that the teacher needs to organise 'low-level' people systems which increase the probability of children being successful.

The organisation of people and the organisation of resources are interdependent. What can nullify them is a lack of confidence in teachers that young children are capable of obtaining necessary paper, sorting out paints, sharpening pencils, using mathematics equipment or using reading corners without the consistent supervision of adults. Some children are not, that is true, but the evidence from classrooms in a range of socially and academically different primary schools is that, given the kind of organisation we have discussed here, children are more capable than many would imagine.

Dangerous equipment should be obviously identified ("If you need to use anything with a red label on it then you must see me first") and stored in areas that will minimise even accidental injury. This is more than common sense; it is career protection.

Other Issues

Many of the other issues about the organisation of equipment in classrooms are common sense. Difficulties can often be resolved not by reading books about it but by wandering into colleagues' classrooms and testing one's own methods of organisation against theirs.

Two issues are worth mentioning briefly. Many classrooms only provide opportunity for the display of two-dimensional art work and it is this lack of display which helps to limit the potential of primary art and craft. Creating the availability of three-dimensional display space can increase the amount of work which takes place.

Finally, all primary classrooms pay respect to the need to display fiction and non-fiction books but occasionally the displays are not as stimulating to children as they might be. As a general rule:

- display fewer books but rotate the displays frequently
- display books cover out rather than spine out
- arrange the books in theme clusters
- organise an effective low-level' system of book care.

Planning Classroom Work -1

Organising the teaching of 30 mixed-ability children across six or seven different 'subject' areas (and, often, integrating two or three of those subjects under one theme) is a complex task and, like all complex tasks, it requires a measure of planning to make it work.

The time taken to produce effective plans should benefit the teacher who has written them and, consequently, the children in that teacher's class. Good plans should enable teachers to answer these questions:

- What are the purposes of my teaching?
- What activities will the children do to achieve those purposes?

- What resources do I need to allow those activities to happen?
- What finished work will emerge as a result of those activities?
- How can I assess the success of my teaching?
- Will my planned work fit into the time I have available?

Good planning does not guarantee good teaching but it is rare to find good teaching which has not been well planned. Let's look at the five key questions good plans should answer.

1. What are the Purposes of My Teaching?

Teaching has purposes. Teachers work in classrooms to achieve certain objectives with and on behalf of the children they teach. If teaching is to be most effective those purposes need to be made as clear as possible.

Defining 'objectives' needs to be precise because the way in which objectives are written will help to define the answers to many of the other questions about planning. Nevertheless, writing effective objectives often causes problems.

Objectives can refer to 'facts', 'skills' and/or 'concepts'.

'Facts' are true statements which children can be expected to learn and recall. 'Henry VIII had six wives' is a fact.

'Skills' are accomplishments which children learn through doing. It is impossible to 'do' a fact but almost impossible not to 'do' a skill. 'Riding a bike' is a skill which is learnt by doing. In the classroom, 'observation', 'hypothesising", 'using evidence' and so on are all skills which children need to 'do'.

'Concepts' are general notions of things which are arrived at after exposure to a range of facts, skills and experiences. Power' is a concept. We cannot "know" power like we know 'Henry VIII had six wives' and we cannot 'do' power as we do 'observation'.

Much of the documentation arising from the National Curriculum contains objectives against which teachers are expected to plan. One of the principal benefits of a well thought-out National Curriculum should be to free teachers from deciding 'what' has to be taught and allowing them to concentrate on 'how'.

2. *What Activities Will the Children Do to Achieve Those Purposes?*

To achieve these objectives children have to do things in classrooms. The objectives themselves don't define those activities although they should make it easier for them to be defined.

Activities need to be appropriate in three different ways. First, they need to be *applicable to different kinds of objectives.* An objective which is essentially factual requires a different level of activity from an objective which is skills-based. Equally, while a factual objective may require only one activity for it to be successfully achieved, a skills-based objective, in which children have to learn to 'do' things, is likely to require a greater number of activities.

Second, the activities need to be *applicable to the different ability levels of children in a class.* Accurate 'matching' of activities to children will continue to be one of the most difficult tasks teachers have to face as children's responses to the activities they are asked to do depend so much on immediate contextual matters such as mood, relationship with the teacher, attitude and so on. Nevertheless, it is important that 'matching' is seen as an important aspect in the definition of classroom activities.

Third, the activities need to be *relevant to the children.* If we accept that we learn by assimilating new material in the light of our past experiences, the activities we plan must enable our children to handle them from within the experiences those children have already had. If we don't do that children are unlikely to learn effectively.

3. What Resources Do I Need to Allow Those Activities to Happen?

There is little point in thinking carefully about objectives and learning activities if the resources are not available to activate them. Being clear about our resource needs in our planning helps to:

- check that activities we want to happen can happen
- provide information on new resources which are required by a class or a school
- ensure that teachers are properly prepared for each series of lessons. (Who wants to rush around frantically at lunch-time unless they have to?)

4. What Finished Work Will Emerge as a Result of Those Activities?

There is nothing wrong with having a reasonable idea at the beginning of a term or half-term of the kinds of work children will be expected to produce at the end. Indeed in some ways it is crucial that this happens.

If we support the view, for example, that language is a cross-curricular subject then we need to know what particular aspects of writing, reading, listening and talking will be covered by any other work we are planning. Only then can we look at the breadth of our language provision for our children and devise compensatory or supplementary activities where they are necessary.

5. How Can I Assess the Success of My Teaching?

Good plans, and particularly carefully defined objectives, help in the assessment of both teaching and learning. Assessment is important. Well-formed objectives often contain within them the evidence that is required about children's achievement. There is little doubt about what children have to do to prove that they know that Henry VIII had six wives; simply answer the question "How many wives did Henry VIII have?"

The problems occur when the objectives are either ill-defined or inappropriate for conventional assessment techniques. Eliot Eisner has drawn an important distinction between 'Instructional' objectives and 'Expressive' objectives.

'Instructional' objectives are those in which what is to be learnt is specified; 'expressive' objectives are those in which the learning which occurs is individual and unpredictable. So to know that Henry VIII had six wives is an 'instructional' objective; to experience the moods created by Holst in *The Planet Suite* is an 'expressive' objective.

Assessing 'expressive' objectives is less a matter of defining clear tasks and more one of judging the appropriateness of response, discriminating, in Stenhouse's words, "understanding from misunderstanding."

6. Will My Planned Work Fit into the Time I have Available?

Teaching takes place within limited time scales. As we write this, the calendar for next term shows that it is only nine and a half teaching weeks long. Planned, purposeful work needs to be completed; work which is left 'hanging' with primary children can rarely be successfully picked up again.

Once you have defined objectives and organised learning activities and resources, it is important to ensure that the planned work fits into the time you have available for it. Given the naturally hectic life of primary schools this suggests that planned work should not fill every available space which appears to be free at the beginning of a term; something unexpected, and time-consuming, always happens!

PLANNING CLASSROOM WORK—2

You may wonder whether there are any curriculum areas which shouldn't be planned. The answer is no: all areas need planning. It is important to understand the difference between 'instructional' and 'expressive' objectives described on the previous page and the implications of choosing one or the other. Defining the work you are planning in wholly instructional terms can destroy much of what some subjects are really about; defining work in wholly expressive terms can deny children access to important information and skills.

It is not a case of planning some curriculum areas and not others. All curriculum areas should be planned. What is important is to understand the nature of the work being planned within a curriculum area. 'Instructional' and 'expressive' objectives help to do that.

Theme Work

Much of the evidence from HMI Reports suggests that thematic work is attempted in most primary classrooms and poorly executed in many. Much of the reason for that can be found in the quality of the planning behind the theme. Organising work thematically has a number of advantages for young children but it also presents much the most difficult planning activity for the teacher. When planning themes you need to be sure:

- of the balance between the various 'subject' components (for example, science, history, geography)
- that the content of each 'subject' is appropriate to the theme
- that the balance of work between the 'subjects' is maintained throughout the year
- that the required objectives can be covered (particularly important with the National Curriculum)
- of the cross-curricular work in other subjects (language, mathematics, art, technology, physical education, music, RE and so on) which your theme is facilitating. This will affect your planning needs in those subject areas and suggests that themes should be planned first.

What Time Span Should Plans Cover?

The answer to this question is dependent upon a number of factors including the range of subject matter covered, the age-group of the children and the time of year.

Plans which cover a shorter time span are more appropriate for younger children or for situations in which the teacher's knowledge of the children is relatively poor.

In general, it seems ineffective to devise plans which work for less than half a term or longer than a whole term.

What Should be in My Plans?

Your plans should contain information which enables you to answer the key questions of planning:

- What objectives do I want the children to achieve?
- What activities will the children need to do to achieve them?

- What resources do I need, to allow those activities to happen?
- What finished work will emerge as a result of those activities?
- Will my planned work fit into the time I have available?

What Do Plans Look Like?

There are numerous ways of devising plans which contain answers to the questions above. Whatever your plans look like, they should:

- be easily accessible. Information should be obtainable from them very quickly
- enable other teachers who might take your class during the year or later to see what you have done
- allow the answers to the key questions to be recorded clearly.

There are arguments which suggest that teachers should each be responsible for their own plans and what they look like, but the need to coordinate children's learning as they move through a school is a strong reason for staff to think carefully about the presentation of plans and their completion. Effective and similar Planning by every teacher in a school can reduce misunderstanding and increase effective information flow about the children and the work they lave been doing.

The sample page illustrated on previous pages is part of one school's attempt to produce just such a coordinated package which answers the key questions. It is not the only way of presenting plans and, we hope, might stimulate others to improve or change radically these designs.

There are nevertheless some criticisms of effective planning. Some staff will be unhappy at having their 'freedom' to plan in their own way (or, to be honest, not to plan at all) taken away from them.

This presents a staff management issue which has to be handled carefully. You might want to look at 'Dealing with Differences' about this. The benefits for the children of effective planning undoubtedly outweigh the disturbance to some colleagues.

Content	*Activities*	*Resources*	*Finished work*
1. Some plants can be grown from their own seed	A) Explore a range of plants to look foor seeds Look for • number of seeds • pattern of • distribution • shape	Tomatoes, Apples, Pears, Chestnut, Water Cress	Drawings, paintings, wax-resist of inside of fruits + particular seeds
	B) Gather a range of seeds from children's homes. Display/discuss Look for • shape • texture • colour Classify	Seeds brought from home Plants/fruit they came from Illustrations of "	Discussion about appearance Drawing + writing comparing two seeds
	C) Discuss conditions required for growth		'How to grow a plant from seed' chart- written and drawn
	D) Plant variety of seeds Look for • growth rate • pattern of growth	Seeds for each group Plant pots, water, John Innes, plastic bags, trays, information books	Measurement of plant growth Close observation Drawing Modelling Written work-'what happened' Poems + story

A sample page from a school planning document

Sometimes plans are criticised because they "never work out like that in real life". This is very true. Nothing succeeds as planned and no one would argue that the plans you create will succeed in their entirety. Sometimes time will run out and sometimes your plans won't have been as appropriate or relevant as you thought. Changes will have to be made.

What plans are about is reducing the degree of uncertainty to a reasonable level and increasing the probability of children being provided with an appropriate education.

Sometimes plans are criticised because "they take a long time to do".

Good planning can (and should) take up some of what has previously been seen as 'holiday' time and/or INSET days. The advantage of planning before the beginning of a term is that it saves considerable time (and tension) as the term progresses.

RECORD-KEEPING

There are times when record-keeping is the bane of teachers' lives. There seems too much, too often, and no one is quite sure what happens to it all anyway.

There are other times when it seems absolutely vital; nothing is more frustrating than the absence of information when trying to organise and plan for a new class.

As the curriculum becomes more complex and demanding both of these views will strengthen. Time to complete records will decrease; the importance of having them will increase.

The problem is simply expressed—how to devote

minimum time to maximum effect and do full justice to each of thirty or so very different individuals.

Who Needs Records Anyway?

Various groups require records of one sort or another.

The LEA will require certain records to be kept on an authority-wide basis. In some local authorities these will be restricted to mathematics and language and may often take the form of the results of standard assessments.

The government, through the guise of the National Curriculum, will want similar information on a national scale, again as an end-product of a series of nationally organised continuous and formal assessments.

Secondary schools require information from primary schools about the children joining them at the beginning of the new academic year. Just occasionally, secondary schools mistrust the quality of information they are given; equally occasionally, primary schools wonder whether the effort of producing it was at all worthwhile.

Parents require information which will help them understand their children's attitudes and abilities. There is a growing feeling that many parents are dissatisfied with bland, generalised comments at open evenings and parents' meetings and that, while unpleasant information is difficult to take, a spread of honest information given consistently throughout a child's school career helps parents to see their child in a more realistic context.

Teachers, most importantly of all, require effective records. Sometimes these may be very specific and linked to learning problems; at other times they may be very general. Some may be a way of responding to national and LEA demands; others may be to help plan on a week-to-week basis which children should be doing what. Without them, teaching becomes impossible.

'Subject'	*Need to Record*
Mathematics	Facts, skills and concepts understood Progress made in scheme (if used) Comments which reveal weaknesses Attitudes
Reading	Reading level Reading progression Attitudes to books and reading Specific weaknesses
Written/Oral (Language)	Level of communication and listening abilities Ability in factual and 'creative' writing Spelling or phonic weaknesses Attitude to talking and writing
Theme work (History, Geography and Science)	Skills practised Level of content learnt and concepts understood Confidence in practical work Social skills in peer group
Creative Arts	Special abilities Serious difficulties
(Music and PE) General Profile	Progression through scheme (if appropriate) Summary of academic ability Attitudes and application Personality and social development.
Parents' evenings	Summary of comments to parents Parents' attitudes, queries or concerns Action taken or reference made
Medical records	Any condition affecting school performance or child's development
Special needs	Full records and reports of case conferences, statementing procedures, psychologists' reports etc.

Which Records Need to be Kept?

If records have to respond to the variety of audiences outlined above and time is short, it is important to be clear

Children's name	Content/skill						Content/skill						Content/skill						Content/skill					
	Activity						Activity						Activity						Activity					
	A	B	C	D	E	F	A	B	C	D	E	F	A	B	C	D	E	F	A	B	C	D	E	F

Above This planning sheet records particular activities.

Below This sheet shows teacher and parent responses to a Home-shared Reading System.

TEACHER			PARENT								
Book	Date	Message	Was the book enjoyed?			Was it understood		Did your child seem confident?			Message
						easily	with help				
Sniff Sniff	14. 9. 87	Please read this to Ann	✓			✓		✓			Much enjoyed
Mog's Mumps	16. 9. 87	To share + enjoy	✓			✓		✓			We like this series
Our dog	21. 9. 87	Ann will read to you today	✓			✓		✓			She read it lots of times

Fig. 16.3

Below This sheet records children's attitudes towards and ability in problem-solving activities.

Below This sheet shows teachers' comments to parents at an Open Evening and parents' responses.

about those which need to be kept. Some of these needs will be statutory; others will be personal to each teacher.

There is no definite answer to this question and the list produced on page 168 can be amended or added to depending upon your situation. Nevertheless, it seems important for the following to be kept by, or be accessible to, each teacher.

What Formats Should the Records Have?

Some of the formats for record-keeping will already be pre-determined. Those developing other formats should bear in mind 'minimum effort for maximum effect'. Record-keeping is time consuming enough anyway. The trick is to devise formats which:

- contain all the information you need
- are easy to complete
- are easy to read.

Record sheets often suffer through being ill-designed. Schools which have taken care to consider in detail the record-keeping they require would find it worthwhile, if there is no in-school expertise, to take advice (voluntary or otherwise) about record sheet design. While most teachers accept the need for comprehensive records, disillusion sets in when the completion process becomes unnecessarily arduous.

PROFILING

What Does it Mean?

Although there are many differences in detail concerning definitions of profiling, the broad features invariably include:

- *recording* achievement
- *reporting* on progress
- *monitoring* progress
- *involving* the child
- *involving* the parents.

What profiling attempts to offer is an all-round balanced view of children and their academic and social development. Many schools will have record-keeping systems, reports for parents, LEA record cards, etc. What a pupil profile sets out to do is bring together all the bits and pieces about the child into one document which will grow as the child moves through the educational system.

Profiling is a formative record of achievement and attainment which can be seen as integral to the child's learning.

Why Profile?

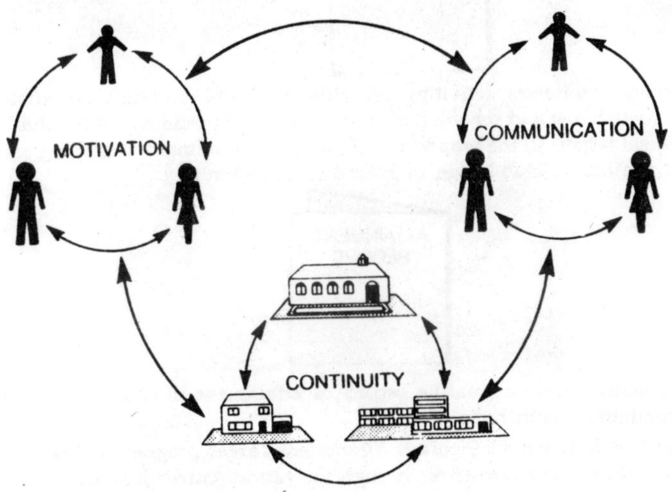

Fig. 16.4

We profile in order to...

Motivate children by involving them in their own goal setting.

Enable the child's experiences, attainments and competencies to be valued and to help the child develop as an individual and encourage a positive self image.

Provide the child, parent and teacher with an expanding source of information which is accessible, available and to which all parties have the opportunities to contribute.

Ensure development of learning and foster effective teaching by providing the school with a record of the child's personal achievements as a way of maintaining continuity/compatibility between and within primary and secondary education.

What Does the Profile Contain?

Evidence of achievement in the form of cross curricular samples of best school work selected by the pupil, together with their teacher. Items may be part of normal course work or produced especially for the portfolio. The portfolio contents to be reviewed and updated on a regular basis.

A record of interests, activities and achievements beyond the main curriculum from both home and school. It also provides an opportunity for the child to set personal targets in the broadest of contexts, be it to improve spelling, gain the next gymnastics club badge, or keep their bedroom tidy.

A formative and summative record of attainment in core and foundation curriculum areas including:

Record of National Curriculum Attainment Target progress and the school's record of the child's progress through the various curriculum areas.

Results of school, LEA and national standardised testing and assessment.

Summative records of attainment including those required by the LEA.

Fig. 16.5

The following are examples of one approach to profiling development in Devon by a group of headteachers. We were impressed by the clear aims and objectives and attention to practical detail. This is management in the sense of setting attainable targets for teachers and supporting them by giving useful, realistic advice.

1. Achievement

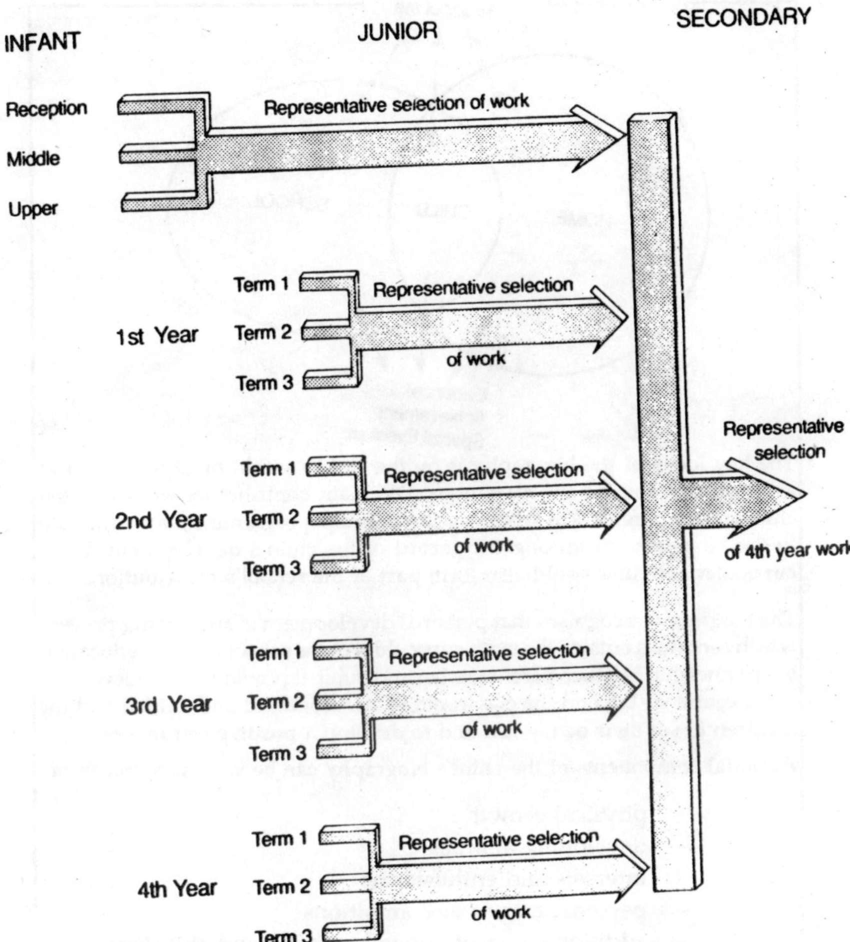

As the child progresses through the primary school, representative work from all the stages is selected, reviewed and retained as appropriate, termly and annually, to provide a formative record of achievement. A final selection of fourth year items providing evidence of achievement would then form the nucleus of secondary transfer documentation.

Fig.16.6

2. *Biography*

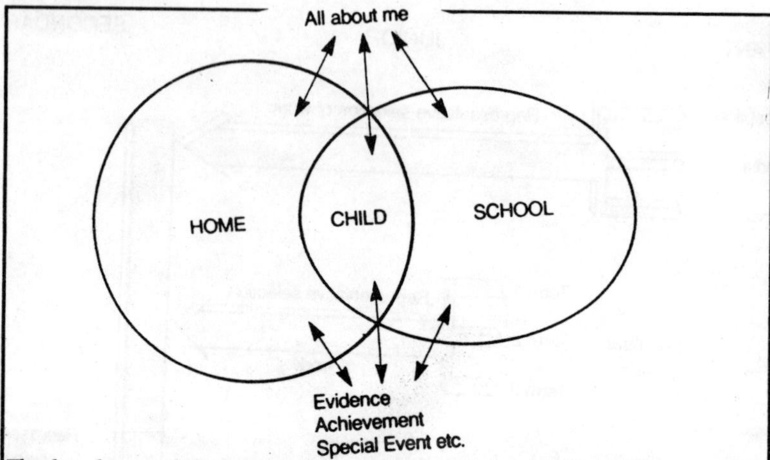

The key locus of the biography is on the child's world of experience and achievement beyond the classroom. The main contributors would be the child and/or parents. The school's science/health programme may contribute to the biography as an ongoing record of the child's development. Extra curricular activities could also form part of the school's contribution.

The biography recognises that personal development is an ongoing process which continues outside the main curriculum of the school and that education is a partnership between parent teacher and pupil. It provides for achievement and experience beyond the classroom to be recognised and valued and for children to set their own goals and to develop a positive self image.

Essential components of the child's biography can be seen as a record of:

— physical growth
— developing abilities
— interests and enthusiasms
— personal targets and ambitions
— additional contributions by parent and child*Profiling*

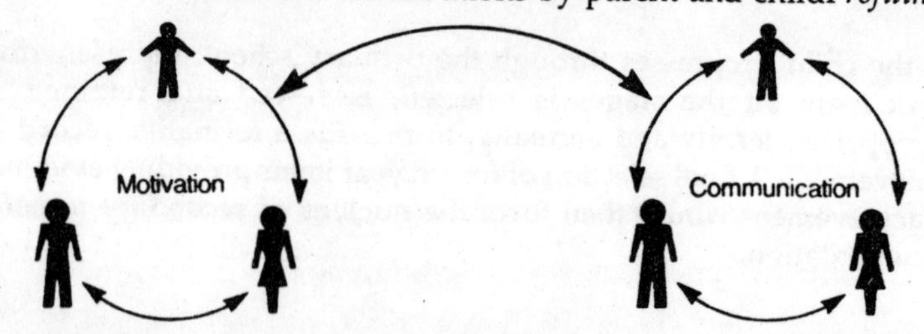

Fig. 16.7

3. Attainment

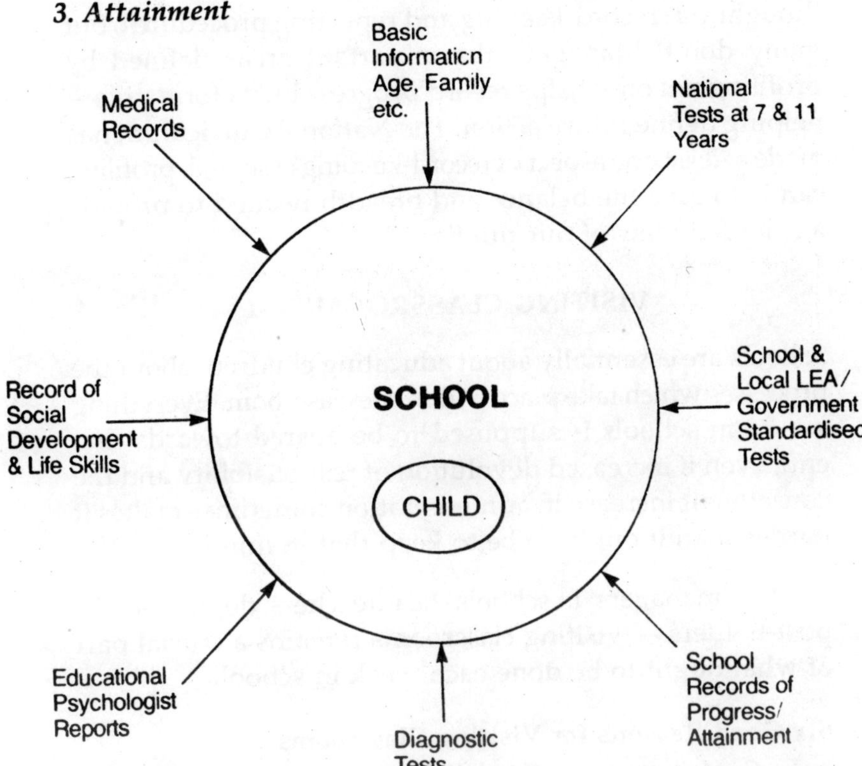

This part of the profile contains records of attainment from the commencement of the children's schooling until the end of their education. To be an effective formative record it must be an efficient means of passing relevant information between successive class teachers and between schools and stages of education. This will require teachers to base on curriculum continuity and common record-keeping approaches.

Fig. 16.8

Profiling and the National Curriculum

With the increased accountability brought about by the legal requirements of recent education legislation the profile offers a very practical way forward for primary teachers. Many schools already have effective and well thought-out record-keeping and reporting procedures, but many don't! Managing the important areas defined by profiling not only helps record progress but is formative—helping define future action. The National Curriculum has made at least one aspect of record-keeping essential; profiling can help give the balance and breadth needed to provide a rounded view of our pupils.

VISITING CLASSROOMS —1

Schools are essentially about educating children, about the processes which take place within the classroom. Everything we do in schools is supposed to be geared towards that end, even if increased devolution of responsibility and the consequent increase in administration sometimes makes it harder than it ought to be to keep that in mind.

For 'managers' in schools -headteachers, deputy heads, post-holders — visiting classrooms remains a crucial part of what ought to be done each week in school.

Six Good Reasons for Visiting Classrooms

1. To Contribute to an Overall Picture of the Life of the School

If classroom life is so central to schooling then it is important for 'managers' to have a view of a school which takes into account the day-to-day practice of teachers and children in classrooms. At this level the impressions one gains are not intended to be judgemental but to contribute to the sum total of the knowledge carried around.

2. To Assess and Evaluate the Quality of the Work Taking Place

In addition to a generalised 'feel' about teachers and children in classrooms there is also a need to make assessments. Such assessments might be about:

- the implementation of agreed school policies
- the atmosphere within classrooms
- the level of independent working shown by the children
- the physical organisation of the classroom
- the management of the children by the teacher
- the use of available resources
- the effect of certain children upon each other.

Assessment and evaluation of classrooms are important if those who work in a school are to plan for the future as effectively as possible.

Equally importantly, the introduction of appraisal procedures over the next few years means that classroom visiting becomes a necessary part of any 'management' orientated activity. Without it, appraisal procedures will be still-born.

3. To Keep a Hand in (And to Make Mistakes!)

Headteachers, in particular, have less opportunity to visit classrooms than they used to have. Even when opportunities were more frequent, one of the justifiable criticisms of headteachers was that they had 'lost touch' with the reality of classroom life.

As the demands upon teachers have grown, as the curriculum has broadened in its scope and as there have been inevitable changes in attitudes towards schooling, it is easy to see why some teachers feel that headteachers just 'don't know what it is like any more'.

Because the headteacher's job is different from that of a class teacher some of this is unavoidable. (Interestingly, it may be that the increased administrative role of the headteacher may soon result in the deputy head being accepted as the 'senior teacher in the school).

For now, though, it remains important that headteachers should experience the range of pressures class teachers are under and open themselves to making the same range of small day-by-day 'mistakes' which are a feature of classroom life. The management of change in schools is made easier if those responsible for the change are aware of the context within which new behaviours are expected to operate.

4. To Pass on Messages of Good Practice

The risk of declining awareness of classroom life is one which grows the longer headteachers stay as headteachers. It doesn't mean, though, that headteachers never have expertise which they can pass on to other colleagues. One of the reasons many teachers, including headteachers, have been promoted has not been their fitness for the job into which they are being promoted but their excellence in the job they are leaving. Headteachers are likely to have been very reasonable teachers.

Headteachers are not the only members of staff with expertise, either. We hope that teachers with specific responsibilities will have some expertise in the areas for which they were appointed.

If it remains true that 'actions speak louder than words' then a classroom visit could be more beneficial to a colleague than an hour-long meeting after school. It almost certainly means, especially given the practical orientation of most primary teachers, that any discussion about practice should, where possible, be supported by practice in action.

5. To Look at Individual Children

Individual children have needs which require

assessment and action. Some assessment has to take place out of the classroom but all assessment should involve in-classroom work as well. What matters about a child's performance is both the raw data of a child's abilities and how that ability is reflected in the reality of day-to-day classroom life.

Looking at children in classrooms may reveal that a problem which seemed to be one of ability was actually one of attitude; it may tell us that some children are not being allowed the conditions under which they can develop certain attributes. It will certainly enhance understanding.

6. To Provide Particular Help to a Class Teacher

Class teaching is a much busier, more intense activity than it used to be. Class teachers welcome specific help from time to time. It is as simple as that.

Getting the Right Balance

If time is limited for both headteachers and post-holders then achieving an acceptable balance between the reasons for classroom visits is important. The weight you attach to each reason will be directly related to the particular conditions within your own school. Beware of certain pitfalls, though.

> "As soon as I went to the school as headteacher I offered to help my colleagues in their classrooms as much as I could. All they had to do was ask.
>
> Well, they did. In no time at all my time was taken up with regular, fixed visits to each member of staff. They felt good about this and so did I.
>
> It was only when a parent came to complain about a teacher that I realised I had never been in that colleague's classroom other than on a timetabled basis. They knew I was coming and

> I really ran the lesson. So I had never seen that class—or any class, I suddenly realised—working normally, without me being in control."
>
> "I think she had the best of intentions, so I'm not grumbling about that, but what happened in practice was that she ended up going into just one or two classrooms a lot and leaving the rest of us alone. I know they asked for help and had one or two difficult children but we were never, and I mean never, visited. It made us feel as though we weren't a real part of the school any more".

All of the reasons for visiting classrooms have their own importance; you have to achieve a balance between them. In doing so, of course, you create a set of messages to your colleagues which can be supportive but can also be counterproductive.

Don't hide the reasons for classroom visiting. Declare them. Let everyone know they exist. Talk about the difficulties of balance but be seen to be trying to get it 'right'. In this way you will minimise any difficulties which might occur.

VISITING CLASSROOMS — 2

Doing It

In the previous section we suggested a number of reasons why visiting classrooms is important. As with much of what we talk about in this book, though, theory and action don't always sit well with each other. Knowing that classes should be visited is no guarantee that the visits will be productive. There are important factors at play.

Atmosphere and Trust

Teaching is a stressful occupation. Dealing with 30 mixed-ability immature children across seven or eight different subject areas and trying to devise, organise and coordinate successful learning experiences for them all is not a job for the faint-hearted. Teachers talking in staffrooms seem to mention three failures for every success. It is hardly surprising that many are not keen at first to be observed as well.

Maximising the advantages of classroom visiting means seeing the classroom operating as normally as possible. Seeing the classroom operate as normally as possible means creating an atmosphere of collaboration and trust. (Of course there will be times when classrooms cannot be observed in this way, such as disciplinary procedures, responding to the complaint of a parent or the report of an inspector. But it is to be hoped that these occasions don't represent the everyday life of a school.)

How you do this is inevitably bound up with your own personality and the relationships you develop. Ideas which have worked in our own experiences and those of others include:

- beginning by asking others to assess and evaluate your own work first. In other words, lead from the front
- making it clear why visits are essential to your job
- not rushing to judgements too soon
- identifying and discussing mistakes in your own teaching first
- declaring your own curriculum strengths and weaknesses

- taking advice from other members of staff
- allowing teachers to start from where they are
- not expecting all teachers to respond equally enthusiastically
- concentrating first on the areas of teaching in which each teacher feels most confident
- staying calm.

Some of the reasons for class visiting are less threatening to class teachers than others. If you are genuinely visiting classrooms to keep your hand in, work with individual children or provide general help then the way in which you carry out those visits will contribute to the atmosphere and confidence you create.

Assessment and Evaluation

It is clear that assessment and evaluation of work in classrooms presents the biggest threat to teachers and that there are understandable reasons for this. Yet assessment and evaluation also present the best opportunity for improving classroom practice, helping children learn better and, ultimately, reducing levels of stress amongst our colleagues. What can be done to alleviate this paradox?

1. Be Clear about the Purpose of the Visit

Any visit to a classroom provides evidence of some form, however subjective. If the purpose of the visit is to make a deliberate assessment or evaluation of what is taking place, however, then this should be declared openly. There can be little more undermining than knowing that the person who has just 'come in to help' is watching every move you make.

2. Focus Down on to Something Particular

The 'feel' of a classroom *is* important and develops over days, weeks and months. Visits which are made specifically for assessment and evaluation need to be more focused; the person making the visit (and the person(s) being assessed) need a clear idea of the purpose of their visit.

This doesn't mean that the purpose has to be defined so tightly as to be a straitjacket. Discovering a class who are all capable of forming the letter 'U' correctly might hide the fact that none of them can form the other 25 at all.

3. Understand the Teacher's and/or Children's Intentions

If it is a colleague's or child's performance we are assessing then we need to know what that colleague or child is trying to do and why. This information should help us to make our judgements more effective by raising two questions:

- Is the colleague/child trying to do something reasonable?
- Is it being achieved?

If the answer to the first question is "No, I don't think so" then the discussion which follows will be much different than if the answer is "Yes".

4. Gather Sufficient and Appropriate Evidence

Assessing and evaluating classrooms has the same difficulties as all other assessment and evaluation.

A 'rush to judgement' is dangerous. Make sure that you have sufficient evidence before any judgements are made.

'Sufficient' refers to quantity. Equally important is to gather evidence of quality. This will partly be touched on below. What it also means is that the evidence we obtain of the often subjective, messy reality of classroom life needs validating before it can be used. Don't rely on one point of view.

5. Choose Appropriate Strategies

There are a range of strategies through which information can be gained — anecdotes, interviews, observation schedules, questionnaires, video and audio recording, photographs, records. Each of them has strengths and weaknesses as both a means of getting information in the classroom (video may be off-putting) or of revealing appropriate information (interviews may not be the best way of finding out about handwriting). Choosing the appropriate strategy is important.

6. Provide Feedback

Most people prefer feedback of one form or another following assessment or evaluation and teachers are no different. What is important is that feedback should:

- be presented constructively at all possible times
- be given in a manner which respects the receiver
- be clear
- contain examples which refer to the points made
- not be judgemental until it is possible to be
- when negative, contain positive suggestions for improvement
- be followed up.

The last point we want to make is this. The most effective form of professional and personal development is that which occurs from within, which we 'own'. One of the purposes of providing feedback on assessment and evaluation of classroom visits is to find areas which colleagues will want to consider for themselves and to improve.

Action-based research about our own practice is the most important development we can make. Well-conceived and sympathetically orchestrated classroom visits can help to move teachers towards that position.

Who does it for the headteacher is another question. Perhaps they have to be open to appropriate assessment and evaluation from colleagues, too.

The Effect of the Observer's Presence

Your presence in a classroom inevitably affects the situation of which you are a part in a number of ways. Three are particularly important.

Projection

Here, the observer imagines they are actually teaching the class and thinks more in terms of what they would do in the circumstances, rather than observing the teacher. The danger is of the observer being projected as a paragon whose lessons never flagged, whose children were never inattentive and who was perpetually kind and understanding. The art of constructive observation is to wrench oneself away from those fantasies and concentrate on helping the teacher.

Compensation

Here, the observer seeks to make up for their own deficiencies. An untidy or badly organised observer may be excessively punitive over this characteristic in others.

When the observer's failings are already known to the person being observed, this form of hypocrisy is not only irritating but also reduces the legitimacy of otherwise credible comments.

The Power Relationship

A powerful headteacher may reduce a newly arrived probationer to a nervous jelly simply because of the huge gap in status. More experienced teachers who nevertheless have a strong sense of hierarchy, will have a different view of a headteacher's visit than others who operate in a more collegial style.

17

Motivating Children

It is not unusual when appointing adults to posts to look for qualities of self-motivation.

Teachers in primary schools cannot rely on self-motivation among their children, many of whom must wonder at their young age why they are there at all. Connie and Harold Rosen, in their book *The Language of Primary School Children* (Penguin, 1976) said

> It is easy to think of many reasons why a young child should not want to write and very difficult to think of reasons why he should.

Every teacher of primary children could, at some stage or another, translate that comment into every curriculum area.

One of the characteristics of poor teaching is to assume that children will bring motivation to their work; some will, but most won't. One of the fundamental tasks of primary teaching is not only to introduce children to a body of facts, or a collection of skills and concepts, but to do so in a way which will encourage children to develop both an intrinsic interest in the subject and a keenness to find out and stay committed.

For some children the subject matter is enough. Every primary teacher will have taught children who, irrespective of ability, seemed sparked and inspired by the very nature of one particular subject. This is not true for the majority, though.

The evidence that is available suggests that children's interests and motivation in the primary school are developed much more through personal interaction with their teachers and others than through anything else.

It is not that other influences are not important. It would be foolish to deny the influence of the home, the media or peer groups but teachers have little control over those. What is important is that we should be aware of what is possible in the classroom. Motivating, enthusing and encouraging children is an important function of teaching.

The Factors

1. Fairness

Children develop a sense of fairness as they move through school. While their own may not always be well-formed they are certainly able to spot fairness or unfairness in others. Their attitude to it is much like the British attitude to speaking French—"I can understand what they are saying but I can't speak it very well myself!"

"It's not fair" is a common phrase in most primary schools. Children are quick to be demotivated by teachers who run unfair classrooms. Children enjoy being in classrooms where:

- the demands made are reasonable
- everyone is treated equably (children will be demotivated by teachers even if they treat otherwise unpopular classmates unfairly)

- teachers sort out squabbles in a reasonable way
- teachers emphasise and practise qualities of fairness continually.

2. *Approachability*

Children enjoy being in classrooms run by teachers who are accessible to them and who are interested in what they have to say. Interestingly, many children are put off by teachers who try and curry favour with their classes. Children seem to expect, almost want, a distance between them and their teachers. On the other hand, the work children have to do is seen as coming 'from the teacher'. There appears to be a common view which says "If she wants me to be interested in her world, then she ought to be interested in mine." Not unreasonable, really.

3. *Clarity*

Children are motivated by teachers who make what they have to say understandable, whether it is a class lesson, individual help, instructions or a reprimand.

It is sometimes difficult for teachers to realise how much of what is being presented to children each day is new; to adults it often seems commonplace. Just as teachers are demotivated at INSET sessions by presenters of new material who talk too fast, assume understandings or badly structure their session, so children are demotivated by teachers.

4. *Excitement*

Many adults have been introduced to new subjects and experiences they might otherwise have ignored by the sheer excitement of friends and colleagues. Children like excitement and commitment from teachers and respond to it. A sense of calm in a classroom is undoubtedly important but calmness doesn't have to mean blandness.

A famous teachers' book about spelling was titled *Caught or Taught?* It is a title which could apply very well to the interests and abilities children develop as they move through their primary school. Enthusiasms should not be hidden.

5. Humour

Not surprisingly children enjoy and are motivated by teachers with a sense of humour. It's hardly surprising when you imagine that they are sitting in the same room with one teacher for up to six hours a day. Once again, though, primary children don't want humour all the time; they seem to have an awareness that school is also a place to work. What humour means in this context is not that of a stand-up comedian!

6. Praise and Success

Like all of us, children are motivated by success; that is no surprise. Successful work is often important, although very young children sometimes don't understand what it is about their work that their teacher has defined as successful. Success in anything is motivational—walking down the corridor properly, putting the gym equipment away, snowing care for others; all of these count.

Praise is obviously the signifier of success and so children are motivated by praise. Unfortunately, there is much evidence to suggest that the ratio between teachers' 'praising statements' and 'critical statements' is heavily weighted in favour of critical statements.

If you dare, tape record yourself working with a class or group of children for 45 minutes and count the praising and critical statements you make. Identify to whom each was aimed, if possible. The evidence will appall you, but might provide the answer to some of your motivational difficulties!

7. Individuality of Response

Children are motivated by teachers who care about them as individuals well as members of a class. Some recent evidence has suggested that "touching and talking" is an effective way of allowing children to understand and feel care for individuals. Children later—and unknowingly—responded more positively to teachers who gently touched their arm or hair when praising or criticising than they did to teachers who did not touch.

8. A Climate of Care

Children respond more positively to teachers who are perceived to care not only about them but also about the class, the classroom and the school in general. Such care is reflected in the teachers' attitude to classroom display, tidiness, their colleagues and so on. What is important about primary children's responses to classroom life is that they confirm numerous cliches, from the medium is the message" to 'it's the way you tell 'em'.

As children move through the primary school their basic motivational attitudes towards themselves as learners and workers are forming all the time. By the time they leave the primary school they will already be able to confirm themselves as 'no good at maths', 'a scientist', 'always lazy" or 'really hardworking". Those attitudes will have a profound effect on the rest of their school lives. It is important to realise that they are formed through the interactions with those who have worked with them more than anything else.

PASTORAL ORGANISATION

Pastoral care can be defined as all of that part of a teacher's responsibility beyond the academic and intellectual development of their pupils. It is primarily concerned with *social, emotional send personal* development.

In primary schools any separation between the curricular and pastoral responsibilities of teachers is usually seen as minimal—and rightly so. Apart from sound educational reasons for viewing the child as a whole person, the 'class teacher" organisational structure encourages the development of individual relationships and understandings in the classroom. Nevertheless pastoral problems invariably take up more time than any other difficulties and we need to have clear management structures in place to deal with them.

The Role of the Class Teacher

The following true story (and you will know many more along the same lines) is an interesting example of one teacher's effective response to a problem in her class.

> Gemma was a fairly bright nine year old who had completely lost interest in school work. She was doing just enough to get by but her teacher, Ms Miles, knew Gemma was under achieving. Ms Miles decided to have a private talk with Gemma; after an indifferent start it began to emerge that friendship groups were one of the problems. She was particularly worried about Louise who had been her best friend but was now in with another group and seemed to be against Gemma joining in.
>
> Ms Miles decided to watch what was happening in class and to get staff on duty to keep an eye on things during breaks and lunch-times. She also contacted Gemma's parents and asked them to come in for a chat about their daughter's progress.
>
> Gemma's parents were equally concerned and had noticed a deterioration in Gemma's approach

to school. After talking together the adults brought Gemma in to let her know their thoughts and to listen to her ideas.

After hearing from other staff and considering all the factors the following action was decided upon:

1. Ms Miles would have a word with the girls about being more positive within the friendship group.
2. At the end of each day Ms Miles would write down all the positive things Gemma had achieved and these comments would go home on a Friday.
3. Gemma's parents would visit Ms Miles on a fortnightly basis to see how things were progressing.

This action was effective and in a very short time Gemma was working hard and enthusiastically again.

The case above illustrates the four key features of the class teacher's role in relation to pastoral care:

- giving time on an individual basis
- gathering accurate information
- involving parent(s), child and teacher in discussion
- taking some sort of positive action.

The Role of the Year-Group Coordinator/Head of Lower School/Upper School Etc.

In the larger primary school there is often the post of year group coordinator or head of Infant/Junior department (or some other similar title) who frequently has a pastoral overview of a number of classes. Although the class teacher is always the first line pastoral adult, this more senior member of staff can, and hopefully does, play a very useful role by:

- leading staff discussion on pastoral matters
- linking personal and social education to pastoral care
- defining management structures for dealing with pastoral problems
- acting as support to class teachers.

The Role of the Headteacher

In many primary schools the headteacher will play a crucial role when dealing with pastoral matters — particularly in the problem sphere! Many parents will want to see the headteacher rather than the class teacher, deputy or coordinator; they often feel that they will achieve more by going to the top.

There is a danger in the headteacher accepting this role and skating on very thin ice when trying hard to be knowledgeable about the child concerned—especially when the headteacher has only taught the child twice that term.

In any but the most special cases, the headteacher should be the final resort in dealing with pastoral problems.

This is one area where delegation is definitely the order of the day. The people who know the child best should usually be the ones to talk with parents, gather information and make decisions about the child.

The Role of Ancillary Staff

All ancillary staff should be briefed about their possible involvement in children's pastoral development. It often happens that an ancillary helper can make a different relationship with a child to that of the teacher; this can sometimes mean that the child will talk more openly with the ancillary.

Ancillary Staff Need to be Aware of

- the importance of listening to children
- the reflective technique (where a child is prompted into talking, perhaps about difficulties, by repeating the last words of a sentence or phrase spoken by the child)
- the need to identify pastoral problems and discuss them with teaching staff
- the importance of confidentiality.

Regular discussions and a high level of involvement with all ancillary staff can greatly assist the development of positive and effective pastoral care.

Safety Nets

No formalised pastoral system is ever perfect and we all know that even the most professional teacher can find an individual child particularly irritating and obnoxious—sometimes with good reason! In accepting this, we do need to devise safety nets for staff. When it's been a wet playtime for the third day and Mr Smith has been up most of the night with his sick child and he suddenly decides he's had enough of Belinda, there should be a strategy in place to help.

Here are some common ones—what actually happens is less important than meeting the main difficulty, which is removing Belinda from the room, and there being an agreed procedure for doing this.

> A 'Paired' support—this is where a reciprocal arrangement is agreed to help deal with the very difficult child. Basically, if a pupil is

provoking you to the point of distraction, you are able to send him along to a colleague who is aware that this may happen. The other side of the coin is that you are willing to accept children from your colleague's class in similar circumstances.

B Senior member of staff support—this is where a year group coordinator or deputy agrees to take responsibility for very difficult children for a short period of time.

C Headteacher support — headteacher agrees to accept responsibility for the child if A and/or B are inappropriate or unavailable.

In B and C above there is often an inbuilt assumption that the adult will carry out some pastoral work with the individual concerned and hopefully begin a process whereby the problem will be at least alleviated if not solved.

The key point when considering safety nets is *to play to individual's strengths.* Some of us have a sympathy and patience with certain children which is lacking or in short supply in other colleagues. Some of us have an authority with certain pupils which others lack. These qualities need to be recognised and used to the pastoral advantage of children and the teacher's effective classroom management.

Parental Contacts

The role of the parent in pastoral care is vital. The relationship between the child, teacher and parent is not one that can flourish if the school sets up barriers which prevent easy parental involvement—and all too often those barriers are quite unintentional!

We need to set down clear advice for parents about communication with school. First, in the *school brochure* (see over), second in *written communication* and third *verbally*.

Special Education Needs	Children who have difficulty with learning are given extra help both in the classroom environment and by specialist teachers. Support is also available from the School's Psychological Service, advisory teachers and ancillary helpers.
Pastoral Care	Apart from guiding your child's academic studies, we are committed to promoting his or her general development and welfare. The key person as far as your child is concerned is the form teacher, to whom any problem should normally be referred initially. Each year group is also co-ordinated by a more senior member of staff called a Year Group Co-ordinator Tutor who will be involved in more serious or complicated problems, as might the Deputy Heads or the Headteacher. At times the school also seeks the advice and assistance of various outside agencies in dealing with more specialist problems. Our Education Welfare Officer liaises at times between home and school and we also have regular contacts with the School Psychological Service, Social Services, the Police and so on.
Discipline	We insist on good standards of personal and social behaviour from all children in the school. If we are particularly concerned about a child's behaviour we will contact the parents. We do have a system whereby a child is put on `report' which means that his/her behaviour and attitude to school work is checked upon at each lesson. In extremely rare cases we do have the right to suspend pupils.

An extract from a school brochure

Outside Agencies

For all children there will be some contact with outside agencies such as the Area Health Authority, Educational Welfare Officer and Social Services. It is important that those in school dealing with these agencies build up trusting and professional relationships with them. The school doctor who has to wait while children from Class 2 get changed from PE and is never offered a cup of coffee will take away a certain view of that school!

ASSESSMENT AND TESTING— 1

The General Situation

'Assessment' and 'testing' are quite different, although both result in the formation of judgements about children's learning.

Assessment is any activity which leads to the forming of a judgement about the abilities, knowledge or attitudes of someone or something.

Testing is a formal, often standardised procedure which aims to provide specific information within a limited area.

Both assessment and testing take place a great deal in schools. In the case of assessment this is hardly surprising as the purpose of education is to develop the 'abilities, knowledge and attitudes' of young children. Teachers in classrooms could hardly be said to be teaching if they were not making continual judgements about these three aspects of children's lives.

Testing, though, is already more prevalent than many believe. It has been reported recently that 79 per cent of LEAs have some programme of standardised testing in primary schools, most commonly in reading but also in mathematics and 'general ability', which was tested using verbal and non-verbal reasoning tests. Additionally, many schools also tested children with formal material of their own choosing.

The growth in testing appears to be continuous, partly

as a response to the increasing democratisation of schools. Pressure has grown on schools to answer two questions from parents:

- What are my child's specific abilities?
- Where does my child stand in relation to other children in the class or age group?

Specific questions have to be answered with specific information. Test results appear to provide that.

Diagnostic or Reportage?

Formal testing can be used for two main purposes. In the first case, teachers learn information about children which helps them to plan work more effectively. Such tests diagnose (or appear to diagnose) difficulties and problems which can be remedied. In the second case, formal tests provide a score or a result which can be used to report information, either to local authorities, the government or, as we saw above, to parents.

Advantages and Disadvantages

Both assessment and testing have advantages and disadvantages and need to be used appropriately.

Assessment

+ uses a variety of approaches to gather information-talking, questioning, observation, work-sampling
+ builds up a rounded picture of a child's abilities
+ allows for specific contextual information to be taken into account
– doesn't provide evidence of progress relative to other children
– doesn't provide information which enables comparison between schools

- – sometimes results in evidence which cannot be easily communicated to others
- – depends on a reasonably sophisticated subjective understanding of the whole situation.

Testing

- \+ can be used for comparative purposes
- \+ can, because of standardised administration procedures, be used at different sites
- \+ can help to reveal information useful for the establishment of national standards
- \+ provides information in an easily communicable and, apparently, understandable format
- – can restrict nature of assessment so that children have to reveal understandings in unfamiliar ways
- – may only be used in areas of the curriculum where formal testing works
- – may encourage curriculum provision to reflect the test rather than allow the test to monitor the curriculum provision
- – may be inappropriate for certain age-groups.

Managing Assessment and Testing in School

Assessment and testing are an important part of the work of a school. In making decisions about their use certain principles are important.

1. Work from the Curriculum to Assessment and Testing and Not the Other Way Round

Tests and assessments are not activities through which children learn, except indirectly as a result of diagnostic testing. Assessment and testing reports or judges the quality of the curriculum offered and children's responses to it. A well thought-out curriculum should precede well-thought-out assessment and testing.

2. *Don't Use Either in the Wrong Context*

When you decide to assess or test understand the advantages and disadvantages of each. Both have limitations; to use them inappropriately simply magnifies them.

3. *Accept the Limitations*

Assessment and testing are often criticised because "they don't tell the whole story". Nothing tells the whole story. The limitations don't render assessments and testing redundant.

4. *Understand the Response of Children*

Rightly, the time when primary school children were fed an unrelenting diet of tests leading towards the 11+ have long gone. The corollary is that many primary children are not as used to taking tests as they were. Test conditions which conflict with the normal mode of classroom work can be disturbing.

5. *Build Assessment and Testing into School Policies*

Notwithstanding that children's work should be curriculum led, assessment and testing are not afterthoughts of a school's curriculum policy. They should be an integral part of it. The decisions you take about assessment and testing should have the same status as the decisions you take about the content and process of the curriculum.

6. *Choose from a Selection of Tests*

There are many tests on the market many of which claim to do a similar job. Trial tests before you buy them. Make sure they provide you with information you want, have been properly validated, are easy to administer, are reasonably easy to mark and contain effective record sheets.

7. *Don't Let Testing Take up Too Much Time*

Primary classrooms are busy places punctuated more than enough by activities other than learning opportunities.

Primary children need time to accomplish much of their work-interruptions affect the final quality. Try not to let testing interrupt the day-to-day flow too much.

8. Use 'INSET Days' to Explore Assessment Techniques

Assessment is important to schools, adding to the information provided by tests and revealing information where tests are inappropriate.

Assessment techniques, being informal and ongoing, can seem non-problematical but subjective judgements need to be as sophisticated as any testing procedure. 'INSET days' and other INSET opportunities should be used to explore the difficulties with assessment and to provide some solutions.

9. Use Children's Self-assessment

There is growing evidence that enabling children to assess themselves in the classroom is not only a good motivator but also enhances the quality of information already available to teachers. A number of packs of self-assessment material for children are being published at the present time.

ASSESSMENT AND TESTING—2

The National Curriculum

The management of the introduction of National Curriculum assessment and testing is to a great extent out of the hands of those who work in schools. At the time of writing an agreed timetable which covers maths, science, technology and English has already been published and made available to schools. Schools will have to statutorily administer the assessment and testing materials which will, inevitably, have to be produced at high speed.

From the point of view of those who work in schools

the 'management' of National Curriculum assessment and testing means understanding what is supposed to happen, which organisation is responsible for what, identifying crucial strengths and weaknesses, supporting and making good use of those strengths, and reporting on the weaknesses through any consultation procedures which might be made available.

What Parts of the Plan have Relevance to Primary Schools?

By Autumn 1989	Attainment targets formulated for Key Stage 1 (age 5—7 years) in maths, science and, probably, English.
By Autumn 1990	Attainment targets for Key Stage 2 (7/8-11 years) in maths, science and English.
	Probably, attainment targets for Key Stages 1 and 2 in technology.
By Summer 1991	Trial assessments (without reporting) for Key Stage 1 in maths, science and English.
By Autumn 1991	Probably, attainment targets for Key Stage 2 in technology.
By Summer 1992	Reported assessments for Key Stage 1 in maths and science and, probably, English.
	Trial assessments (without reporting) for Key Stage 1 in technology.
By Summer 1993	Reported assessment for Key Stage 1 in technology.
By Summer 1994	Trial assessments (without reporting) for Key Stage 2 in maths, science, English and, probably, technology.
By Summer 1995	Reported assessments for Key Stage 2 in maths, science and English.
	Either trial assessments (unreported) or reported assessments for Key Stage 2 in technology.
By Summer 1996	Possibly reported assessments for Key Stage 2 in technology.

Who is Responsible for What?

The National Curriculum Council (NCC) is responsible

for advising the Secretary of State on the curriculum content of each subject area and on the production of attainment targets, statements of attainment and programmes of study.

The *Task Group on Assessment and Testing (TGAT)* was responsible for advising the Secretary of State on the pattern of testing to be implemented in schools in England and Wales. (At the time of writing, Scotland was not included in the National Curriculum proposals. It seems inconceivable, despite some opposition in Scotland, that something very similar won't be imposed there as well).

The *Schools Examination and Assessment Council (SEAC)* is responsible for advising the Secretary of State on the production of assessment and testing material. It aims to produce this material by commissioning outside organisations to devise and trial it.

What Form of Testing is Recommended?

TGAT suggested that:

- both informal (assessment) and formal (testing) procedures should be used
- reporting to parents should be based on a combination of both methods
- moderation panels should be created so that schools could unify their subjective procedures as much as possible (although quite how this will work in practice remains to be seen)
- the reporting of tests should be progressive across year groups; in other words that the tests should not be restricted to children of a single year
- the testing should be linked closely to National Curriculum targets to provide overall profiles of attainment

- much of the formal testing and assessment at Key Stage 1 (age 5-7) should be based on tasks which replicate classroom activity as closely as possible and which can be administered as part of the normal classroom day. This will not apply at Key Stage 2.

What are the Likely Problems?

First, that the timetable will not be adhered to. It depends on agreement about the attainment targets being reached by the deadlines, the production of implementable assessment and testing material by the deadlines and the provision of INSET for all teachers.

Second, that the consultation procedures will become a sham in order that the deadlines can be met. The targets require some of the most sophisticated thinking to take place over very short periods of time. If it appears difficult to do this, political expediency may overtake the real needs of schools, parents and children.

Third, there will be overload on teachers. This could mean that the assessment and testing simply won't get done. It could mean a greater drain on the profession as more teachers leave. It could also mean that other forms of assessment and testing teachers might want to use are put to one side.

Fourth, public acceptability of the scheme could encourage inappropriate testing. There are already doubts over testing at seven because of the different amounts of time children have spent in school and their different range of pre-school educational experiences. Political pressure could force testing on even younger children or could cause testing in areas of the curriculum often thought to be untestable.

Fifth, the INSET load will be too great to organise. The testing and assessment will be carried out by teachers unprepared for it.

So much is still unknown of the core that it is difficult to perceive it in 'management' terms at the present time. What will have to be managed without doubts are:

- the school's INSET programme
- information to parents
- teacher morale.

Much that is good could result from a well thought-out programme of assessment and testing. To achieve this some in-school management is necessary but, for once, the responsibility lies as much out of schools as it does within them.

18

Financial Management and Buildings

LOCAL MANAGEMENT OF SCHOOLS

Local Management of Schools (LMS) came about as a result of the Education Reform Act 1988. For most primary schools it means the passing of budgetary control from the LEA to the individual school. Not all the money for running the school is handed over, as some finance is kept centrally by the LEA, but the major finances are the responsibility of the governors and head teacher.

Aims

The major aims of LMS are:

- to give greater flexibility in the spending of the school's budget
- to let the school respond more readily to the changing needs of its pupils and the local community.

Although the financial side of LMS is fundamental, LMS has much wider implications than the allocation of resources.

Three areas of particular concern are these:

- appointments
- dismissals and disciplinary procedures
- marketing.

The first two areas have, in the past, had a high level of LEA involvement, but LMS puts them squarely in the governors' court.

The third, marketing, is concerned with the school's links with the local and wider community — again something not traditionally part of the management function.

The Timetable

There are two groups of primary schools affected by LMS—those with more than 200 pupils and those with less than 200. For the smaller school the LEA *may* decide to delegate the budget or keep it centrally. If the LEA doesn't delegate it, it must still run the school's budget to the formula as set up by the LEA and approved by the Secretary of State. The timetable is as follows:

<table>
<tr><th></th><th>30the Sept 1989</th><th>1st April 1990</th><th>1st April 1993</th><th>1st April 1994</th></tr>
<tr><td>Formula Funding</td><td rowspan="2">Schemes put forward for approval by LEAs</td><td>All schools in scheme plus transition arrangements</td><td></td><td>End of transitional arrangements</td></tr>
<tr><td>Budget Delegation</td><td>Schools may receive budges</td><td>All schools above 200 pupils must receive budget</td><td></td></tr>
</table>

The timetable for the introduction of LMS

How is the Formula Decided?

This can be shown by the following flow-chart:

The Lea Budget-Setting Process

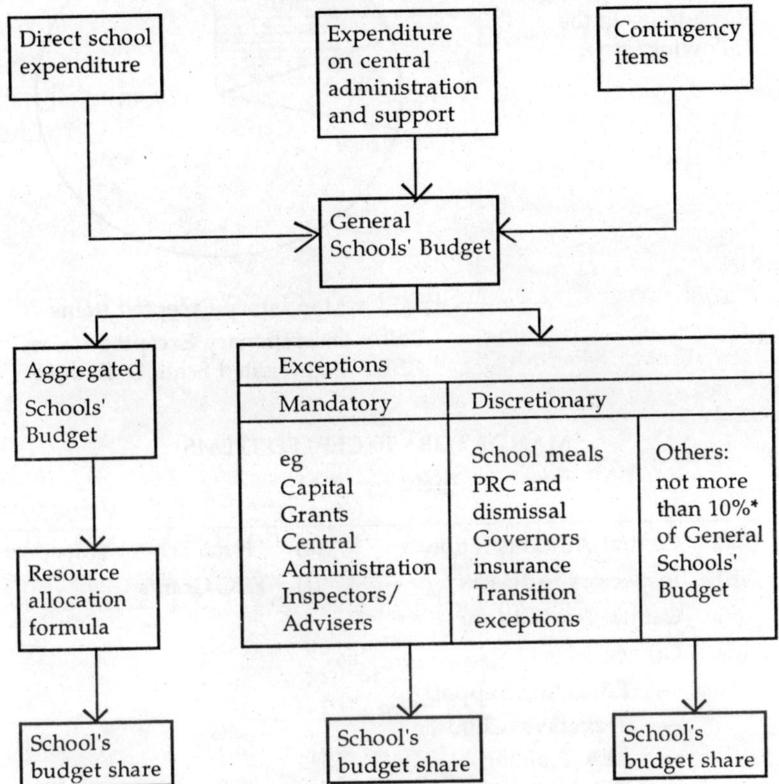

* Expected by the Secretary of Stateto reduce to 7% after the LEA's 3 year review

General Schools' Budget (GSB)

The whole 'cake' is known as the *General Schools' Budget* and is made up in the following way:

The whole 'cake' is known as the General Schools' Budget and is made up in the following way:

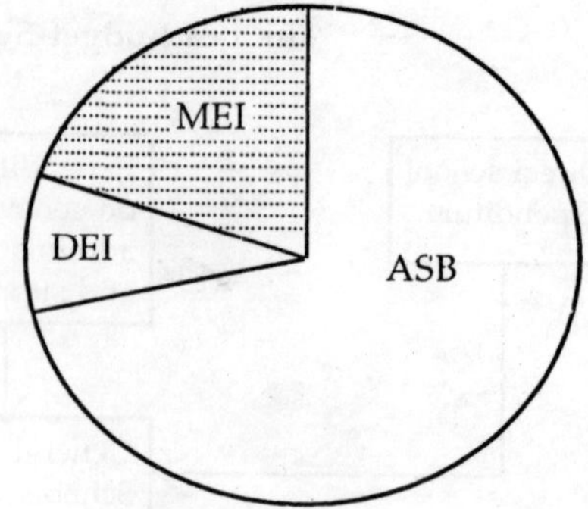

MEI = Mandatory Excepted Items
DEI = Discretionary Excepted Items
ASB = Aggregated Schools' Budget

MANDATORY EXCEPTED ITEMS

(held by LEA)

(a) Central Administration
(b) Inspectors/Advisers
(c) Capital Expenditure
(d) Grants:
— Education Support
— Travellers' Children
— LEA Training
— Section 11

(e) Home School Transport
(f) EEC Grants

The Aggregated Schools' Budget (ASB)

The ASB is the important bit! It's what's left after the LEA's formula has been applied. These resources are under the governors' control in schools where the budget has been delegated and under LEA control where it hasn't.

At least 75 per cent of this budget is determined by how many children you have in your school and by their ages—this is known in the jargon as *the age-weighted pupil number*.

DISCRETIONARY EXCEPTED ITEMS

	Not subject to 10%		*Subject to 10% (7% after three year)*
(a)	Transitional arrangements	(a)	LEA initiatives
(b)	Early retirement	(b)	Structural repairs
(c)	Governors' insurance	(c)	Statemented pupils + Ed. Psych
(d)	School meals	(d)	EWOs
		(e)	Premises insurance
		(f)	Peripatetics
		(g)	Pupil support
		(h)	Special staff costs (cover, safeguarding)
		(i)	Library/museum services
		(j)	School specific contingencies
		(k)	Other approved items

As formulae vary from authority to authority you cannot say definitively the total items in the ASB but some things are common to all schools. For example:

- teaching and non-teaching salaries
- day-to-day running costs of the premises
- equipment, books, goods and services used by the school
- supply teaching budget
- midday supervision.

Management Implications

LMS has created pluses and minuses for all teachers who are involved in the management of their schools.

+ flexibility
+ choice
+ independence

+ accountability
+ opportunity
+ freedom from bureaucracy
– additional management tasks
– additional responsibility
– diversion of teacher time from pupils/curriculum
– formula funding based on pupil numbers ignores individual schools' problems.

To make the most of LMS and cushion the negative points we need to manage the total resources effectively. Looking at the area of finance, here are some ways of approaching this task:

A Decide on	**B Cost out**
• basic expenditure/set costs	• school development plan
• likely expenditure/estimated costs	• resource requirements
• unpredictable expenditure/ contingency costs	• new services.

Compare totals for A and B—in other words *match your overall plan to your budget.*

1. Do this before you begin the year.
2. Keep a close watch on real expenditure v. planned expenditure.
3. Vary the plan if necessary.
4. Involve governors, and all staff.
5. Make sure someone is responsible for an overview.
6. Don't be afraid to seek advice from the LEA.

Conclusion

LMS is hard work, full of challenges and problems,

has significant training implications, needs the support of costly technology and has yet to be proved a boon or a burden; it will probably turn out to be a bit of both!

> The telephone bill in the school was about £80 a year over the amount allocated. Since the new system of extensions had been installed the bills had rocketed. You see, anyone could dial out and staff were just not putting down all of their private calls. It mattered now because the school had its delegated budget—before the LEA had simply paid the bill. The headteacher decided to solve the problem; he took the telephone out of the staffroom and locked it away in a cupboard!
>
> Result: disaffected teachers, saving of £35.
>
> This story illustrates one of the conceptual difficulties of LMS—the difficulty of looking at the WHOLE before analysing the parts. In the overall budget the saving on telephone calls was negligible *and* caused negative feelings among some staff—a less drastic solution was always possible. If the whole budget had been in deficit looking at every part and going for savings might have been appropriate.
>
> *Remember: look at the totality before tinkering with the constituent parts.*

SITE AND BUILDING

At the centre of the management of primary schools are people; but it would be foolish to underestimate the importance of the physical environment. Cold, uninviting class or staffrooms have an obvious effect on staff and pupils, and the wider community make any number of judgements based upon their perception of the way in which a site and building are used:

Responsibilities

Since the Education Reform Act (1988) responsibility for the site and building of a school is divided up as follows:

- cleaning and caretaking—LMS (governors)
- internal maintenance—LMS (governors)
- school grounds and playing fields—LMS (governors)
- structural repairs and maintenance—discretionary (could be kept at LEA level or delegated)
- major refurbishments—discretionary (as above)
- overall responsibility—governors.

On a day-to-day level it will usually be the caretaker (sometimes referred to as the custodian) or headteacher who will deal with problems relating to the fabric of the building. You need a clear procedure for reporting damage or deterioration to the site or building -usually a standard form or log book will be adequate. Whatever system you devise make sure everyone is aware of it.

Community Use

Increasing use is being made of schools for community use; some have a long tradition of evening classes, societies, youth groups, etc. and under LMS such use is set to increase. We all know of the difficulties community use can bring (well, all those of us who have actually worked in schools), but properly managed you can gain great benefit from such use.

Benefits

- Helps to develop a positive image of the school
- Gives members of the community a chance to see something of the school's work through displays
- Provides income
- Helps security (although see *Problems* below)
- Gives an opportunity for contact with groups and individuals from the local community.

Problems

- Classrooms, hall, etc. can be left in disarray
- Security can be difficult with strangers in the school
- Caretaking, locking up, etc. can create difficulties depending on caretaker's contract
- Parking problems when large functions are on
- Some groups may be 'controversial'
- Double booking.

Bookings for community use are the responsibility of the governors although this is usually delegated to the headteacher. This means that you have to be careful about lettings. Often it is the secretary who is the first to receive a request so she needs to be clear about the conditions for groups using the school premises—costs, timings, room availability and so on.

Points to Watch Out For

- Make sure your school has the right facilities for the hirer—for example, if you only have a small hall with lots of display boards the local five-a-side football club might do better to find another venue
- Make sure your booking form is clearly explained to the hirer. If midnight is the latest locking-up time you don't want a wedding reception that is just getting in full flight as the caretaker comes to turn the key!
- Inform local police if there is going to be a really big function and you anticipate parking problems
- Keep your own simple booking record to avoid double booking and to inform the caretaker
- Discuss and review community use with your caretaker and secretary
- Ensure valuable school items are locked away
- Check that community users are aware of fire exits, access to first aid equipment and emergency telephone
- If you get a request to use the school premises by a group that might be conceived as controversial—for example, a political group advocating racial hatred—make sure you discuss the request with the governors.

You may think "most of this doesn't apply to our school," but be prepared! Under LMS you are positively encouraged to increase, where possible, the community use of your site and buildings.

Making the Best of Things

Imagine an infant school set in a town but with a good sized field as well as the usual playground and an ornamental garden; the staff decide that some sort of wildlife sanctuary would help the science curriculum. They manage to get some sponsorship and PTA money and construct a small pond—a successful use of the school's environment.

A class of 11 -year-olds want to improve their classroom which has high windows, poor display space, crowded tables, etc. Their teacher turns it into a problem-solving exercise and within two weeks the room has been rearranged, plants brought in, windows cleaned and so on. Another improvement in the environment.

We can all think of many such examples but there are some underlying principles when trying to improve the school's site and building:

- set attainable targets
- involve others in identifying areas for improvement
- if a number of areas are identified, draw up a priority list
- make sure the reason for the change/ improvement is clear
- if appropriate, get the governors' and/or LBA's permission.

Caring Attitudes

Whatever sort of building you work in you need to try

and develop a caring attitude towards it from adults and children. Overcrowded and unattractive working conditions are very poor motivators and can inhibit all manner of positive moves in such things as teaching styles, curriculum innovation and shared resources.

As referred to in other sections of this book, *ownership* is a key concept of effective management in the primary school. So you have to make sure that children and teachers feel that they have some stake in the building. Responsibility for designated areas is one way of doing this: another is to allocate resources in such a way that staff have the flexibility to make their classrooms more attractive places.

In one school where graffiti was a problem, a policy of instant cleaning off was begun and in a very short time the scribbling stopped. A clean environment does seem to help perpetuate itself!

Perhaps the best way we develop a caring attitude towards our work place is by example. When everyone begins to bother, care becomes part of the school culture and so we hardly notice the effort being made.

BUDGET ALLOCATION

What are We Talking About?

For the purposes of this section, *budget allocation* refers to the allocation of monies specifically designated for such items as books, stationery, consumable stock and equipment. In many LEAs this is known as 'capitation' as in the past it has been the amount provided by LEAs on a 'per capita' basis.

How Does Local Management of School Fit in with This?

Clearly LMS has radically changed the finances given to schools but, in reality, much of the increased devolution is fairly tightly targeted — for example, staff salaries. What might be termed 'curriculum funding' will remain a crucial sum to be divided up.

Who has the Responsibility?

The short answer is 'the governors'. There are three common ways in which governors might handle this:

- by forming a sub-committee to oversee all finance and allocate funds themselves
- by delegating 'capitation' funding to the head teacher and working in consultation with him/her
- by delegating 'capitation' funding to the head teacher and keeping a watching brief.

However, the bottom line is that this money can be spent at the discretion of the governing body.

Experience to date indicates that the responsibility invariably falls to the headteacher. Bearing this in mind it is worth ensuring that the governing board, and in particular any finance sub-committee, is kept well informed about capitation spending.

Allocation Systems

Four systems of allocation are commonly used in primary schools:

- at the headteacher's discretion
- the 'bids' system
- the 'allowance' system
- the 'bids/allowance' system.

Each has advantages and disadvantages and it will depend on your school's context which is the most appropriate, although you will see from the chart set out on below that we tend to favour a version of the bids system based on a collegial management style below. Only in very exceptional circumstances would we see the first system as a positive managerial position.

CAPITATION ALLOCATION SYSTEMS—PROS AND CONS

System	*Advantages*	*Disadvantages*
Headteacher's discretion	Headteacher has control	Lack of staff involvement. No sharing of expertise. Encourages patronage.
Bids	Everyone is involved. Needs are identified by staff. Priorities can be drawn up based upon an observable rationale.	Difficulties with long-term planning. Staff cannot be sure of definite allocation.
Allowance	Staff can plan easily. Careful expenditure is rewarded. Long-term planning is easier.	Staff expectations-at least as much as last year! Major initiatives are more difficult. Financial power can be put in the hands of a few teachers.
Bids/Allowances	Flexibility. Mid-term planning help. Basic stock can be taken out of budget before allocation.	Confusion among staff. Major initiatives can be inhibited.

You can add your own points to the chart on the left. Which method is used will depend on the size of school,

Capitation Commitment Record

Dept: Humanities Year: 1988/89 Sheet No: 1

Date	*Order No.*	*Supplier*	*Est. Cost*	*Actual Cost*	*Variance* +	*Variance* —	*Credits* —	*Balance*
14.5.88	W 20824	London NAP Centre		119.74				119.74
9.6.88	W 20829	Philip Green ED.		29.95				149.69
28.7.88	W 40464	G. Foster, Yorkshire T.V.		82.61				232.30
28.7.88	W 40465/6	Foyles	677.85					910.15
28.7.88	W 40467	London MAF Centre	49.00					959.15
28.7.88	W 40468	George Philip		31.50				990.65
26/29.7.88		Travel Exp.	c.Fwd 13.10	19.20				1009.85
27.1.89	W 40529	Taskmaster DLM	14.90					1024.75
10.2.89	W 40536	Philip Green		47.50				1072.25
	W 40465/6	Fovles				220.92		851.33
	W 40467	London NAP Centre				42.81		808.52
		C/FWD To 1989/90						191.80
								616.72

the relationships, personalities and priorities within that school — not to mention the role of the governing board!

Accounting Procedures

In most LEAs the accounting requirements are laid down centrally, and under LMS this is likely to increase, but frequently there is a need to design systems to keep track of spending. In most schools the secretary carries this responsibility but it is, of course, vital that the headteacher and deputy are aware of the budgetary implications of their actions. A readily accessible format for capitation spending is therefore essential. Set out at the top of p. 387 is a sample of one school's Capitation Commitment Record; this school bases its system on subject areas—although this sheet is called 'Humanities', and includes history, geography, social studies, environmental studies and graphicacy.

School Fund

There are two key points to remember about School Fund accounts:

- they are mainly 'through' accounts
- they need to be audited every year.

The first point means that usually the School Fund is used to hold money for trips, theatre groups, PTA items, etc., the second point is important because the School Fund is outside the LEA's budget to the school and is, therefore, more open to abuse.

Managing the School Fund should be seen as a very important financial responsibility and a prudent safeguard is to make sure that any cheque account requires two signatures.

GROUND RULES

- Be open about capitation allowance and its procedures for allocation. Involvement of staff leading to a sense of fairness in distribution helps towards achieving shared goals
- Have an overall strategy for spending based upon discussion of the school's needs
- Set up accounting systems that will give you ready access to financial information.

EXTERNAL RELATIONS

Involving Parents in School

The range of parental involvement is very broad. It includes:

- helping in class (ranging from washing paint-brushes to almost teaching)
- working with a group of children around the school
- helping on outings, visits and school journeys
- getting involved with the PTA or Friends of the School Committee and events
- designing newsletters and brochures
- attending at curriculum evenings
- consultating on specific areas of the school's life
- open evenings
- personal interviews
- sport
- bringing special interests or expertise into the school
- helping children at home.

No doubt you can add examples of your own. You

must make your own decisions about the extent parents can be involved at any one time, based on three important factors:

- the school's need to receive feedback from parents and to develop an understanding of the parental view
- the school's requirements for extra help not obtainable elsewhere
- the school's capacity to absorb parents into the school in a variety of ways.

The Problems

Despite the undoubted benefits of parental involvement there are problems. In a management sense these are more important since they are the issues which have to be understood, prepared for, accommodated and dealt with.

1. The Development of Cliques

Some parents see their involvement in school as a special position and talk about it as such outside the school building. Inevitably, such attitudes create resentment amongst other sections of the parent body, bringing difficulties to the school of a different kind.

Even when no clique appears to exist amongst the parent helpers, the group can often be perceived as such by those parents who are not involved.

2. Misuse of Information

By definition, parent helpers are allowed 'behind the scenes' of a school to some degree. Sometimes the information that they acquire can be misused. Snippets of confidential information about children, teachers or other parents dropped into conversations over a cup of tea with friends, or misunderstood events of the school being re-interpreted outside, are not uncommon occurrences.

3. Inappropriate Behaviour

People who work in a school full-time develop an ethos which works for them. Occasionally parents who come into the school on a voluntary basis may behave in ways not appropriate to that ethos.

4. Poor Allocation of Tasks

Most teachers and schools are grateful for any help parents can offer. Just occasionally that 'help' may be counter-productive. The parent washing the paint-brushes may leave the brushes and the sink in a worse mess than the six-year-old children; the parent asked to mount a little work may smear glue or paste over everything; the volunteer chairperson of the PTA may not be able to control a meeting and so on.

5. Misuse of Staff Space

A school which is successful in attracting parental involvement may often have more parents in school during a day than staff. This can result in staff not being able to relax, to talk freely amongst each other or even to grab a cup of coffee before break ends. Some staffs willingly accept parent helpers as they would supply teachers; others are more reticent. This doesn't make them anti-parent necessarily; they are entitled to their own professional privacy. It can, however, make them less enthusiastic about having parents in school.

6. Children of Involved Parents Appear to be Favoured

Consciously or unconsciously it is possible to favour in small ways the children of parental helpers in school. Where such favouritism occurs it is quickly noticed by other children and can rebound on the favoured child. Equally, and in the same way as nonexistent cliques can be perceived, so some children and parents will believe that the children of involved parents are being favoured whether they are or not.

7. Children Can be Unduly Pressured

The inside knowledge which involved parents pick up isn't only about the staffer other children; it can also be about their own. Such information can be used to pressure children.

These problems may be enough to put anyone off having parental helpers in their school again. The point is that the problems have to be managed; when they are the benefits of parental involvement far outweigh the difficulties which remain.

What Can You Do?

1. Establish Ground Rules

If common policies in the school apply to children, staff and supply teachers then they ought to apply to parents, too. It is worth establishing your own particular set of ground rules for parental involvement and then communicating them effectively and pleasantly in a booklet or as a news-sheet. Every parent who offers help should be given a copy; every parent should expect to abide by the rules. Don't be embarrassed by this; most parents will want to fit into your school as well as they can. You might want to specify, amongst other things:

- whether parents announce their arrival in school and how
- what parents should do if they can't appear at a meeting or in a classroom
- to what extent they are expected to discipline children before handing over to a class teacher or the headteacher
- how the school tries to instil discipline in children
- which resources are freely available for use and which are not
- what happens at breaktime
- the need for confidentiality.

2. Arrange the First Involvement on a Temporary Basis

Don't commit yourself to accepting help on an open-ended basis until you know the qualities of the offering parent reasonably well or until you are sure of your joint relationship. A half-term time limit or even shorter is quite reasonable.

3. Value Help Given But Always Keep New Opportunities Open

Parents who are involved in school life should be thanked for it but not to the apparent exclusion of everyone else. At the same time that a particular involvement is being valued, the door should always be left open to others.

4. Accept Involvement at Any Level

Some parents, often through their own experiences of school, are still nervous of becoming involved. This does not necessarily signify lack of interest. Others can perhaps only become involved to a very limited extent. Try to accept that parents who offer only very limited involvement usually have good reasons.

5. Take Some Criticism as Inevitable

Not all criticism can be 'managed away'. Parental feelings towards their own child and their child's school often run deep. The involvement of parents at a particular level in the school, or the involvement of particular parents, is always going to create strong feelings amongst a few people. Provided you have done everything in your power to create a fair system and to explain it carefully then ride any other criticisms with a clear conscience.

6. Don't be Afraid to Interfere

Where you can identify weaknesses in parental involvement in school don't be afraid to interfere. Our experience suggests that the majority of parents want to 'do it right' and are more concerned if problems are not fairly discussed than if they are.

DEFINING THE SCHOOL'S IMAGE

'Image' can be Negative word for many people.

> "The problem with these clothes is that they are all image no quality."

Just two comments from members of an INSET discussion about what image' meant to them. Yet turning the discussion round in that same meeting it became clear that we all respond to images and carry banks of images around with us.

> "I bought this jacket because I thought I looked good in it. It made me feel good."
>
> "These pop stars are all the same. They just give

> them whichever image is fashionable. They are not real."
>
> "I am looking for another job, yes, but Id never go and work in that school. You know what it is like as well as I do!"
>
> "I don't like him very much. I never think he is telling the truth."

Images are everywhere. We all have them and we all respond to them. The evidence is overwhelming. Sales of books with redesigned covers rise dramatically; we look aghast at the family abum which shows us wearing flared trousers or platform shoes; we like some houses and not others; we present certain wines to friends and drink other, cheaper, wines ourselves.

If images are so prevalent, indeed so normal, it is unlikely that schools exist in a state of suppposted purity, image-free. The reality is that your school or classroom will have an image whether you like it or not; that the various groups which form the constituency of your school or class will carry round with them ideas-images-of what it is like, and what its strengths and weaknesses are, what they like about it and what they don't.

As a manager of your school or class you have two options. The first is to allow those images to be formed without input from you. The second is to see defining the image of the school or class as an important and active part of your work. Our attitude is clear. As images are going to form anyway then, as managers, we ought to be as purposeful as we can about defining them.

The Compromise

Inevitably, defining the image of a school or classroom results in a compromise. On the one hand you may have your own personal view of what you would like that image to be; on the other hand you have the perspectives of your colleagues, the children, their parents, the governors, the LEA, their inspectors and so on. As we saw in the early part of this book, there is no such thing as a 'parent's' or 'governor's' view either; there are differences within groups as well as between them.

It is important that we have a clear idea of the 'image' we want our school to reflect. Do we want it

- to be authoritarian and/or democratic?
- to provide a practical education and/ or a didactic one?
- to appear confident and/or open to doubt?
- to be professionally and/or personally orientated?

and so on.

It is also important that we understand the images our constituency would prefer since meeting those images will create confidence in the school. A recent survey of parental attitudes at one school suggested that parents wanted their children

- to be happy
- to work hard
- to be treated fairly
- not to be bullied
- to receive help when they needed it.

Following this survey, the school felt that the difficulties it had been experiencing in gaining parental confidence in new curriculum methods being introduced was a direct result of their failure to create positive images in the areas their parents appeared to value the most.

Responding to a series of images of your school or classroom on a broad rather than a narrow front is bound to create compromise, but compromises can be effective.

> "We had introduced a more practical maths curriculum into the school and the children were doing really well, much more confident and genuinely making better progress. But the parents kept coming up and saying `Why have you stopped teaching children their tables? The irony was we hadn't. We were just doing it differently but we couldn't get most of the parents to see that Some of them started to become critical of the whole maths approach then and we really began to lose their confidence in it and us.
>
> At a staff meeting someone suggested that twice a week, just before the children went home, we all spent ten minutes doing some very obvious work on learning tables. Some of us were very sceptical but we gave it a go. Sure enough, as soon as the children got outside the door they told their mums they'd just been doing tables. It took about three weeks of this before all those who grumbled were coming in saying how pleased they were. Just two lots often minutes a week for a term or so and the criticisms of the mathematics stopped. Amazing."

Defining the School or Class Image — What to Do

1. Know What You Would Like

Your own image of your school or class important. Think about what you would like and how best those messages can be transmitted.

2. Understand Others' Points of View

Find out what images others concerned with your

school have, too. Yours will have to work alongside theirs. Don't assume you know; spend time really finding out.

3. Think Particularly about Others' Negative Images

Are they based on any evidence? Can you do something positive to change them? Are they important enough to worry about?

4. Identify Areas of Compromise

The images your school or class have are important to you and others. Where are the areas of compromise between your preferred images and those held by others?

As far as possible, it is important to meet the needs of the various groups to whom you are responsible.

5. Think of Areas Over Which You have Immediate Control

Some things you can affect quite quickly. You might be able to change the appearance and style of your letters, alter the way children come into school from the playground, govern which books are sent home from classroom, increase or decrease the involvement of certain governors in the day-to-day life of the school.

6. Identify Other Important Factors in Defining the Image of Your School

Some things may take longer to change. You may want to increase or decrease the amount of community involvement, alter the presentation of school concerts, redesign and rewrite the brochure, begin to run effective parents' meetings, change the way individual teachers move children about the school and so on.

Create a priority list and work towards it.

7. Work to the Strengths of Your Own Personal Style

Your personal style will say a lot about your school or classroom. You can't hope to please everyone or to have all the attributes of a perfect human being. Be honest about your strengths and weaknesses and work to your strengths.

8. Make Sure that the Image Reflects the Reality

'Image' is a negative word when the gap between it and reality is huge. That is the moment when everyone realises that the image exists on its own, that it doesn't bear any relation to what is really happening. Ironically, at that point, the image has no substance; everyone loses confidence in it.

One of the important images of schools is their honesty. Trade on this. Declare existing weaknesses as professionally as possible and ensure that everyone is aware of all the existing strengths.

MARKETING THE SCHOOL

We spoke in the previous pages about the inevitability of your school having an image of one sort or another and the consequent importance of being positively involved in its definition. Defining an image of the school which accords with the reality behind it is, in many ways, the first stage of a marketing approach. The second, and equally crucial stage, is communicating that reality and image to anyone likely to be interested in it or helpful to you.

'Marketing'—or approaching it in a structured way— is a very new concept to many primary schools; one with which we are all having to come to terms. Because of that this section of the book is probably the most exploratory of all; there are so few examples in the real world on which to base good judgements.

The independent sector of education has understood the need for marketing for a long time. The need to go out and find customers, maintain their financial security and increase resources or 'go out of business' has concentrated minds wonderfully.

Until recently, most state schools did not share those concerns. Catchment areas, annually guaranteed money from the LEA and resources bought from central supplies allowed, quite rightly in our view, schools to concentrate on the education being provided for children.

All that has changed in recent years and those who work in primary schools find themselves sharing the same concerns as their colleagues in the independent sector. Open enrolment, the weakening of catchment areas, financial devolution and open purchasing markets have suddenly broadened the responsibilities of primary school head-teachers to a degree which many are finding uncomfortable.

What is certain is that primary schools will no longer be able to rely on either a flow of children into the school or an equable redrawing of catchment areas when enrolment patterns change.

What this means is that those who work in primary schools will have to develop plans and strategies for marketing that which they have to offer. What is this likely to mean in practice?

1. Presenting the School Differently

Different interest groups which surround the school will be interested in it in different ways. The marketing of the school, through its image, will have to respond to those different needs. Parents will differ from inspectors, inspectors will differ from local business and so on. Some parents will differ from each other, too.

'Presenting the school differently' doesn't mean

presenting conflicting messages about the school. That would be totally counterproductive. It does mean working out how to present the same image or message in a way that can be understood by different groups so that the school benefits throughout its constituency.

> "When parents come to visit the school I sit them down, give them a cup of coffee, task them a few questions and listen. I'm "trying to find out what they are interested in and what matters to them.
>
> Later, when I take them around the school I show them as much as possible but I concentrate on those areas of the school which I think will be of particular interest. There is no point spending enormous time in the gym with someone who has just talked to me for ten minutes about pottery. It's the kiln they want to see. If I didn't listen over coffee, though, I'd never find this out.
>
> Is it worth it? Well, it impresses people I suppose. What it does best, I think, is make sure that parents send their children here with some enthusiasm, confidence and support.'

2. Understanding the Purpose of the Marketing Exercise

Planning is as important in marketing as it is in everything else. Once the perspectives of the targeted group have been identified we have a better idea of the approaches they might prefer. Additionally, what we give, show, send to or talk about to those people has to be focused on the particular purpose we had in mind.

Asking for sponsorship monies from local companies requires a different approach from asking for one of their employees to come and talk to children.

In the first instance companies will need to know

- how much money is required
- over what time scale
- what the money is to be used for
- whether the use is compatible with their own operation
- what publicity might be gained for the company.

In the second instance they might want to know

- what support the employee might receive from the school
- what audio-visual facilities are available
- how long their employee will be away from work
- whether any publicity is possible
- some background information on the work children have done already.

3. Developing a Strategy

Successful marketing is rarely the result of a one-off operation. It depends on a combination of the appropriateness of the particular marketing exercise coupled with existing confidence in you and your school.

As this section was being written Marks and Spencer had just announced the successful introduction of a unit trust fund at the same time as other such launches had failed. There will be a number of reasons for this but one will almost certainly be the stock of goodwill Marks and Spencer had created long before they thought of involving themselves in unit trusts.

It is a lesson schools might have to learn. The chances of obtaining money from local companies are likely to be increased if some positive involvement with that company has occurred before the request for sponsorship is made. The chance of maintaining high enrolment into the school will be increased if parents of pre-school children in the area have been aware for some time of what the school stands for and what its achievements are.

4. Learning New Skills

Developing marketing ability over the next few years will require new skills, particularly in areas such as the media. The importance, for example, of presenting local newspapers and free-sheets with press releases is likely to grow. Writing those press releases in a way which the local papers can use is no more time-consuming than talking to a reporter on the telephone, but it does require the investment of a little time talking to the papers to find out what they want. Good press releases

- free reporters from having to rewrite copy
- increase the chance of exposure in local papers
- maintain some of the control in the hands of the school.

Other skills which could become important in the future include

- responding to media interviews, particularly on local radio
- creating opportunities for local radio and television involvement
- preparing documentation for specific target audiences—some governors, inspectors, local companies
- preparing a marketing plan
- researching the results.

From our present viewpoint the growing importance of marketing seems both exhilarating and appalling at the same time. Few teachers entered the profession with the thought that marketing our schools might become one of our most important activities.

As with everything else, though, situations, ideas and demands change. We do have to respond to those changes as best as we can. If we don't, both we and the schools we work in will suffer. The truth is that it may be the next but one generation of teachers and headteachers who are fully at ease with marketing strategies and marketing language. Those of us at the sharp edge of the changes must still take it seriously.

THE SCHOOL AND ITS GOVERNORS

In a time of uncertainty and doubt one thing we can say for sure is that the role of school governors has changed. The effective management of the new role has got to be a high priority for headteachers and many other staff as well. A clear definition of the new responsibilities is essential knowledge for all teachers and ways of realising the positive potential of governors are a must for all educational managers.

The Legal Framework

Education (no. 2) Act 1986

- Gives size, constitution and functions of governing body
- Defines *composition*—basically, this gave parents and non-political governors a majority on governing bodies (see 'Constitution of Governing Bodies' overleaf for details)
- Defines the ground rules for *becoming a governor.*

— minium age of 18

— a governor serves for four years—parent and teacher governors are elected by secret ballot
— parents may complete four years even though their children have left school
— teachers cease to be governors if they leave the school
— travel and subsistence expenses are allowed.
— Defines *responsibilities of governors.*

1. Appointment of Staff

- Headteachers are selected by an LEA and governors' panel which has at least equal numbers of governors
- other staff appointments are the governors' responsibility although they can delegate
- deputy head appointments can be as for headteacher or as for other staff
- job descriptions for redeployed teachers can be written by governors, and the LEA must take this into account.

[NB: some minor changes to this in 1988 Act-see p. 217.]

2. *Curriculum*

Governors should:

- record and update aims of the school
- consider LEA curriculum guidelines and possibly modify them
- note that headteachers are responsible for delivery of the curriculum and for reconciling any differences between the LEA and governors
- assume responsibility for the existence of sex education in schools
- assume responsibility for the provision of a balanced political education

- ensure that all curriculum documentation is available to parents
- ensure that community and police views are taken into account.

[NB: 1988 Act increases these powers and makes some changes-see pp. 217-218]

3. *Finance*

Governors should:

- require LEAs to give a statement of overall running costs of the school
- assume responsibility for a large part of 'capitation'; this can be delegated to the headteacher.

[NB: 1988 Act changes this significantly -see p. 217.]

4. *Discipline*

- there are strict rules for dealing with suspensions
- only the head teacher has the power to suspend a pupil
- governors may draw up guidelines for pupil discipline
- staff may be temporarily suspended by the head teacher or governors
- dismissal and early retirement may be recommended by governors—only LEA can do this in County Schools
- voluntary aided schools' governors are employers so they undertake formal procedures concerning staff.

5. *Governors' Meetings and Procedures*

- no governor can be on more than four boards
- the chairperson is to be elected annually; he/ she cannot be an employee of the school

- a quorum is three or one third, whichever is the greater
- any three governors may call a special meeting
- all governors' papers (minutes, reports, etc.) must be available for anyone to consult (except for items deemed 'confidential')
- others may be invited to meetings
- personal involvement in an issue precludes a governor from taking part in discussion
- decisions must be by majority vote
- the clerk must be appointed or dismissed in accordance with published procedures or in agreement with governors
- if the clerk is absent, a governor may step in
- an adjourned meeting with incomplete business must be completed at a later date
- governors' meetings require seven days clear notice unless the chair rules otherwise.

6. Annual Meeting for Parents

- governors must give an annual report to parents on what they have done during the year and hold a meeting to discuss the report
- resolutions for consideration can be passed if the number of parents present is equal to 20 per cent of the school roll.

Constitution of Governing Bodies

(Sections 3,4, and 6 of the Education (No. 2) Act 1986)

County, Controlled and Special Schools

(i) *Under 100 pupils:* 2 parent governors 2 LEA governors 1 teacher governor
The headteacher if he/she wishes *Either* 2

foundation + 1 co-opted (controlled schools) or 3 co-opted (county and special schools)

(ii) *100 to 299 pupils:* 3 parent governors 3 LEA governors 1 teacher governor

The headteacher if he/she wishes *Either* 3 foundation + 1 co-opted (controlled schools) or 4 co-opted (county and special schools)

(iii) *300 to 500 pupils:* 4 parent governors 4 LEA governors 2 teacher governors

The headteacher if he/she wishes *Either* 4 foundation + 1 co-opted (controlled schools) or 5 co-opted (county and special schools)

(iv) *Over 600 pupils:* 5 parent governors 5 LEA governors 2 teacher governors

The headteacher if he/she wishes *Either* 4 foundation + 2 co-opted controlled schools) *or* 6 co-opted (county and special schools)

LEAs have the option to drop the largest *category* (iv) and treat schools of over 600 pupils the same as those of 300-600, thus establishing 16 as the top size of governing board. This is the only flexibility allowed on numbers.

In making co-options, governors must bear in mind the need for representation of the business community.

Aided and Special Agreement Schools

Regardless of size:

At least 1 LEA governor

In primary schools, at least 1 representative of the minor authority, if any

At least 1 parent governor

At least 1 teacher governor in schools of under 300

At least 2 teacher governors in schools over 300
Foundation governors sufficient to secure majority set out below
The headteacher if he/she wishes.
There shall be a majority of foundation governors of 2 over all other interests in boards up to 18 members and 3 in larger boards. One foundation governor must always be a parent of a pupil.
Commencement dates: county and special schools by September 1st 1988 and voluntary schools by September 1st 1989.

Education Reform Act 1988

This Act did not replace the 1986 Act—in fact most of the 1986 Act has remained unaltered. What has changed is an *increase* in the power of school governors (and central government).

Sections most affecting school governors are concerned with:

1. Finance

- eventually all schools (initially those over 200 pupils) will have control over a major part of their budgets
- the LEA, working within strict governmental guidelines, will produce a formula which determines which budgetary items are kept centrally and which devolved to schools (see Local Management of Schools pp. 195-199)
- major items for governors to decide are: teachers, books, stock, equipment and maintenance.

2. Staffing

- governors make all appointments with advice

from the LEA — they may or may not decide to involve the headteacher

- governors recommend dismissal of staff

3. Admissions

- to reduce the 'standard number' (i.e. admissions in 1979-80) governors and LEA must obtain the approval of the Secretary of State
- raising admission numbers does not require this approval.

4. Grant Maintained Status (Opting Out)

- governors of schools with over 300 pupils may apply to be financed directly from the Secretary of State
- this can only be done following a ballot of parents equal to 20 per cent of the school roll and a majority of those voting are in favour
- a second ballot is required if less than 50 per cent vote in the first. The second ballot is binding whatever the turn-out.

5. The National Curriculum

- governors, LEAs and headteachers have a joint responsibility to comply with the requirements of the National Curriculum (see Primary Schools and the National Curriculum pp. 77-79).

6. Religious Worship

- schools must have a daily collective act of worship
- it can be at any time and not for the whole school at once
- it should be broadly 'Christian'

- governors and staff may apply for partial or total exemption from the 'Christian' requirement if the catchment area reflects another or other faiths.

Major Point

- The 1988 Act has two major areas where governors are crucially concerned *-Finance* and *Curriculum*.

Involving Governors

Peoples' perceptions of what happens in our schools are as important as *what* happens. Governors are no exception to this view. They bring the *perspectives* of the business person, the parent, the politician and so on — given their new powers it is vital that their understanding of what goes on in school is as full and accurate as possible.

When involving governors it is important to recognise the two ways in which we operate with them: informally and formally.

1. The Informal

- Even though these may be formally set up, informal functions are relaxed occasions which allow governors to meet informally with staff, parents and other members of the local community. They should provide opportunities for relationships to be deepened and the basis of mutual respect and trust to be laid down.
- It's a good idea to arrange an informal monthly or half-termly meeting between the chairperson of governors and the headteacher to keep communication lines open.
- Some examples of informal governor involvement are as follows:

  (a) school plays, concerts, parties, Christmas lunch

(b) sports day, prize giving, competitions, etc.
(c) social occasions with staff, for example, wine and cheese, retirement of long serving staff member
(d) PTA type functions, for example, discos, barn dances, 'fairs', etc.

2. The Formal

- The termly *governors' meeting* is the most crucial structure for involving governors; this is where much of the decision-making takes place and so head teachers and teachers need to be well-prepared, be seen to be efficient and effective managers and learn new skills in terms of cooperating with non-professionals.
- The *sub-committee* structure adopted by many governing bodies (for example, for curriculum, finance, site and building, etc.) is another formal set-up whereby governors can become professionally involved with staff.
- Staff appointments will invariably involve governors.
- Visits to the school (which can be informal) when governors can see staff and children at work.

All these situations give opportunities for governors to gain insight and make contributions to the life of the school. At all of them staff, and head teachers in particular, need to be:

- well-briefed with the necessary information
- clear about their view on issues
- aware of governors' perspectives.

No one is sure how the governors' new powers will

affect schools. In some cases their impact may be minimal, in others it may be radical. Many governors are worried and concerned about their new responsibilities and they need the constructive support of the head teacher and staff.